GRAPH WINDOW ICONS

Icon	Name	Description
	Arrow	Draws lines with arrowheads
	Line	Draws lines
	Ellipse	Draws circles and ellipses
	Polygon	Draws multisided shapes
	Rectangle	Draws squares and rectangles
	Text	Adds text of variable font and point size
	Freehand	Draws freehand shapes and lines
	Line Chart	Uses the selected range to display a line chart
	Bar Chart	Uses the selected range to display a bar or 3D bar chart
	Horizontal Bar Chart	Uses the selected range to display a horizontal bar chart
	Mixed Chart	Uses the selected range to display a combination bar and line chart
	Pie Chart	Uses the selected range to display a pie or 3D bar chart
	Area	Uses the selected range to display an area chart
	High-Low-Close Chart	Uses the selected range to display a HLCO chart
	3D Line Chart	Uses the selected range to display a 3D line chart
	3D Bar Chart	Uses the selected range to display a 3D bar chart
	3D Pie Chart	Uses the selected range to display a 3D pie chart
	3D Area Chart	Uses the selected range to display a 3D area chart
	Select Chart Type	Lets you select or change the type of graph
	Delete	Deletes the selected object(s)
	Replicate	Replicates the selected object(s)
	Rotate	Turns the selected object(s) or graph 90 degrees
	Flip Horizontal	Flips the selected object(s) to look backwards
	Flip Vertical	Flips the selected object(s) to look upside down
	Bring to Front	Moves the selected object(s) in front of other overlapping objects
	Bring to Back	Moves the selected object(s) behind other overlapping objects

Computer users are not all alike.
Neither are SYBEX books.

We know our customers have a variety of needs. They've told us so. And because we've listened, we've developed several distinct types of books to meet the needs of each of our customers. What are you looking for in computer help?

If you're looking for the basics, try the **ABC's** series. You'll find short, unintimidating tutorials and helpful illustrations. For a more visual approach, select **Teach Yourself**, featuring screen-by-screen illustrations of how to use your latest software purchase.

Mastering and **Understanding** titles offer you a step-by-step introduction, plus an in-depth examination of intermediate-level features, to use as you progress.

Our **Up & Running** series is designed for computer-literate consumers who want a no-nonsense overview of new programs. Just 20 basic lessons, and you're on your way.

We also publish two types of reference books. Our **Instant References** provide quick access to each of a program's commands and functions. SYBEX **Encyclopedias** and **Desktop References** provide a *comprehensive reference* and explanation of all of the commands, features and functions of the subject software.

Sometimes a subject requires a special treatment that our standard series don't provide. So you'll find we have titles like **Advanced Techniques, Handbooks, Tips & Tricks,** and others that are specifically tailored to satisfy a unique need.

We carefully select our authors for their in-depth understanding of the software they're writing about, as well as their ability to write clearly and communicate effectively. Each manuscript is thoroughly reviewed by our technical staff to ensure its complete accuracy. Our production department makes sure it's easy to use. All of this adds up to the highest quality books available, consistently appearing on best-seller charts worldwide.

You'll find SYBEX publishes a variety of books on every popular software package. Looking for computer help? Help Yourself to SYBEX.

For a complete catalog of our publications:

SYBEX Inc.
2021 Challenger Drive, Alameda, CA 94501
Tel: (510) 523-8233/(800) 227-2346 Telex: 336311
Fax: (510) 523-2373

SYBEX is committed to using natural resources wisely to preserve and improve our environment. As a leader in the computer book publishing industry, we are aware that over 40% of America's solid waste is paper. This is why we have been printing the text of books like this one on recycled paper since 1982.

This year our use of recycled paper will result in the saving of more than 15,300 trees. We will lower air pollution effluents by 54,000 pounds, save 6,300,000 gallons of water, and reduce landfill by 2,700 cubic yards.

In choosing a SYBEX book you are not only making a choice for the best in skills and information, you are also choosing to enhance the quality of life for all of us.

THE ABC's
OF 1-2-3
FOR Windows

THE ABC's
OF 1-2-3®
FOR Windows™

Robert Cowart

SYBEX®

SAN FRANCISCO • PARIS • DÜSSELDORF • SOEST

Acquisitions Editor: Dianne King
Developmental Editor: Christian T. S. Crumlish
Editor: Brendan Fletcher
Technical Editors: Nick Dargahi, Dan Tauber
Word Processors: Scott Campbell, Ann Dunn, Susan Trybull
Book Designer: Suzanne Albertson
Chapter Art: Suzanne Albertson
Screen Graphics: Cuong Le, Thomas Goudie
Typesetter: Elizabeth Newman
Proofreaders: Rhonda Holmes, Dina F. Quan, Hilda van Genderen
Indexer: Ted Laux
Cover Designer: Thomas Ingalls + Associates
Cover Photographer: Mark Johann

To Jennifer and Molly,
for making it bearable

ACKNOWLEDGMENTS

Many thanks to all the people at SYBEX who keep on keepin' on despite the high-speed perils of the computer book publishing industry. Their efforts played a key role in bringing this book to you.

Thanks in particular to the editorial staff associated with this book: Editor-in-Chief Dr. Rudolph Langer; Acquisitions Manager Dianne King; Developmental Editor Christian Crumlish; of course my editor, Brendan Fletcher; and for technical review, Dan Tauber and Nick Dargahi. Additional thanks to Jeff Kapellas and to Word Processors Scott Campbell, Ann Dunn, and Susan Trybull for their help in getting this book out ahead of schedule.

Next, the production staff who put the pages together and shipped them out the door to the printer, under incredible deadlines: Book Designer Suzanne Albertson; Typesetter Elizabeth Newman; screen-capture queen Delia Brown and Screen-Graphics Artists Thomas Goudie and Cuong Le; and Proofreaders Rhonda Holmes, Dina Quan, and Hilda van Genderen.

Then, I want to thank the people almost nobody sees—the sales crew. SYBEX has its own independent force of salespeople who pound the streets and the phones, to get my books (and the many other SYBEX books) on the shelves of stores around the world—from the small, independent book stores to enormous supermarket chain stores, from Poughkeepsie to Portugal.

And finally, thanks to my friends—to Steve Cummings and family for helping with the writing (XOXO); to Kathy G., Beverly, Colleen, Julie, and Karen F. for your patience with my schedule (and my answering machine!); and to Kim for the "Bob" jokes, the coffee, the late-night video escapes, and the Breyer's ice cream.

CONTENTS
AT A GLANCE

CONTENTS

INTRODUCTION

FEATURING

- What Is a Spreadsheet?
- What Can 1-2-3 Do?
- How to Use This Book

IF YOU'VE NEVER USED LOTUS 1-2-3 AND WANT TO LEARN how, *The ABC's of 1-2-3 for Windows* is the book for you. In 68 simple and practical lessons, you'll learn all the skills a beginner is likely to need. Using everyday examples, you'll create worksheets, modify them, print them, and graph them. Once you have a firm grasp of the fundamentals, you'll learn how to build a database, how to use functions, and how to create macros.

I've written this book with the beginner in mind, using an easy-to-understand style that explains all the essentials of 1-2-3 for Windows in plain English. I've also designed the book to get you started working with 1-2-3 immediately. As you follow the exercises step by step, you'll be told exactly which keys to press and which commands to use, so you'll learn by doing. Then, additional explanations will make it clear how to apply the techniques you're learning to your own worksheet needs.

This book is written for a particular version of 1-2-3, Lotus 1-2-3 for Windows. If you are using another version of 1-2-3, such as version 2.2 or 3, you should refer to books covering them specifically. Being non-Windows products, they differ substantially.

What Is a Spreadsheet?

If you have ever seen an accountant poring over a wide notebook of green-ruled paper that has lots of columns and rows, you know what a spreadsheet is. Many businesses use spreadsheets for keeping records of transactions, budgets, receivables, payables, general ledgers, and the like. Just as the word processor is the computer counterpart to the typewriter, the computerized spreadsheet is a version of an accountant's or manager's multicolumn accounting paper.

Most spreadsheets (or as Lotus calls them, *worksheets*) are used to store numbers, and those numbers are usually part of some overall mathematical formula. Take a column of expenses, for example. Chances are the column is to be added, with a total appearing at the bottom. To arrive at the total, an accountant would normally sit down with a calculator and manually punch in the numbers to arrive at a total. But since a computer likes nothing better than to sit around adding, subtracting, and multiplying numbers, why not have the computerized worksheet do all the calculations? With 1-2-3 for Windows, you can.

Some History

When spreadsheets were introduced on personal computers in the late 1970s, they caught on like wildfire. The first spreadsheet program, VisiCalc for the Apple II, was an overnight success, and it set the standard for other spreadsheets for some time. VisiCalc was largely responsible for the success of Apple Computer, in fact. Soon other, more advanced spreadsheet programs, such as SuperCalc, Microplan, and PerfectCalc, appeared. With the 1982 release of Lotus 1-2-3 for the IBM PC, the third generation of spreadsheets was well underway.

Since its initial release, millions of copies of 1-2-3 have been sold, and people worldwide have learned to use it for their business and engineering needs. Several versions of 1-2-3 have appeared over the years, as have many add-on products that enhance the operation of 1-2-3. It's not stretching the truth to say there is an entire multimillion-dollar industry formed around 1-2-3 users.

Now, with the acceptance of Microsoft Windows as the most popular graphical user interface (GUI) for IBM PC's and compatibles, Lotus has released a Windows version of their product. The advantages of the Windows interface are significant. Windows makes 1-2-3 for Windows easier to learn and use than its predecessors, and once you've learned 1-2-3 for Windows, you can do more with it in less time since the commands are simpler. And you can manipulate many features of the program with your mouse.

Columns and Rows

A spreadsheet appears on the computer as a table of columns and rows. Each intersection of a column and a row creates a box called a *cell*. Cells are referenced by their location on the spreadsheet, such as A1 (column A, row 1) or G3 (column G, row 3). Each cell can hold a number or a formula. The formula is used to calculate the cell's numerical value by reference to other cells in the spreadsheet. Consider the model spreadsheet in Figure I.1. If you were to enter the formula shown into cell A6, 1-2-3 would calculate the total of cells A1 through A5 and place the result into cell A6.

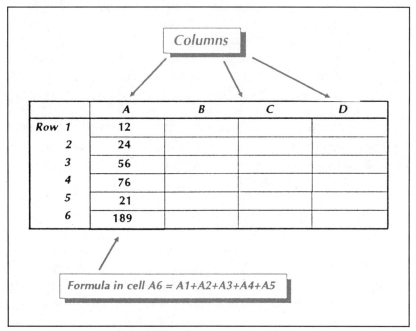

Figure I.1: A model of a spreadsheet

What Can 1-2-3 Do?

You will probably use 1-2-3 most often to perform mathematical calculations like the one shown above, though as you gain experience your calculations are likely to become a good deal more complex. However, creating spreadsheets is only a small part of what you can do with 1-2-3. Over the course of this book, you will also learn to take advantage of the 1-2-3 capabilities described in the following sections.

Rapid Business Calculations

Even using 1-2-3's most basic computational tools, you can quickly and easily create home and business budgets, sales reports, and other business documents. Creating such spreadsheets is made easier by 1-2-3's built-in *functions,* which allow you to use spreadsheet data in analytical, financial, and statistical modeling computations.

Once created, your spreadsheets can easily be altered to reflect changes in income, expenses, or any key variable. For example, if you were to change the data in any of cells A1 through A5 in Figure I.1, the total in A6 would automatically change to reflect the alteration. Similarly, by altering key variables in a complex spreadsheeet containing many cells and formulas—say, a proposed annual budget—you can quickly experiment with the bottom-line results of various scenarios. This what-if capacity can be an invaluable aid in the corporate or even small-business decison-making process, and it is precisely what has made 1-2-3 so popular.

Formatting Your Worksheets

The formatting commands 1-2-3 for Windows offers give you great flexibility in the way your worksheets look, both on the screen and on paper. For example, you may want dollar amounts to display the dollar symbol ($). Or you may want figures to display in boldface. You can achieve either of these effects with a few clicks of your mouse.

Cells can also contain text information (called labels) rather than just numbers. With 1-2-3's text-formatting capabilities, you can change the font (typeface) and display size and style of text, create fancy effects such as boldface and italics, change the color of your text, and more. If you have a high-resolution printer, you will be amazed at the quality and diversity of the reports and graphs you can generate with 1-2-3 for Windows.

Sharing Data between Worksheets and Other Programs

Since Windows lets you run a number of programs simultaneously, you can easily "cut and paste" information from one worksheet into another worksheet or into other types of documents generated by another application (a word processor, for example). In addition, 1-2-3 for Windows allows you to have as many as 256 worksheets within each file, and these worksheets can interact with each other. Cells in one worksheet can be used in formulas for another worksheet. This lets you keep various types of information segregated on separate worksheets while allowing you easy access to them.

Graphing and Databases—the "2" and "3" of 1-2-3

But 1-2-3 is more than just a spreadsheet program—the name 1-2-3 actually has a meaning. There are three parts to the program, only the first of which (1) does worksheets. The second portion of the program allows you to create a variety of attractive graphs from your spreadsheet data to give your data more visual impact. Finally, 1-2-3 has a database feature that lets you create and organize *tables* of information, much like a telephone directory lists names and addresses. With a 1-2-3 database, you can rearrange your information easily, and search for needed data quickly.

Printing

You can print out anything you create in 1-2-3. Printouts can include all or just part of a given matrix of cells. You can also incorporate titles or descriptive phrases in your reports and graphs, use various typefaces and font sizes and styles, and combine information from a number of linked spreadsheets.

How to Use This Book

Don't be alarmed if some of the details just discussed went over your head. The purpose of this book is to explain and give you hands-on experience with the most important features of 1-2-3. In the following lessons, you'll be introduced to these 1-2-3 features and given a chance to use them yourself. In the process, you'll build a few worksheets that you may even end up using later.

At this point, you have at least a general idea of what 1-2-3 can do, and may already have some ideas about what you want it to do for you. However, if you're like the many users who are intimidated by the supplied manuals, you may not have even installed 1-2-3 on your computer yet. If this is the case, you should turn to Appendix A, "Installation," which will take you through the steps of setting up 1-2-3 for your system. If you have already installed the program according to the instructions in the manual supplied by Lotus, just move ahead to the first lesson.

From the first lesson to the last, each lesson in this book will take you further in the direction of becoming a proficient 1-2-3 user. The more advanced lessons assume you have read earlier lessons, so it is best to work through them in order. Once you have finished all the lessons and built the worksheet examples, you'll have a pretty thorough understanding of the concepts involved, and when and where to use them. Then you will find this book a valuable resource for reminding yourself how to do a particular task. Since I've broken up the book into small discrete lessons, you can use the Table of Contents to easily look up the topic you're interested in.

Conventions Used in the Book

To pack all of this information concisely into a book of this size, we've had to devise some rules for differentiating between the things you type, the things 1-2-3 displays, and the instructions you are being given by me. The rules are as follows:

- Explanatory notes or discussion are presented in standard paragraphs.

- When I want you to actually do something specific on your computer, I will tell you in a series of numbered steps:

etc.

- When 1-2-3 shows something on the screen in response to something you have done, I will generally say "1-2-3 responds with:" and then show you the response printed in a different color, like this:

1-2-3 response

- When I ask you to type something on the keyboard, I will show you what to type either in boldface type, as in "Type **THIS** and press Enter," or, if what you are to type is on a separate line, it will look like this:

What you type

About the Default Worksheet Directory

When you save and retrieve worksheet files from and to your hard disk, 1-2-3 assumes you want to use a particular directory. This is called the *default directory.* The default directory your system will use will vary depending on how you installed 1-2-3. If you followed the instructions in Appendix A of this book, the default directory will be C:\123W\WORK. Accordingly, the instructions and figures in this book assume that C:\123W\WORK is your default directory.

If you installed your system differently, 1-2-3 may show another directory, such as C:\123W\SAMPLE or C:\123W, as the default directory. If you want the figures and instructions in this book to match your screens, you should change the default using the steps outlined below. If you don't know how to perform some of the operations these steps require, complete Lessons 1 through 9 and then return to these pages to change your default directory.

① Make sure you have a directory on your disk called
    C:\123W\WORK. Use DOS, Windows File Manager,
    XTREE, or another file management program to create the
    directory if it doesn't exist.

② Run 1-2-3.

③ Open the Tools menu and choose User Setup.

④ Alter the Worksheet Directory setting to read

    C:\123W\WORK.

⑤ Click on OK.

Now whenever you go to open or save a file, C:\123W\WORK
will be displayed as the default directory in the File Save and File Open
dialog boxes.

PART

1

Getting Started

1 LESSON

Starting Your Computer

FEATURING

- Booting Up
- Running Windows
- Quitting 1-2-3 for Windows

IN THIS LESSON, YOU'LL START YOUR COMPUTER AND bring up Windows. Both 1-2-3 for Windows and Windows version 3.0 or later should already be properly installed on your hard disk. If you have not yet installed 1-2-3 for Windows, please turn to Appendix A, "Installation," or consult the *Before You Begin* booklet that came with your software.

You can skip this lesson if you already know how to turn on your computer and bring up Windows.

How to Start Your Computer

Let's assume you are seated at your computer and ready to get working.

 Find the power switch to the computer. It is usually on either the front of the computer box or the left side near the rear of the box. Don't confuse the screen (monitor) with the computer itself. Although portables and laptop computers have built-in screens, in most cases the computer is a metal box separate from the screen. When you've found the power switch, flip it on.

② If the screen doesn't come on by itself when you've turned on the computer, then activate it by turning on its power switch. Location of the switch will vary from model to model.

The computer will take a few seconds to perform a diagnostic check, and then it will "boot up." Once this process is complete, either the DOS prompt will appear, or if the command to start Windows has been added to your AUTOEXEC.BAT file, Windows will run automatically. You will know Windows has loaded when the large Windows sign-on screen appears (you can't miss it!).

If Windows doesn't load, you will see a few words about your type of computer. Then you will see the *DOS prompt,* which looks something like this:

C>

To the right of the greater-than sign, you will see a small flashing box. This is the *cursor.* The cursor marks the point at which you can type in commands to your machine. To start Windows, type in the following command:

WIN

Then press Enter.

The Windows sign-on screen will now appear, followed by the Program Manager window. The exact arrangement of the Program Manager window will vary depending on how you saved it last, but it should look something like Figure 1.1. Your Program Manager may also be "iconized" at the bottom of your screen, or obscured by another program.

Since 1-2-3 for Windows is a Windows program, it will not run without Windows. That is, you can't run it from the DOS prompt by typing

123W

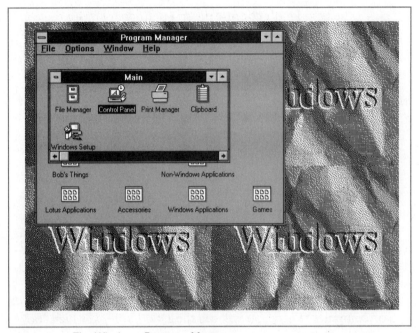

Figure 1.1: *The Windows Program Manager*

As with any Windows program, doing so will produce the message:

This program requires Microsoft Windows

This means that you have to run Windows first, then run 1-2-3 from there, as explained in the next lesson.

LESSON 2

Starting 1-2-3 for Windows

FEATURING

- Using the Mouse
- The 1-2-3 Icon
- The Run Command

NOW THAT YOUR COMPUTER IS RUNNING AND YOU'RE IN Windows, you're ready to start up Lotus 1-2-3 and work with a blank worksheet.

Using the Mouse

First off, find the mouse on your desk. Move the mouse across the desk, and notice that as you do, the little arrow on the screen moves too. This little arrow is called the *mouse pointer.* You use the mouse pointer for most activities within 1-2-3.

The most basic operation using the the mouse is called *pointing.* As you might expect, pointing means positioning the pointer on top of an item on the screen.

Notice that your mouse has two (or possibly three) buttons that you can press. Generally, once you point at something, you have to press the left mouse button for 1-2-3 to take any action. (Your mouse buttons may be reversed, meaning that you'll have to click on the right button, but this is not likely.) This procedure is called *clicking*. Often I'll give an instruction, such as "click on the Cancel button." This would mean to point at the Cancel button and press the left mouse button quickly, instantly releasing it. If I want you to hold down the mouse button while performing a task such as moving the mouse, I'll tell you explicitly. Holding down the button while moving the mouse is called *dragging*. Normal clicking means just to click and release.

Some procedures require you to *double-click*. Double-clicking means to click the left mouse button not once, but twice—in rapid succession. Double-clicking may take a little practice. How fast you have to click depends on how Windows is set up on your computer. (Double-click speed is set through the Windows Control Panel.) You may have to experiment a bit to get the hang of double-clicking. A normal double-click takes about a second, and shouldn't be difficult to do.

Starting 1-2-3

Since 1-2-3 for Windows is a Windows application, you have to run it from within Windows. There are a number of ways to run 1-2-3 within Windows; in this lesson, I'll explain the two most common: clicking on the 1-2-3 icon, and using the Windows Run command.

Running 1-2-3 by Clicking on Its Icon

The most direct way to start 1-2-3 is by clicking on the 1-2-3 icon in the Lotus Applications group in your Program Manager. The Install program added this icon and the group when you installed the program. Here's how to get to it:

① You should now be in the Program Manager, since you just entered Windows (by default, the Program Manager always appears first). If the Program Manager is iconized (that is, if it appears as a tiny box, or *icon,* at the bottom of the screen), double-click on it to open it into a window. If it's already open, skip to step 2.

② Locate the Lotus Applications Group icon and double-click on it to open it. The icon opens to reveal the contents of the Lotus Applications group. Your screen should now look something like Figure 2.1.

③ Double-click on the 1-2-3 for Windows icon to run 1-2-3.

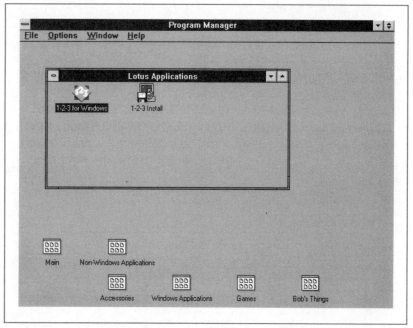

Figure 2.1: The Lotus Applications group window

Running 1-2-3 Using the Run Command

Another way to run 1-2-3 is via the Run command on the Program Manager's or File Manager's File menu. This may be the easier way if you don't want to use the mouse, if you are in the File Manager, or if you are using a replacement for the File Manager or Program Manager (such as the Norton Desktop) that allows you to run programs by typing their names.

① Open the File menu. You can do this by clicking on the word *File* in the menu bar or pressing the Alt and F keys simultaneously.

② Choose Run. Again, you select it by clicking the word *Run* or pressing the R key.

③ Now you will see a small window, or *dialog box,* entitled "Run." As you work with 1-2-3, you will encounter dialog boxes that give you warnings, provide information, or present you with options. I will explain how to respond to these dialog boxes as we go along. In this dialog box, type in the full path name of the 1-2-3 program, including the directory it is in, in the Command Line box. Figure 2.2 shows an example that assumes 1-2-3 is on the C drive in a directory called 123W. Note that the directory where the program is stored has to be typed in too, as does the extension (.EXE).

If you type in the name incorrectly, you will see a dialog box that reports

Cannot find file; check to ensure the path and filename are correct.

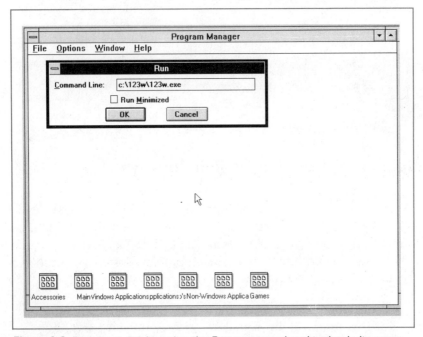

Figure 2.2: Running 1-2-3 by using the Run command and typing in its name

or

The specified path is invalid.

Click on OK, and try again after checking the path and file name.

*W*hich Way Is Better?

There is no particular advantage to running 1-2-3 from the icon as opposed to running it with the Run command. Obviously it requires less typing to use the icon, but feel free to use the Run command if you feel more comfortable with it.

Regardless of the technique you use to run 1-2-3, the same thing happens. You first see the 1-2-3 for Windows program title screen briefly, and then, in a few seconds, 1-2-3 comes up on your screen, displaying a blank worksheet. Turn to Lesson 3 to learn about the parts of the 1-2-3 screen, and how you use them.

*Q*uitting Lotus 1-2-3 for Windows

You may find that rather than working through all the lessons in this book at once, you'll want to do a few lessons at a time. The steps below explain how to leave 1-2-3 safely.

① Open the 1-2-3 File menu.

② Choose Exit.

③ If you have any spreadsheets open, you will be asked if you want 1-2-3 to save the file (and any changes you made) before exiting 1-2-3, with the message

   Save all files before closing?

   Since we have not made any changes to the worksheet yet, you can simply click on No to exit 1-2-3. (If by chance you do want to save your worksheet, turn to Lesson 9 for instructions.)

If you want to leave Windows as well, follow these steps:

(1) Activate the Program Manager. The easiest way is to press Ctrl-Esc, which brings up the Task List. Then highlight Program Manager and click on Switch To or press Enter.

(2) Open the File menu and choose Exit Windows.

(3) Click on OK in the dialog box.

LESSON 3

The 1-2-3 Window

FEATURING

- The 1-2-3 Window
- The Worksheet Window

WHEN YOU START 1-2-3, IT DISPLAYS THE 1-2-3 STARTUP screen, also known as the *1-2-3 window*. Within this window is the *worksheet window,* which contains one blank worksheet.

In this lesson, we'll look at the parts of the 1-2-3 screen. Once we know our way around the 1-2-3 screen, we'll be able to begin experimenting with 1-2-3's menus, buttons, and the worksheet itself.

Parts of the 1-2-3 Window

The 1-2-3 window, shown in Figure 3.1, is the window that you work within while in 1-2-3. The size of this window determines the maximum size of your worksheet windows, since they must fit within the boundaries of the 1-2-3 window.

Each of the parts of the 1-2-3 window is described below.

SmartIcons   The SmartIcons are "buttons" that you can click on with the mouse. Each icon represents a different, commonly used command.

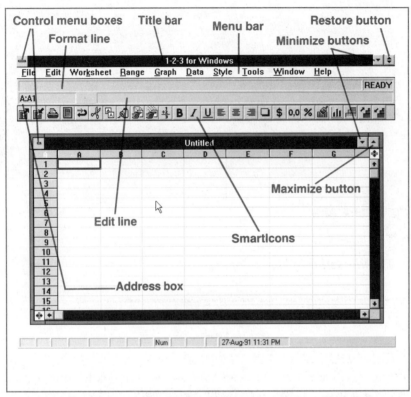

Figure 3.1: The 1-2-3 start up screen, with a blank worksheet displayed

Clicking on an icon is a shortcut for executing commands from the menus. You can also assign new icons from a supplied list for tasks you perform regularly.

Control menu box
: The control menu box is something that all Windows programs have in their upper left corners. Clicking here opens the window's control menu, from which you can choose to close or resize the window.

Title bar
: As with all Windows programs, the title bar simply states the name of the program running within the window. In the case of the 1-2-3 window, this will read "1-2-3 for Windows."

Maximize button	Clicking on this button enlarges the window to its maximum size. Worksheet windows can't be larger than the 1-2-3 window, so to see as much of a worksheet as possible, click on the 1-2-3 window's maximize button first, then on the worksheet's.
Minimize button	Clicking on this button "minimizes" the 1-2-3 window or the worksheet window to an *icon* (a tiny square at the bottom of the screen) to get it "out of the way" for the moment. Double-clicking on the icon restores it to its former size and lets you continue working.
Menu bar	The menu bar is very important, because it is from here that you tell 1-2-3 what to do. Each word on the menu bar represents a series of commands you can choose from. Clicking on a name in the menu bar displays the choices on that menu.
Address box	If you look at the worksheet window, you'll notice that the worksheet is a grid of rows and columns. The intersection of a row and a column is called a *cell*. Each cell in a worksheet has a unique "address," called the *cell address*. The cell address is composed of the column and row of the cell, such as A19, B5, or C7. The address box always indicates the address of the cell you are working on, so that you don't have to look at the row and column markers.
Edit line	The edit line is where you enter or edit data into a cell. As you type in your data, it appears here. The edit line also contains the address box.
Restore button	When the window is maximized, the maximize button changes to display a two-headed arrow. This is the restore button. Clicking

on the restore button restores the maximized
window to its previous size and location.

Format line   The format line indicates (through cryptic
hieroglyphics) what the formatting of the
active cell is. It also displays the current
column width.

Parts of the Worksheet Window

The worksheet window is the window that contains and displays
your worksheets while you are working on them. With 1-2-3 you can
have many worksheets open at the same time. If you do have more
than one open, each will create a new worksheet window within the
perimeter of the 1-2-3 window.

Though the 1-2-3 window and the worksheet windows have
some elements in common, some of the items pointed to in Figure 3.1
pertain only to the 1-2-3 window. Figure 3.2 shows some details of
worksheet windows.

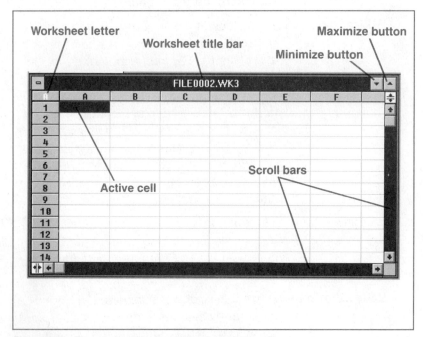

Figure 3.2: Elements of the worksheet window

Here are their descriptions:

Active cell

You're always working with at least one *cell* in a worksheet. A rectangular highlight indicates which cell you're working with.

Scroll bars

If you are familiar with Windows, you should already know about scroll bars. Scroll bars allow you to see parts of a document that are "off screen." Worksheets in 1-2-3 are always larger than the screen area. In fact, by default, 1-2-3 worksheets are 8192 rows by 256 columns, which amounts to more than 2 million cells. By clicking on the arrows at either end of the scroll bars, you can cause the worksheet to scroll vertically or horizontally.

Worksheet title bar

Each worksheet window also has a title bar indicating the name of the worksheet displayed in it.

Worksheet letter

When using multiple-worksheet files (explained later), each worksheet gets a letter that appears in the corner, beginning with *A*.

Minimize and maximize buttons

As with the 1-2-3 window, these buttons let you enlarge the worksheet window to its maximum size, or minimize it to an icon.

4 LESSON

Experimenting with Menus

FEATURING

- Using Menus
- Dialog Boxes
- The Classic 1-2-3 Window

BEFORE MOVING AHEAD TO CREATE A WORKSHEET, IT'S a good idea to start working with 1-2-3's pull-down menus. If you are already familiar with Windows and other Windows programs, you probably already know how to use pull-down menus. If this is the case, you might want to skip this lesson and move to the next one. If you aren't familiar with pull-down menus, you should work through these steps.

Using Menus

Most of the common tasks you'll be doing while in Windows and in 1-2-3 are accessed through menus. As I mentioned earlier, menus contain commands that you use to do your work. When learning a new program, it's always a good idea to take a look at all the menus and the choices each gives you, even if you don't understand them all at first.

*C*hoosing a Command

You can choose a command from a 1-2-3 menu by following these steps:

① Click on the first name up in the menu bar (File). If you prefer to use the keyboard, you can press Alt-F (press Alt, hold it down, and then press F—pressing Alt plus the underlined letter of a menu always opens that menu). The File menu appears, as you see in Figure 4.1.

② Note that the first choice in the menu is already highlighted. This is always the case when opening a menu. Press the ↓ key to highlight the next choice. Notice that the title bar (top of the screen) changes as you highlight each command, telling you what each command can do for you.

③ Highlight each command with the ↓ key or the ↑ key, and read the description on the top line.

④ Using the arrow keys, highlight Import From. Notice that it has a little triangle next to it. This means there is a menu associated with it. Press Enter. A smaller menu opens with a few more choices. Menus such as these are called *cascading menus.*

⑤ Cancel the menu selection by pressing Esc. Escape almost always succeeds in canceling a command you are in the middle of.

⑥ Press Alt to close the File menu.

⑦ Now open the other menus, by clicking on the menu name, or by using the Alt-key method explained above. If a menu is already open, you can move to the next menu to the right by pressing the → key. You may notice that some commands are in a dimmer color or intensity on your menus. Dimmed commands are ones you can't use at the current time.

Notice that some commands have key combinations displayed to their right. For example, on the Edit menu, the Undo command has

LESSON 4

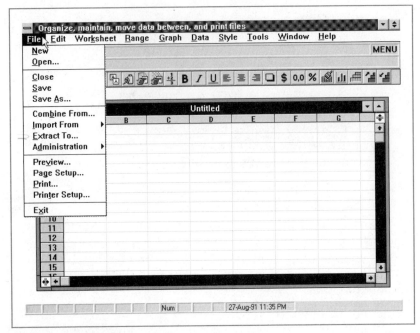

Figure 4.1: Clicking on File opens the File menu

the key combination *Alt + Bksp* displayed after it. These key combinations are shortcut keys you can use to have the same effect as opening the menu and choosing the command. To invoke the command, simultaneously press the two keys listed, just as you pressed Alt-F to open the File menu. As we go through using menus, you'll want to keep an eye on these shortcut keys and memorize them to speed up your work.

Working with Dialog Boxes

Notice also that some commands have an ellipsis (...) after them. Choosing these commands will bring up a *dialog box,* which will ask you to make choices, alter settings, or type in information. The Global Settings command is a good example of a command that brings up a dialog box. Let's experiment with this command.

① Choose Worksheet/Global Settings. (That's shorthand for "open the Worksheet menu and choose the Global Settings command." I'll be using this type of shorthand from now on to describe multistep choices I want you to make.) A dialog box appears with several settings you can alter displayed there.

② Click on the large rectangular "button" labeled Format. Another dialog box appears (the ellipses should have indicated to you that this would happen). Between these two dialog boxes, you're looking at the most common examples of items you'll see in dialog boxes. Your screen should look like that in Figure 4.2, though the boxes may be overlapping each other.

③ Click on the *check boxes* and notice that an X appears or disappears with each click. When a check box contains an X, the option listed beside it is in effect.

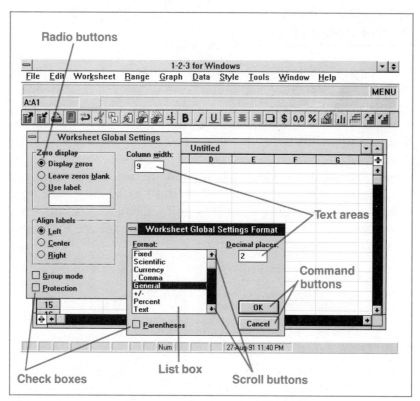

Figure 4.2: Example dialog boxes and typical dialog box elements

④ Click on the little *scroll buttons* in the list box, to scroll the choices.

⑤ Click in one of the *text areas* and notice that the cursor changes to the I-beam, allowing you to type in information.

⑥ Cancel the Worksheet Global Settings Format dialog box by clicking on Cancel or pressing Esc.

⑦ Click on the round *radio buttons* with the mouse pointer. Notice that within each group of settings, (such as Zero Display or Align Labels), only one can be set on at a time.

⑧ Cancel the other dialog box by clicking on Cancel or pressing Esc.

The Classic Commands—For Experienced Lotus Users Only

Because of the large number of experienced Lotus users who have memorized the commands used with versions of Lotus previous to the Windows version, the programmers at Lotus built something into 1-2-3 for Windows called *the Classic window*. The Classic window contains a menu system that acts identically to the one in 1-2-3 version 3.1. If you are already familiar with Lotus 1-2-3 slash (/) commands, you can enter them in 1-2-3 for Windows, and they will perform just as they do in version 3.1. I won't be covering the Classic commands in this book, as we'll be using the new Windows-based menu system. However, if you want to use the Classic commands instead, here's how:

① When you want to give 1-2-3 a command, press /.

② The Classic window will pop up, as shown in Figure 4.3.

③ Type in the commands you are used to using.

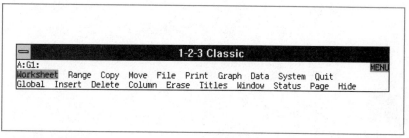

Figure 4.3: The Classic window, for using the tried and true 1-2-3 commands

You can drag the Classic window to a more desirable spot on the screen so that it doesn't obscure your work. Click and hold down the mouse button while positioning the pointer on the top line of the window. Once moved, it will reappear in the new spot next time. If you need to, you can remove the window from the screen until its next use by pressing the Esc key. Normally, though, it will vanish after you execute a command.

Now let's move to the next lesson to learn about getting help when you need it.

5 LESSON

Getting Help

FEATURING

- The F1 Key
- The Help Menu
- The Help System

NOW THAT YOU KNOW THE BASICS OF USING MENUS AND dialog boxes, you're probably wondering what all those choices were, and how you're ever going to learn everything you need to know just to start getting your work done. Well, hold on and don't panic. We'll start working with a worksheet in the next lesson. But before going ahead, you should know about the built-in help system that comes with 1-2-3 and Windows.

Most Windows programs have a help system that is *context-sensitive,* which means that the help system knows what commands you are working with at all times. The 1-2-3 Help system is no exception to this rule. If you get stumped while working with a particular command, 1-2-3 Help can quickly provide more information about the command.

If you're not familiar with how to operate the Windows Help facility, follow the instructions in this lesson carefully. Even if you are familiar with Windows Help or with help systems generally, you may want to browse through this lesson for assistance with 1-2-3 Help.

Using Help, you can actually learn a great deal about 1-2-3 without even cracking a book or the manual!

Using the Built-In Help System

Here's an example. Let's say you want to open a new worksheet, and you're not quite sure how to do it. You surmise that the File/New command (remember, that means the New command on the File menu) may be the way, but you're not sure. So, you use the Help facility to remind you. Try these steps:

1. Open the File menu and highlight New. (Don't click on it, just highlight it using the arrow keys. Clicking on it actually chooses it, and for now we don't want to do that.)

2. Press F1. This is the Help key; pressing it will call up information relevant to the command you are using. Since you have highlighted the New command, the Help facility comes up with some information about it, as you see in Figure 5.1. If the Help window that appears is not maximized (in its largest size) click on the maximize button in its upper right corner. Notice that some of the words on the screen are underlined and others have a dotted underline.

3. Click on one of the words with the dotted underline, and hold the mouse button down. As long as you do so, a definition of the word will appear on the screen.

4. Click on one of the solid underlined words. These words are cross references. When clicked on they will bring up related information.

Note the large buttons at the top of the Help window (Index, Back, <<Browse, Browse>>, and Search). You can click on the Index button at any time to bring up an index of topics you might be interested in looking up. Then clicking on a word in the index jumps immediately to the pertinent information. Choosing the Browse buttons moves through the Help topics one by one, either forward or backward, depending on the button.

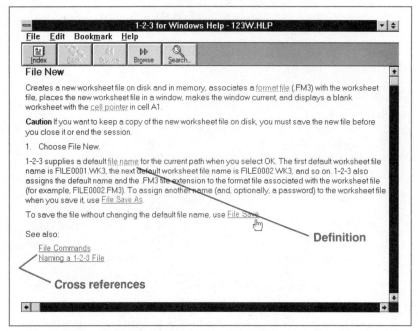

Figure 5.1: Pressing F1 brings up Help on the command you're using

Clicking the Search button brings up a box that lets you specify the topic you want to search for. Type in the word or the first letter of the topic, or scroll through the list, and click on Search. Related topics appear in the box below. Then double-click on the topic you want to read about, or highlight it and click on GoTo.

If you want to backtrack through one or more topics you've recently read, click on the Backup key. Each press backs you up one topic through the list of topics you've already traversed.

The thing to remember is that the Help facility is context-sensitive, and that in addition to letting you easily look up a subject of interest, it will present information relevant to a command you are using. Thus, you can save time searching for a given topic by first selecting the command and then pressing the F1 key.

Using the Help Menu

You can also choose Help topics from 1-2-3's Help menu at the top of the 1-2-3 window. Just open the Help menu, and choose a

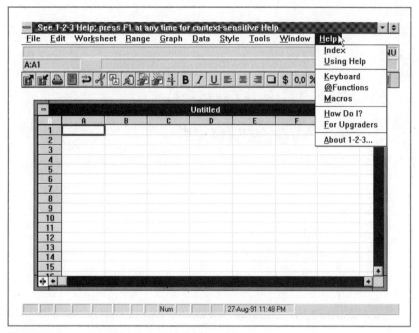

Figure 5.2: You can use the Help menu instead of F1

topic. Notice that some of the topics on the Help menu are also listed when you press the Index button on the Help screen. Figure 5.2 shows the menu and the commands listed on it.

For example, try the following:

① Open the Help menu.

② Choose Using Help. This menu item explains the Help system if you have forgotten how to use it or have questions about it. You will be presented with some basic information about the Help system. If you want some even more basic information, such as an index to topics about Help, press F1.

Since F1 always brings up Help about the program you're using, naturally enough, pressing F1 while in the Help system (which is actually a separate program) fetches some helpful information about it.

6 LESSON

Moving around the Worksheet

FEATURING

- The Active Cell
- Moving between Cells
- Scrolling

NOW THAT YOU KNOW YOUR WAY AROUND THE 1-2-3 window and how to get help when you're stuck, let's start experimenting with a worksheet. If the uses of some of the elements described in the last few lessons aren't clear to you yet, don't worry. Now you're ready to start learning through doing.

Rows, Columns, and Cells

Before we actually start moving around the worksheet, let's talk about worksheet structure. As I mentioned in the introduction, a worksheet consists of a series of columns and rows, with columns running vertically and rows running horizontally. Each column is named by a letter, and each row by a number. The spot where a column and row intersect is called a *cell*. A cell is a bit like a pigeonhole or a Post Office box. It has an exact location and address, and can store information. Thus, the cell in the upper left corner of Figure 6.1 is called

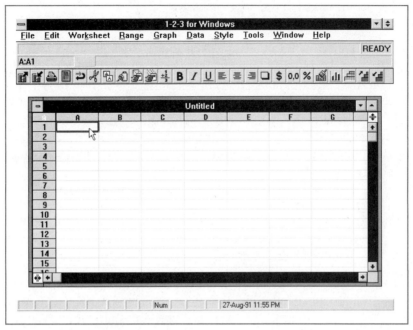

Figure 6.1: A blank 1-2-3 worksheet

cell A1 because it sits at the intersection of column A and row 1. Cell names and contents are the basis for all worksheet activities.

Rows are numbered from 1 to 8192, and columns are lettered from A to Z, then AA to AZ, BA to BZ, and so on to column IV (that's *eye-vee,* not Roman numeral 4). A worksheet that used every row and column would be over 2 million cells in size. If printed, this worksheet would require a piece of paper 21 feet wide and 130 feet long! Practically speaking, though, you would never create such a worksheet. The real number of cells you can have is determined by the amount of memory in your computer, the number of other documents you have open in Windows at the time, and the amount of information you put in each cell of your worksheet.

With so many variables, it's really impossible to say how large your worksheets can be, but suffice it to say that for typical worksheets, there is ample space. Obviously you need some means for moving around within your worksheets if you're going to get much work done.

*N*avigating through the Worksheet

As you work in 1-2-3, you will view your work through the worksheet window. Notice that in the upper left corner of the worksheet window cell A1 is highlighted. This means it is the *active cell*. There is always one active cell, and its address is indicated in the address box. Unless a cell is active, you cannot enter data into it.

Before beginning to type data into the new worksheet, try "navigating" through the cells, rows, and columns by following these steps:

① Move the active *cell pointer* (the highlight) around the spreadsheet using the ↑, ↓, →, and ← keys. If you have a mouse, you can just move the pointer and click on the cell you want to activate. Notice that the address box contents change to indicate the active cell.

② Press Ctrl-→ to "pan" right one screen at a time. The far left column letter jumps from A to I (on a standard VGA screen). Press Ctrl-← to pan to the left again. Now try pressing the Tab key and Shift-Tab for the same effects.

③ Press PgDn to scroll down to the next screenful of rows. PgUp has the reverse effect.

④ Now try using the scroll bars to move around worksheet. Click on the scroll arrows in the bars, or drag the scroll buttons in both scroll bars to their opposite ends.

⑤ Press End, then ↓. Then press End →. This takes you to the lower right corner of the entire matrix of cells. The address box should say IV8192, meaning column IV, row 8192.

⑥ You can move directly to a cell by choosing Range/Go To. Choose the command now. When the dialog box appears, type in A1 and click on OK (or press Enter). The highlight will jump to A1. Note that lowercase letters are OK when entering cell addresses. Incidentally, a shortcut to the Go To dialog box is to press F5.

When referring to a cells by name, type the letter first: C1, or FF23, not 1C or 23FF. If you reverse the order, you may get an error message, or sometimes you will get no response at all. Also, if you have more than one worksheet in your file (recall that you can have up to 256 per file), you can specify the sheet letter in advance of the cell address. For example, you would use the cell address B:A1 to get to cell A1 of sheet B. Since we're only using one worksheet at the present time, 1-2-3 assumes you want to go to A1 in worksheet A if you omit this part of the cell address.

7 LESSON

Entering Data

FEATURING

- Entering Labels
- Entering Values
- Entering Formulas

IN THIS LESSON, YOU'LL FINALLY GET TO BUILD A SMALL worksheet. This worksheet will contain each of the major data types in 1-2-3: labels, values, and formulas.

Elements of a Worksheet

Before we begin entering data into the worksheet, let's take one last look at the worksheet window in order to identify some of its parts, and consider what kind of information can be entered into a worksheet.

The Mode Indicator

Notice that just below the minimize and maximize buttons on the right side of the 1-2-3 window, there is a word that probably reads READY. This is the *mode indicator*. Whenever you're working in

1-2-3, the word here will keep you apprised of which of thirteen modes you're in. As you'll see, the current mode limits which options you have, or allows you to perform certain tasks that you otherwise couldn't.

READY mode means that 1-2-3 is waiting for you to choose a command or enter some data into the worksheet. 1-2-3 will be in this mode more often than other modes.

Cell Contents

Cells can contain two types of data: *labels* and *values*. Labels consist of nonmathematical information and cannot be used in calculations. Labels are typically used to make a worksheet easier for the viewer to comprehend. Row and column names are typical examples of labels, as are words like *Subtotal* and *Total*. Though labels usually consist of words, they can be numbers as well. For example, 1993, 10/12/93, or July 4 could all be labels. However, to instruct 1-2-3 to use a number as a label, you have to precede it with a single quotation mark (for example, '1993).

In contrast to labels, values consist of data to be calculated. Values also show the results of calculations. The numbers in a list to be added to get a total would be considered values, as would the total itself. Additionally, there are two types of values: *constants* and *formulas*. Constants are directly stated numbers, such as 149 and $369.99. Formulas are equations that produce numbers as a result of the formula, such as A1 + A2 + A3. In either case, the cell displays a numeric value. This is why formulas are considered values even though they may not look like values.

The meaning of constants is self-evident; however, unless you are familiar with spreadsheet programs, the formula described above may seem a bit mysterious. It's not really. Formulas have three possible parts to them:

Operators	Mathematical statements that perform calculations. For example, the addition, subtraction, multiplication, and division symbols (+ , − , *, /) are operators.

Functions	"Canned" equations that perform common calculations for you, such as trigonometric, financial, and date calculations. 1-2-3 has many built-in functions called @functions to make complex calculations easier for you.
Cell references	Notations that refer to the values in other cells. For example, the formula A1 + A2 + A3 uses references (joined by operators) to sum the values stored in cells A1, A2, and A3.

Experimenting with Cells

If you've just brought up 1-2-3, you'll already have a new, untitled worksheet waiting for you. If you've been experimenting with the one you have there, you'll want to open a new one by following step 1 of the exercise below. Otherwise, skip to step 2.

① Choose File/New. A new worksheet opens. Note that the name of the new sheet is something like FILE0002.WK3. We'll change the name later. This is a temporary naming convention 1-2-3 uses to create new files.

② Activate cell A1 if the cell pointer isn't already there.

③ Type in the words

   This is a test to see what can be typed into a cell

   Notice that as soon as you start, the mode indicator reads

   LABEL

   1-2-3 has figured out that you are entering a label rather than a value. Also, as you typed the words, those words appeared in the edit line. However, the words are not entered into the cell yet.

④ You may have noticed that two little squares, one with an X and one with a check mark, appeared to the left of the edit line. These are buttons you can click on to either OK or cancel your entry for the cell. Your words aren't entered into the cell until you either click on the check mark, press Enter, or press an arrow key to move the cursor to another cell. Do one of these to enter the data into the cell.

Once you do this, the words will appear on the worksheet, beginning in cell A1. Assuming you haven't entered anything in other cells of row 1, the whole line of words should now appear across the top line of your worksheet. Notice that the edit line now shows a single quote mark as the first character of the cell's contents. When 1-2-3 recognized the first character of your entry as a letter, it assumed that you intended this cell's contents to be a label, not a value. It then added the quote mark to identify the entry as a label. The quote mark is called a *label prefix character.* We'll discuss label prefix characters in more detail in Lesson 8.

You may also have noticed that the line you entered was longer than the cell's width and thus it now overlaps columns B, C, and D. 1-2-3 will always try to display the contents of a cell, regardless of how long it is. The entire contents of a cell will display on the screen as long as it doesn't run into another cell's data.

⑤ Now move to cell B1.

⑥ Type in **25** and enter it using one of the above techniques.

Notice that the edit line does not add a quotation mark. Also notice that only the words *This is a tes* remain visible in cell A1. Since B1 now has some data in it, A1's contents will not overlap it. But if you select A1 again, the edit line will still show the entire contents of the cell.

⑦ Move to A1. The edit line shows the entire contents of cell A1.

⑧ Move to C1.

⑨ Enter **+B1*4**. This is a formula which means "calculate this cell to equal the contents of B1 times 4." (In 1-2-3, the * sign signifies multiplication and, incidentally, the / sign is used for division.)

The first character you type tells 1-2-3 whether you're entering a value or entering a label. Typing in a number, or certain symbols such as

+ , -, (, ., @, #, or $, informs 1-2-3 that you're entering a value. Any other characters indicate a label. The plus sign tells 1-2-3 that you are not entering a constant value, but rather a formula, and that you want 1-2-3 to do some calculating for you. Notice that 1-2-3 calculates the cell as soon as you finalize the formula. The number 100 (the result of multiplying the value in cell B1—25—times 4) appears in cell C1.

(10) Move to B1, type **35**, and press Enter. In an instant, C1 recalculates to 140 since a cell in its formula has been altered.

(11) Just for fun, let's add one more formula in cell D1, which will multiply the cell C1 times 4. Move to D1.

(12) Type in **+C1*4** and enter it. The value 560 appears, which is 140 times 4.

Now try altering B1 by highlighting it and entering different numbers. Cells C1 and D1 will always recalculate to reflect the changes. This is the basic technique for doing "what-if?" calculations. If you enter some large numbers in B1, note that C1 and D1 may display the results of the multiplication in scientific notation such as

1.975E + 13

The E means that the answer has exceeded the mathematical accuracy of 1-2-3 (i.e., that the number has been rounded off), and the 13 means "to the 13th power." Rounding off occurs at 18 digits.

(13) Finally, move the highlight to cells C1 and D1 and notice what the edit line shows. Although the cell's contents is a calculated number (such as 560), the edit line doesn't show this number. Only the cell does. The edit line shows the formula in the cell, not its currently computed value.

(14) Move to cell B1. The edit line *does* show the same value as the cell. This is because B1 does not contain a formula but rather a constant numeric value.

If you'd like to take a break, exit 1-2-3 and Windows according to the instructions at the end of Lesson 2. Don't worry about saving the worksheet you just created; over the next few lessons we'll create a more detailed worksheet to be used throughout the book.

PART
2

Creating
a Worksheet

8 LESSON

Adding Labels to a Worksheet

1-2-3 WORKSHEETS ARE USED IN MANY BUSINESS AND engineering situations, but they are probably most commonly used to create business budgets. This is because you can quickly see the "bottom-line" effects of altering key variables in an annual or quarterly financial scenario. Most of the examples in this book, then, will focus on budgets. If you intend to use 1-2-3 for other purposes, that's OK. The budget worksheets you create will serve as a good learning experience. In the process of creating them, you'll learn all the essentials of 1-2-3 that you'd need to know for most other jobs.

Starting a New Worksheet

We're going to start with a rather simple quarterly budget worksheet, and as we progress to more advanced commands and operations, we'll expand upon it.

If you've just finished the previous lesson, you've been typing things into various cells on the worksheet. You'll want to clean up any cells you've typed into before we continue. You can do this by choosing File/New, or by following these steps:

① Activate any cell with a label or value in it.

② Press Del. This erases anything in the cell.

③ Repeat this process for all cells containing values or labels.

Entering Labels

One good way to get started with a new worksheet is to type in the labels approximately where you want them to be. This will help you decide if the layout of the worksheet makes sense and serve as a reminder of where you want the values entered. If you postpone entering the labels until you've entered some values, chances are good that you'll put some values in the wrong place.

Use these steps to enter the labels (we'll be moving them around and altering their looks later, so don't worry if you're not entering them in the same style or location you see in Figure 8.1):

① Click on the maximize button of the worksheet Window.

② Move to cell A1.

③ Type

   ABC INC.

and enter the data into the cell by pressing Enter or clicking on the check mark on the edit line. You may have noticed that as you typed, the mode indicator switched from READY to LABEL. This is because 1-2-3 automatically recognized your entry as a label. For the same reason, after you entered the label into the cell, 1-2-3 added a quote mark as the first character in the cell's data. This quote mark, which you can see by looking at the edit line, identifies the entry as a label.

④ Move to cell A2, and enter

   1993 Quarterly Budget Projection

Notice that the mode indicator displays VALUE rather than LABEL. This is because 1-2-3 recognizes that 1993 is a number, and it assumes you want to enter a value since the first character of the label is a number. Recall that 1-2-3 looks at the first character of an entry to determine whether it is a label or a value.

⑤ Try to finalize this cell's entry by pressing Enter or clicking on the check mark. You should hear a beep from your computer, and the mode indicator will switch to EDIT. EDIT mode allows you to make changes to the contents of a cell (we'll cover editing later). You're going to have to add one of the label prefix characters as the first character in this cell before it will be accepted as a label.

There are a number of possible label prefixes we could use. Each prefix affects the way the cell's contents will be displayed on screen and when it is printed, as listed below:

Label Prefix	Effect
'	Entry is left-aligned within cell.
"	Entry is right-aligned within cell.
^	Entry is centered within cell.
\	Repeats the characters to fill up the entire cell.

⑥ The mode indicator should read EDIT. (If it doesn't, press F2, the Edit key.) Now press the ← key. Notice that with each press the I-beam cursor (the blinking vertical line) moves left through the cell's data by one character. Keep pressing until the cursor is to the left of the 1 in 1993.

⑦ Type in a quote mark, since we want the text to be left-aligned within the cell.

⑧ Press Enter or click on the check mark to accept the modified cell data. Now the label appears in A2 as originally intended.

⑨ Move to cell A5 and type

Sales

and press ↓ to enter it. Notice that pressing the ↓ key enters the data and moves down to the next cell with just one key press. The other arrow keys work similarly.

⑩ Now go ahead and enter the other labels in column A, as shown in Figure 8.1. Press the ↓ key after making each entry to confirm the label and move down a cell.

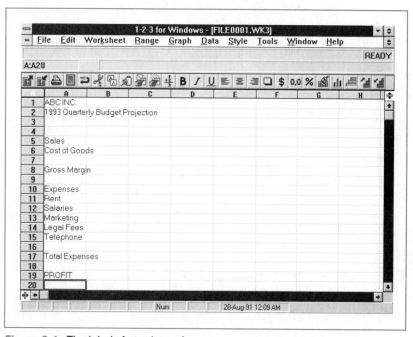

Figure 8.1: The labels for column A

*A*dding the Labels for the Remaining Columns

Next you're going to add the labels for each of the remaining five columns (B through F). Refer to Figure 8.2 to see what they'll eventually look like.

① Move the cell pointer to cell B3 and type

   "First Quarter

Notice that this time we used a double quote, so the label will be right-aligned. When we enter numbers in the column below the text, they will also be right-aligned.

② Press the → key to enter that data, and advance to cell C3.

③ In C3 enter

   "Second Quarter

④ In D3 enter

   "Third Quarter

⑤ In E3 enter

   "Fourth Quarter

⑥ In F3 enter

   "Total

⑦ Check the cells for errors now. Did you make any spelling errors, or enter any labels into the wrong cells? If you did, you can fix the errors by moving the highlight to the cell in question and retyping the correct label. When you press Enter, the old label will be replaced with the new one.

*F*illing Cells with a Repeating Character

You've probably noticed by now that some of the entries are within their cell boundaries. As a result, cells are starting to overwrite each other. Also, it looks as though the labels in column A are going to bump into the values that will eventually appear in column B. We'll take care of these spacing problems soon. First let's add the equals signs under each column head to illustrate how you enter repeating text. Then, having entered all labels for this worksheet, we'll move on to spacing adjustments.

① Move to cell B4. Type

   \ =

and press Enter. Immediately upon pressing Enter, the equals signs fill the cell's width. This is because the backslash is the label prefix that causes a character to be repeated across the cell.

② Repeat this process for cells C4, D4, E4, and F4.

Now your worksheet should look like Figure 8.2.

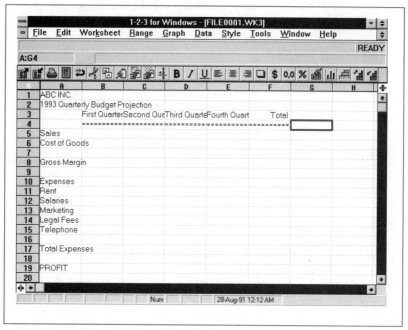

Figure 8.2: The Budget worksheet with all labels entered

If You Want to Take a Break

If you want to take a break at this point, or after any other lessons in this book, you should save your work first. To learn how to save your work, turn to the next lesson.

9 LESSON

Saving and Retrieving Files

FEATURING

- Naming a Worksheet
- Saving a Worksheet
- The File Save and File Open Icons

THE WORKSHEETS YOU CREATE WHILE IN 1-2-3 ARE NOT stored on your hard disk as you work. The operating system (DOS), along with Windows, programs you're running (such as 1-2-3), and the data files you might be working on, are all at least partially stored in your computer's RAM (Random Access Memory) while your computer is on.

It's important to understand that RAM, unlike a floppy disk or hard disk, loses the information in it when you turn off the computer. So, in order to save your work so that you can use it the next time you run 1-2-3, you must actually tell your computer to store your work safely on a floppy disk or hard disk. As a friend of mine once put it, RAM is like the blackboard in a classroom. If you don't take notes in class, you're going to lose the information on the blackboard when it's erased at the end of the day.

It's good practice to save your work often. Computers do malfunction from time to time, and occasionally the power to your workplace may go off unexpectedly, both of which can cause loss of data. If you save your work frequently, you stand less of a chance of losing it—whatever the reason. As a rule of thumb, I like to save my work about every 15 minutes or whenever I make changes that I would not easily remember how to recreate.

Saving Your Worksheets

The first time you save a file, it has to be given a name. The name tells DOS and your computer where to find the file the next time you want to use it. If you do not supply a name, 1-2-3 will assign one, but it will be a cryptic, meaningless name like FILE0004.WK3. This kind of name won't be much of a memory jogger when you're trying to reload a particular file later.

Each time you save a file, it is stored in a directory. If you had the install program copy the sample worksheet files onto your hard disk when you installed 1-2-3, the default directory will be 123W\SAMPLE. If you didn't install the sample files, your default directory will be 123W\WORK. The examples in this book assume your default directory is 123W\WORK. If your default directory is different, just substitute your directory name for the one used in the examples and figures.

Saving a File the First Time

Here's how to name a file the first time you save it. As an example, you'll save the worksheet you began working on in the last lesson. We'll call it BUDGET. You can use the same steps to save your future worksheets.

① Choose File/Save As. A dialog box appears, asking for the name of the file, as you see in Figure 9.1.

② Whenever you go to save a file, the default file name is highlighted. When text is highlighted in Windows dialog boxes, any key pressed will replace all the highlighted text. Thus, you want to be careful which keys you press. Since you probably don't want to retype the entire file and path name (the full path name of this worksheet would be C:\123W\WORK\BUDGET.WK3), it's better to just press

LESSON 9

the ← key, which removes the highlight and lets you edit the file's name.

③ Now press → again to move the cursor to the end of the name.

④ Use the Backspace key to eliminate the default file name (back to the \ after WORK), and type **BUDGET**, the worksheet's new name. You don't have to enter the extension of WK3 since 1-2-3 will add it automatically. The line should now read

C:\123W\WORK\BUDGET

⑤ Click on OK, and the worksheet file is saved and renamed as BUDGET.WK3. You can see the new name in the worksheet's title bar.

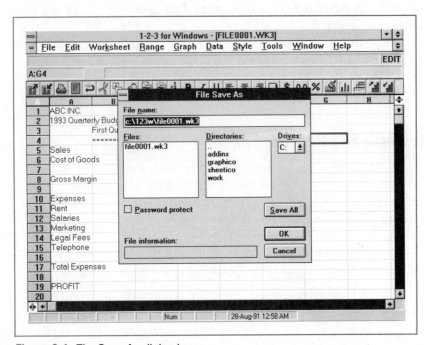

Figure 9.1: The Save As dialog box

If you need to change the directory you wanted to save to, you can type in the whole file name and path name. For example, the name

\EMILY\BUDGET.WK3

would put the file in the EMILY directory.

Another way to store a file in another directory is with the directory box, which is the large box on the right side of the Save As dialog box. You can move through your disk's directories by using this box. When you change directories this way, 1-2-3 types the directory's name for you up in the file name line, so you don't have to type it in. Also, when a directory is selected in the right-hand box, the worksheets in the directory are displayed in the left-hand box, so it's a way of seeing what files are already there. Double-click on the two dots (..) to back up one level in the directory tree, or double-click on a directory name to switch to it.

Saving Your Worksheet After It's Already Named

If you've already saved the file and given it a name, then saving is a simpler process. You don't have to deal with the file's name or the Save As dialog box.

Here's how to save a file once it's already named and saved once:

- Click on the File Save icon shown in Figure 9.2. The file will be saved.

Or

- Choose File/Save. This has the same effect.

File Save icon

File Open icon

Figure 9.2: The File Save and File Open icons

*A*utomatic Saving When Exiting 1-2-3 or Windows

If you want to quickly save your file and exit 1-2-3 at the same time, you can. If you choose File/Exit to close down 1-2-3 and you haven't saved your worksheet since making changes to it, 1-2-3 will ask you if you want to save your worksheets before it closes down.

① Choose File/Exit.

② 1-2-3 asks if you want to save changes to open worksheets that have changed since they were opened. Click on the Yes button to save the changes, or the No button to abandon them. Click on No if you don't care about changes you made, or if you definitely want 1-2-3 to ignore the changes you made and leave the file as it was before you started work on it. If you change your mind about exiting, click on Cancel.

*O*pening an Existing File

Once a file is stored on disk and you've shut down your computer, you'll have to reload it when you start up again. Here's how to open the Budget file. Use the same procedure for future files you create.

*O*pening a File with the File/Open Command

Here's how to open a file using the Open command from File menu:

① Bring up Windows, open the Lotus Applications Group window, and double-click on the 1-2-3 icon (or start 1-2-3 for Windows in some other way).

② Choose File/Open. The File Open dialog box appears, as you see in Figure 9.3.

③ Files in the default directory will appear in the file box. The default directory is normally C:\123W\WORK. Your drive

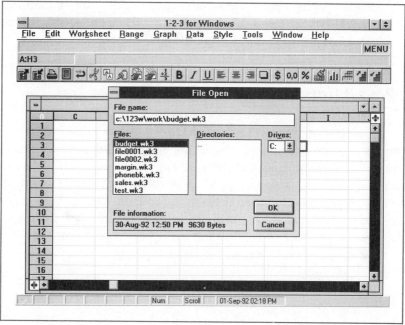

Figure 9.3: Opening a file

letter may be different, depending on which drive contains 1-2-3.

④ Among the files shown in the box should be your Budget file, BUDGET.WK3. If it isn't in view, scroll the file box until it is. If the wrong directory is being displayed, double-click on the correct directory in the directory box. If the drive is wrong, open the Drives list box by clicking on the small down-arrow to its side. Then you can choose the correct drive.

⑤ Click once on BUDGET.WK3. Notice that the File information box (bottom of the dialog box) indicates the file size, as well as the date and time when the file was last modified.

⑥ Click on OK or double-click on BUDGET.WK3 to open it. In a few seconds it will come up in the 1-2-3 window.

Since opening files is a common operation, there's an icon for doing it without the menu. Clicking on the File Open icon shown in Figure 9.2 has the same effect as choosing File/Open.

Taking It from Here

For the duration of this book, lessons will continue from one to the next as though you were working straight through without a break. You'll be building and using several worksheets in the process of the lessons, and of course, you'll probably want to stop from time to time. If you want to take a break at the end of a lesson, you should save your worksheet (unless told not to bother), and then retrieve it when you come back to the next lesson. If you forget how to save or retrieve files, just refer back to this lesson.

LESSON 10

Adjusting Column Widths

FEATURING

- The Column Width command

NOW THAT THE LABELS ARE CORRECTLY ENTERED, WE can make some adjustments that will allow you (and others) to see the labels clearly.

By default, column widths in a new worksheet are set to 9. As you know, if a cell contains text that exceeds this length, the complete text will still display so long as the cells to its right are empty. If the cells to the right are not empty, however, some of the text will be hidden. If the cell in question has numbers instead of text, the numbers will not show at all. Instead, asterisks will fill in the cell.

You can solve column-width problems in several ways. If you want all the cells in your worksheet to be wider, you can set the default width for all columns to a number larger than 9. This is done with the Global Settings command on the Worksheet menu. Or, if you only want to alter a few columns, you can do that manually, either from the Worksheet Column Width dialog box or by using the mouse. So that you get the hang of the basic techniques, we'll try them both in this lesson.

Changing a Column's Width Manually

We'll start by resetting the width of column A with the manual approach. First we'll use the mouse, then the Width dialog box.

Using the Mouse

Here's how to adjust column widths using your mouse:

① Each column has a left and a right border. Move the mouse pointer up to the column headings (above row 1) and position the pointer right on the border between the *A* and the *B*. The pointer should change into a left/right arrow.

② Press the left mouse button, keep it down, and move the mouse to the right. As you do so, column A widens. Release the mouse button when the size is approximately the same as you see in Figure 10.1. All the columns to the right of A will be pushed right, and the cells in column A will now have more room to display their contents.

Using the Worksheet Column Width Dialog Box

Now try using the dialog box method to adjust column A.

① Make sure the cell pointer is on any cell in column A.

② Choose Worksheet/Column Width. A dialog box appears, as you see in Figure 10.1. Type **12** in the Set Width To box and click on OK.

The column is now adjusted to 12 characters in width.

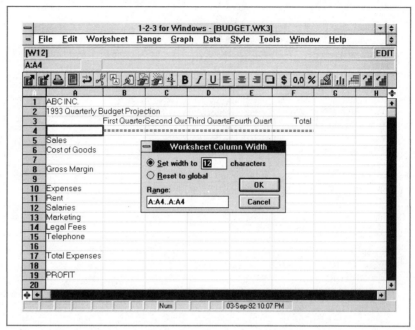

Figure 10.1: Setting the field width with the Worksheet Column Width dialog box

*C*hanging Column Widths *Globally*

If you know in advance that you want columns to all be a certain minimum width, you can set this "globally." Global settings are settings that affect the entire worksheet.

Let's set all the columns in the worksheet to 12 characters.

① Choose Worksheet/Global Settings. The Worksheet Global Settings dialog box appears.

② Type **12** into the Column width area. Look over the other areas of the box. As you see, you can globally preset other cell characteristics, such as label alignment, treatment of zeros, and format. We'll discuss these options in later lessons.

③ Click on OK, and the columns widen to appear as shown in Figure 10.2.

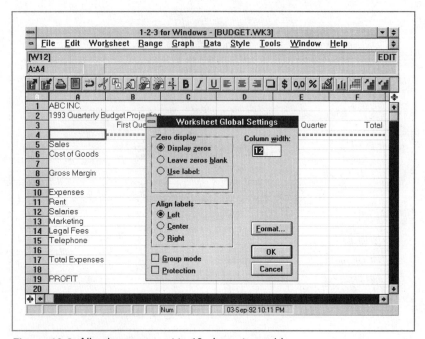

Figure 10.2: All columns are set to 12 characters wide

LESSON 11

Changing the Alignment of Text

FEATURING

- Selecting a Range of Cells
- Right Alignment of Labels
- Center Alignment of Labels
- SmartIcons

BY DEFAULT, 1-2-3 DISPLAYS LABELS WITH A LEFT alignment. This means that usually a label will abut the left side of its cell. You can see this state of affairs if you look back to Figure 10.2. All of the labels you entered in column A are aligned to the left. This is because you didn't precede these labels with one of the label alignment prefixes described in Lesson 8, so the default alignment is still in effect.

Adjusting a Single Label's Alignment

If after entering a label you decide you are dissatisfied with the default alignment, you can still change your mind. Let's adjust some of the cells we've already entered to improve their readability.

① Move the cell pointer to A5, which holds the label *Sales.* By highlighting cell A5, you are telling 1-2-3 that A5 is the cell you're going to adjust.

② Choose Style/Alignment. The Style Alignment dialog box appears.

③ Click on the Right radio button to activate it. Then click on OK.

Sales jumps to the right side of the cell. The alignment has been changed. Note that the edit line now reads *"Sales* instead of *'Sales.*

Changing the Alignment of a Range of Cells

You could use the above technique to alter the format of each cell you want realigned. However, if you have a block of contiguous cells to alter, there's an easier way.

A series of adjacent cells is called a *range.* A range can consist of as few as two cells or as many as two million, as long as the cells are adjacent. Just as a word processing program will let you select a series of words or sentences to copy, delete, or otherwise modify, 1-2-3 allows you to select a range of cells to modify in various ways. Changes you make will then affect all the cells in the selected range. Thus, if you need to alter the alignment of a series of adjacent cells, it's much faster to select the range first and then issue the applicable alignment command.

Since we want to right-align all the cells from A5 through A19, we can select them as a range and do it in one fell swoop.

① Move the mouse pointer to cell A5.

② Click and hold down the mouse button. Now drag the pointer vertically down the column, highlighting cells along the way. Notice how each cell touched by the pointer is included in a box. These cells become part of the selected range. Recall that this is called *dragging* the mouse.

③ Continue dragging until all the cells from A5 to A19 are selected, as shown in Figure 11.1. Then release the mouse button. Now cells A5 through A19 are a range.

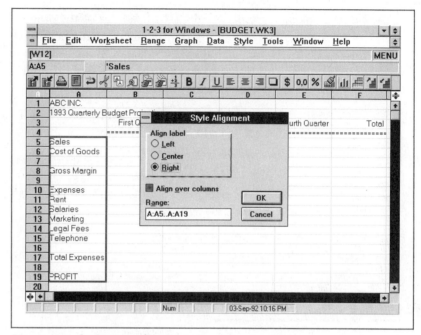

Figure 11.1: Setting the alignment of a range of cells

④ Choose Style/Alignment. From the dialog box, choose Right, just as you did before.

Notice that the Range box reads *A:A5..A:A19*. This line, which indicates the selected range, is entered in the dialog box automatically by 1-2-3. (Note that the *A:* means that all the cells in question are in the A worksheet. Recall that each worksheet file can hold 256 different worksheets, labeled A through IV.) Note, however, that ranges are always indicated by two cell names separated by two dots, such as A:B14..A:F29.

If you wanted, you could type in a different range yourself at this point, altering which cells would be affected by the alignment settings. This is useful if you don't have a mouse, or if you are selecting a range too large to be easily selected with the mouse.

⑤ Click on OK. The range realigns.

⑥ Now, as an example, let's realign the headings of the other five columns, even though we right-aligned them when we entered them. These headings are contained in the cells in the range B3..F3. This time, we'll select the range from the dialog box. Choose Style/Alignment again.

⑦ Click on the Range section of the dialog box (or use the Tab key to advance to it). Type in **B3..F3**. You can omit the worksheet letter; 1-2-3 will assume you are referring to the currently active worksheet, which is A.

⑧ Choose Left from the dialog box and then click on OK. Cells B3..F3 should become left-aligned.

⑨ Repeat steps 6 and 7 above and right-align the cells B3..F3 again.

Using the SmartIcons for Alignment

There is a third technique you can use for changing the alignment of cells, and it is the easiest if you have a mouse. This technique uses the icon palette. Try these steps as an experiment:

① Select the range A5..A19.

② Make sure your icon palette is showing. If it isn't, choose Tools/SmartIcons and click on the check mark in the Hide palette button. Then click on OK. The icon palette should now appear. (Its location on the screen depends on how the other buttons in the dialog box were set.)

③ With the range still selected, click on one of the three icons shown in Figure 11.2. Figure 11.2 also shows the effect of clicking on the Center icon. Try each one, just to see the effect. Each time you click on one of these icons, the range (or the current cell, if no range is selected) will be reformatted.

④ Leave the labels right-aligned when you're through experimenting.

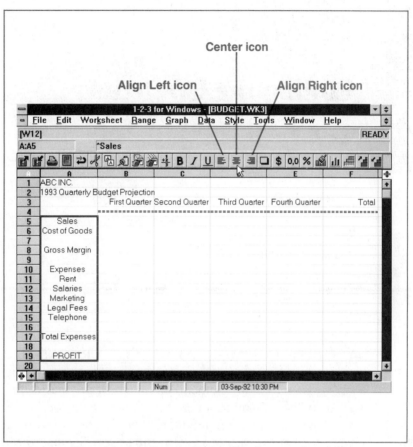

Figure 11.2: Changing cell alignment using the alignment icons

⑤ Save your work now by choosing File/Save. Then take a break or proceed to the next lesson.

12 LESSON

Editing the Contents of a Cell

FEATURING

- EDIT mode
- The I-Beam Cursor

IT'S QUITE COMMON TO DETECT ERRORS IN CELL contents after they've been entered, or to decide you want to modify a label for one reason or another. Perhaps the label doesn't fit into its cell and you don't want to widen the column, so you decide to abbreviate it. As you'll see, it's common that you'll want to develop and edit formulas as your worksheets evolve and as you "debug" them.

Up to now, you've made corrections to the labels you've input by simply retyping the entire label. However, retyping an entire cell just to make a few changes to a formula, a value, or label can be tedious and introduces chances for additional typing errors.

Therefore, 1-2-3 has an EDIT mode, which you toyed with briefly when attempting to enter the label in cell A2 that starts with the number 1993. When you tried to enter this label, 1-2-3 automatically went into EDIT mode. You also used EDIT mode to add the ' label prefix. This lesson describes EDIT mode in a little more detail.

Using EDIT Mode

Using EDIT mode is simple. You highlight the cell you want to work with and press F2. As an alternative, you can double-click on the cell. An I-beam text cursor appears in the edit line, allowing you to edit the contents of the cell. In EDIT mode, the arrow keys on the keyboard change function: They no longer allow you to move between cells; instead, they let you move between characters on the edit line. You can also use the Backspace and Del keys to eliminate unwanted letters and numbers. As you type in new characters, all characters to the right of the cursor are pushed to the right. When you're finished, pressing Enter or clicking on the check mark accepts the changes. Pressing Esc or clicking on the X leaves the cell's contents as it was before you started editing.

To demonstrate EDIT mode, let's abbreviate the column headings in columns B, C, D, and E. You may have noticed that the labels in these cells are a little tight, especially in cell C5, which runs right up against its neighbors. Of course, we could globally widen the columns to 12, but then we wouldn't be able to see the entire worksheet at once (on a VGA screen using the default font of 10-point Arial).

Editing Labels, Numbers, and Formulas

Editing is the same whether you're changing a value, formula, or a label. We haven't created any formulas yet, but just keep in mind that editing them is the same as editing labels and values. You'll be modifying formulas later.

Let's say we want to abbreviate the column headings to read as follows: *1st Quarter, 2nd Quarter, 3rd Quarter, 4th Quarter.* Follow these steps:

① Activate cell B3.

② Press F2, the Edit key. The mode indicator changes to EDIT. The I-beam cursor appears at the end of cell B3's contents. (Notice that 1-2-3 has changed the usual single quote to a double quote. It did this when you realigned this cell to right-aligned.)

③ Press the ← key eight times, which puts it just to the right of the word *First*.

④ Now use the Backspace key to erase *First*. Take care not to erase the double-quote mark, since that's needed to prevent 1-2-3 from thinking you're entering a value.

⑤ Type in **1st**. The edit line should now read *1st Quarter.*

⑥ Press Enter or click on the check mark to finalize the change. The mode indicator changes back to READY.

Additional Editing Tricks

1-2-3 also recognizes several editing tricks drawn from the standard Windows repertoire for text editing. For example, you can select a word by double-clicking on it. Then whatever you type next will immediately replace the highlighted word. You can also select a portion of text by dragging the mouse cursor over it, or by holding down the Shift key and pressing the → or ← key to extend the selection from the point where the cursor is positioned.

Try these steps to illustrate:

① Move to cell C3.

② Press F2 to switch to EDIT mode.

③ In the edit line (not in the cell), double-click on the word *Second. Second,* along with its label prefix character, becomes highlighted.

④ Whatever you type in at this point will replace the high-lighted text. Type

2nd

Now the edit line reads *2nd Quarter*. Notice that the cell does not yet change.

⑤ Accept the changes by pressing Enter, pressing an arrow key, or clicking on the check mark. (From now on, whenever I say "Accept the changes," take one of these three actions.

At other times, I may just say "Enter _____ in cell _____" to mean you enter the data and accept it.) The change now registers in the cell.

⑥ Move to D3.

⑦ Press F2. In the edit line, position the I-beam between the " mark and the word *Third*. Instead of using the arrow keys, this time use the mouse to position the I-beam. Just position the cursor and click. The I-beam will drop into the text at the point where you click.

⑧ Press the Del key. Each press gobbles up one letter to the right of the I-beam. This is just like Backspace, only backwards. (Backspace gobbles to the left.) Press the Del key enough times to eliminate *Third*, then type

3rd

⑨ Accept the changes.

⑩ Move to E3 and press F2. In the edit line, position the cursor just before the word *Fourth* (after the "). Press the Shift key and hold it down. Now press the → key several times. As you do, letters are highlighted. Keep the Shift key down and press → enough times to highlight all of *Fourth*. Then release Shift.

⑪ Type:

4th

This replaces the highlighted text.

⑫ Accept the changes.

Instead of using the Shift-key approach, you can drag the I-beam cursor over the text you want to select. As long as you hold the mouse button down, dragging the cursor over text selects it. Once selected, you can delete it with Del, or replace it with text you type in. You can also press Shift-Ctrl-→ to select text one word at a time.

Your worksheet should now look like Figure 12.1.

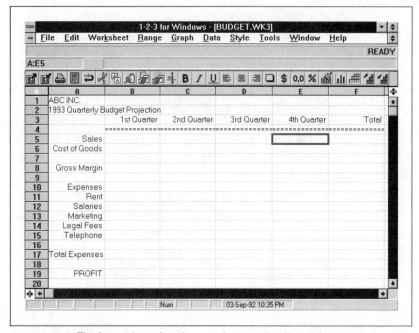

Figure 12.1: _The four column heads now shortened to fit comfortably in the cells_

LESSON | 13

Oops! Using Undo to Reverse a Mistake

FEATURING

- The Edit/Undo Command
- The Undo Icon
- Disabling Undo

HOW MANY TIMES HAVE YOU DONE SOMETHING ON your computer that you instantly realized was a big mistake? Maybe you just deleted the contents of a cell (or even a whole range of cells), or edited the wrong cell. Luckily, these and even more catastrophic mistakes you unwittingly make to your worksheets can be reversed using 1-2-3's Undo command.

Reversing mistakes isn't the only thing you can do with Undo. You can also try out an option, make a formatting change, or try a numeric value, just to see the results. If you don't like them, you can just issue the Undo command and whatever you were working on will be returned to its previous state. This is obviously more convenient than typing the old value or formula again or resetting the formatting.

You can access the Undo command in three ways: from the icon palette, from the Edit menu, and by typing Alt-Backspace. Undo will reverse most commands, though there are some it won't. The most important exceptions are the commands on the File menu. For example, once you make changes to a worksheet file and use File/Save to save it on disk, the old file is overwritten. This can't be reversed with Undo, although if you've made a backup file, you should be able to retrieve the old file.

To work through this lesson, you must enable the Edit/Undo command. To see if Undo is enabled, open the Edit menu. If Undo is dimmed, follow these steps to enable it:

① Choose Tools/User Setup.

② Turn on the Enable Undo button.

③ Click on Update.

④ Click on OK.

Experimenting with Undo

Try these examples of undoing mistakes:

① Move the cell pointer to B5.

② Enter **5000** into the cell.

③ Move the cell pointer to another cell.

④ Choose Edit/Undo. Undo removes the value from B5.

Notice that even though the cell pointer was moved to another cell, 1-2-3 remembered what the last important action was (moving the cell pointer doesn't qualify).

① Now enter **45000** into B5.

② Enter **Hello** into the same cell.

③ Choose Edit/Undo. Notice that B5 is returned to its previous value of 45000.

④ Try to choose Edit/Undo again. You can't, because it is grayed out. Alas, you can't undo the effects of the Undo command. Only the latest action you performed can be undone. Once you use another command, including Undo, or enter or edit a cell, you've lost the chance to undo the previous action.

Now let's try another example, one potentially more cata-strophic. Before doing this exercise, save your work with File/Save, just in case.

① Select the range from A1 to F19.

② Choose Edit/Clear. This command is used to clear the contents of the highlighted cell or range. In this case, all our work will be erased from the worksheet.

③ Click on the Undo icon shown in Figure 13.1 this time (or, if you are not using a mouse, choose Edit/Undo). All the labels should now reappear.

④ Click on any cell or press one of the arrow keys to deselect the range.

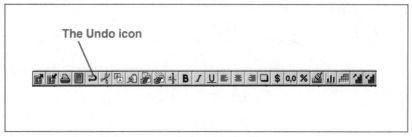

The Undo icon

Figure 13.1: The Undo icon

About Undo and Dialog Boxes

In addition to reinstating cell data that has been changed or deleted, Undo can remember the settings in the many dialog boxes of 1-2-3. Whenever you make changes in a dialog box, 1-2-3 stores a copy of the old dialog box settings in memory, just in case you decide you want to undo them. Then, if you choose Undo, all the changes you just made in the dialog box are undone. This is just like clicking on Cancel in the dialog box, only in this case you've accidentally clicked on OK and said, "Oops! I shouldn't have done that."

LESSON 13

Turning Off Undo

Undo uses your computer's memory area to store information. For example, when you deleted all the cells in the worksheet, they were temporarily stored in your computer's memory chips (RAM) so that you could change your mind and recall them. However, holding this information slows down 1-2-3 a little bit and consumes more memory. If you're getting low-memory messages from 1-2-3, you may want to disable the Undo feature to see if there is any improvement. Adding memory is really the better solution, but disabling Undo may help. If you do disable Undo, keep in mind that once you make a mistake, there's no fixing it.

① Choose Tools/User Setup.

② Turn off the Enable Edit Undo check box by clicking on it with the mouse.

③ Click on Update if you want Undo to be disabled in future 1-2-3 sessions.

④ Select OK in the dialog box.

To reenable Undo, open the dialog box once more and turn the check box on.

LESSON 14

Entering Numbers

FEATURING

- VALUE Mode

NOW YOU ARE READY TO ADD NUMBERS TO YOUR worksheet. You'll be adding formulas in Lesson 15, but we'll start with "constant values" (unchanging numbers) first, so that the formulas have numbers to work with.

Take a look at Figure 14.1 to get an idea of where you're going to enter the numbers. These values are the various first quarter earnings and expenses for ABC Inc.

Entering the Values

Enter the values for the first quarter by following these steps:

① Move to cell B5. Enter **8000.**

Notice that as you type, the mode indicator changes to VALUE, since the first character you typed was a number. Typing any number, the symbols +, −, (, ., @, #, $, or any other currency symbol signals 1-2-3 that you are entering a value.

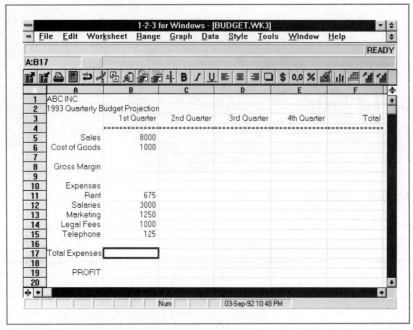

Figure 14.1: Constant values for the first quarter

② Move to B6 and enter **1000**.

③ Go ahead and enter the other cells as you see them in Figure 14.1.

Notice that even though these are dollar amounts, 1-2-3 displays them as plain numbers, with no commas or dollar signs. Obviously 1-2-3 doesn't know that you are entering dollar amounts. By default, 1-2-3 uses a simple format of no commas and no decimal places for numbers. Later, we'll change these cells to a format more appropriate for currency.

If you want numbers in your own worksheets to have another format, such as scientific notation, fixed decimal length, or currency, you can change the default format with the Worksheet/Global Settings/Format command. Then any values you enter will use that format. However, for most uses, the default setting (called General) works fine. In General format, numbers are right-justified with no assumed decimal places. Additionally, very large and very small numbers are shown in scientific notation.

So far, you've entered all the constant values for the first quarter. As for the other three quarters, we'll deal with them soon by copying the cells from the first quarter over to the other columns. In the meantime, notice that the Gross Margin, Total Expenses, and Profit cells are still empty. That's because those cells will contain totals to be calculated by 1-2-3. Thus, they need formulas in them. You'll see how to add formulas to the worksheet in Lesson 15.

15 LESSON

Entering Formulas

FEATURING

- Numeric Formulas
- The @SUM Function
- The Sum Icon

SO FAR, YOU HAVEN'T DONE MUCH WITH YOUR worksheet that couldn't have been done with a word processor: You've created a table containing a series of columns and then added a few numbers and a few labels. The real power of 1-2-3 only becomes evident when you begin entering formulas or @functions that calculate the values you've entered into your worksheet. Then the worksheet begins to operate like a big, customized calculator.

Formulas resemble mathematical equations, and thus look different from labels. You can create formulas that perform operations as simple as adding a column of numbers or as complex as calculating a loan amortization table or the net present value of a series of future cash flows.

You've already experimented a bit with some simple formulas in Lesson 7. You may recall that, unlike labels or constant values, the formulas aren't displayed in their cells, but rather the results of the formula's calculations are. The formula itself appears only on the edit line.

The Elements of a Formula

Numeric formulas are the formulas you'll work with most often. You've already experimented with some numeric formulas using cell data. For example, the formula +A1*A2 multiplies the value in cell A1 by the value in cell A2. You can also enter constant values into formulas: 6+2, for example, would be a valid formula.

Numeric formulas use a combination of arithmetic operators (+, −, *, /, and ^, for addition, subtraction, multiplication, division, and exponentiation, respectively). They can also contain @functions, which are formulas built into 1-2-3 that perform common calculations automatically.

To enter a formula into a cell, you always follow the general steps listed below. For now, just read these steps to get a feel for entering formulas. Don't worry about entering specific values just yet; we'll get to that in a moment.

① Enter a plus sign (+). This signals 1-2-3 that you are going to enter a formula. The mode indicator changes to VALUE.

② Type in the first *operand*. Operands, which can be either numbers or cell addresses, are the values that you want to calculate.

③ Then enter an operator (such as +, −, *, or /). Operators tell 1-2-3 what mathematical operations it should perform.

④ Enter the second operand.

⑤ Repeat this process until the formula is complete. Figure 15.1 shows a model formula constructed according to these steps.

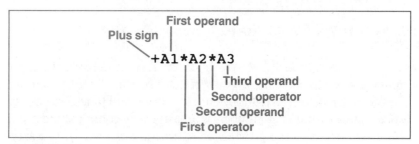

Figure 15.1: A model 1-2-3 formula

Once you enter a formula, the result will be calculated immediately and displayed in the cell containing the formula, down on the worksheet. If the result won't fit in the cell, 1-2-3 will display the number in scientific notation (if possible) or as a string of asterisks. You'll have to widen the column to see the value of the number.

Entering Simple Formulas

With that understanding, let's enter the simple formulas that will calculate the gross margin, total expenses, and profit.

① Begin by selecting cell B8, the Gross Margin cell. Since gross margin means "the difference between the income from sales and the cost of the products sold," we need to subtract the Cost of Goods cell (B6) from the Sales cell (B5) to determine what the gross margin is. Type in

+ B5 − B6

and confirm the entry.

② As soon as you confirm the entry, 1-2-3 calculates the gross margin at 7000, since that's 8000 minus 1000. Now move to cell B17. Since this cell is going to show total expenses, we need to add cells B11, B12, B13, B14, and B15. The formula should be

+ B11 + B12 + B13 + B14 + B15

so enter that formula there. The sum of those cells is quickly calculated when you confirm the entry, totalling 6050.

Using the @SUM function

For illustration, I had you enter the last formula in the most cumbersome way. Imagine if you were adding a really long column. Typing in the all the cell names would be boring and time-consuming. Since adding columns of numbers is an extremely common operation within worksheets, 1-2-3 provides an @function to make writing such calculations simpler.

This function is called the @SUM function, and it simply adds a list of values that you specify. You can specify a series of cells by listing just the first and last cells in the series, as long as they are in a row or column. (Recall from Lesson 11 that this is called a *range*.) This beats typing in each cell's name as you just did. You can enter the @SUM function through the keyboard or with the mouse.

*E*ntering an *@SUM Function Manually*

To enter an @SUM formula through the keyboard, you type in the characters *@SUM* followed by the reference of the range you want to sum. Thus, the cells you used in your last formula, B11 through B15, would be written as range *B11..B15*. Let's go ahead and try it.

① Move back to cell B17.

② Type

   @SUM(B11..B15)

and confirm the entry. Notice the sum of 6050 is the same, even though the edit line now shows the new formula.

Keep this trick in mind. Remember that when specifying a range of cells to sum that they must be contiguous—all in a row. There can, however, be blank cells in the range.

You can sum a horizontal range of cells, a vertical range, or a larger rectangular range of many cells. For example, the following @SUM formulas are acceptable:

@SUM(A1..A10)	vertical range summation
@SUM(A1..F1)	horizontal range summation
@SUM(A1..F10)	rectangular range summation

*U*sing the Summation Icon

Though the @SUM function is a pretty nifty time-saver when working with columns, you can use an icon to add values even faster. The

Sum icon is the icon that displays the equation $1 + 2 = 3$, as shown in Figure 15.2. Clicking on this icon adds the column of numbers nearest the current cell. You don't even have to type anything in. Let's try it.

① Move to cell B17.

② Delete the formula there by pressing Del. Cell B17 should now be blank.

③ Position the mouse pointer on the Sum icon in the palette. (If the icon palette isn't showing, turn it on with the Tools/ SmartIcons command.)

④ Click and hold down the right mouse button, and read the text that appears in the title bar (top line) of the 1-2-3 window. It reads:

    Sum the nearest adjacent range

⑤ Release the right button. Now click normally (left button) on the icon.

Notice that the edit line immediately shows the formula

@SUM(B11..B15)

1-2-3 was smart enough to guess that you wanted to add up the nearest column of numbers. It also left out cell B16, since that cell is empty.

Obviously, using the Sum icon is the easiest way to enter formulas for adding columns of numbers. The Sum icon will sum the nearest adjacent range containing values, whether the cells are arranged horizontally or vertically (vertically arranged cells will take precedence if two ranges are adjacent to the current cell). To avoid

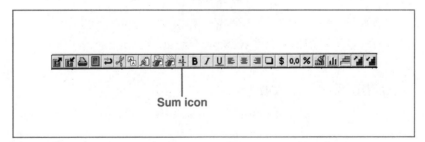

Sum icon

Figure 15.2: *The Sum icon*

ambiguity in a case like this, select the range you want to sum, including the blank cell at the end of the range, and click on the icon.

Calculating the Profit

The last step in completing the 1st Quarter column is to calculate the profit made. This is figured by subtracting the total expenses from the gross margin.

① Move to cell B19.

② Since B8 contains the gross margin and B17 contains the total expenses, you should enter the formula

   + B8 – B17

③ Confirm it. The value 950 now appears in B19. Looks like the company cleared only $950 in the first quarter.

Note that even though B8 and B17 have formulas in them, their calculated values are what is used by the formula in B19. In this way, cells can reference other cell's calculated values in a sort of "domino effect."

Worksheets containing hundreds of cells that are dependent on each other in this way are not uncommon. But, as you can imagine, it's of critical importance that your formulas be correct. If a formula near the top of the chain is wrong, all cells further down the chain will display erroneous calculations.

Now that the first quarter's column is finished, your screen should look like Figure 15.3.

LESSON 15

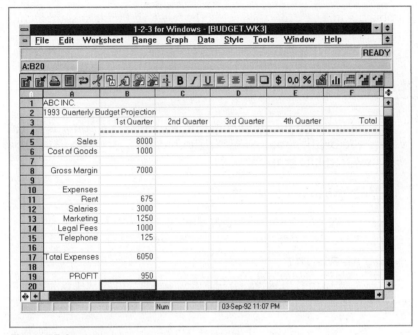

Figure 15.3: *The first quarter's column completed*

PART
3

Manipulating
Your Worksheet

16 LESSON

Moving and Copying Cells

FEATURING

- Copying a Range
- Moving a Range
- Relative References
- Converting to Values

AT THIS POINT, THE ABC INC. BUDGET HAS ONLY ONE OF four quarters' figures entered and calculated. That's the bad news, since it took quite a few operations to get that far. The good news is that the bulk of the remainder will mirror what's in column B. So, with a little sleight of hand, you can capitalize on what you've already done.

Copying a Range to a New Location

Now we're going to fill in the data for the 2nd, 3rd, and 4th Quarters columns by copying the existing column, complete with its formulas and values, to three new positions.

A short discussion of copying is in order first, though. There are two different ways to copy material in 1-2-3. The Edit/Copy technique uses the Windows Clipboard. The advantage of using the Clipboard is that it allows you to copy material from a 1-2-3 worksheet into documents created with other programs, such as word processing programs, database programs, or even other spreadsheet programs.

The other technique, called Edit/Quick Copy, does not use the Clipboard. Its advantage is that it's faster. If you don't need to transfer information from your worksheet into other types of documents, then it's best to use Edit/Quick Copy.

Both commands work in about the same way. You just select the range or cell you want to copy and invoke the appropriate copy command. You then tell 1-2-3 where to place the copied data. Let's try copying the data in the cells in column B to column C.

① Select the range from B5 to B19 by dragging over it with the mouse.

② Choose Edit/Quick Copy, and the Edit Quick Copy dialog box appears. Notice that the mode indicator changes to POINT. When in POINT mode, 1-2-3 is waiting for you to indicate a cell location for some operation such as copying or moving.

③ Notice that the From text box contains the range you just selected, A:B5..A:B19, but that the To text box reads A:B5. If you clicked OK now, you would copy the range of cells to their current location, in essence replacing the range with itself. (Only the cell in the upper left corner of the destination range need be indicated when copying or moving ranges: 1-2-3 figures out the rest.) So, delete B5 from the To text box and enter the upper left cell of the destination range:

C5

If you prefer, you can type in the entire range:

C5..C19

Incidentally, if you don't have a mouse you can enter both the From range and the To range through the dialog box, skipping step 1 above.

④ Click on OK. The contents of B5..B19 are copied to C5..C19, as shown in Figure 16.1.

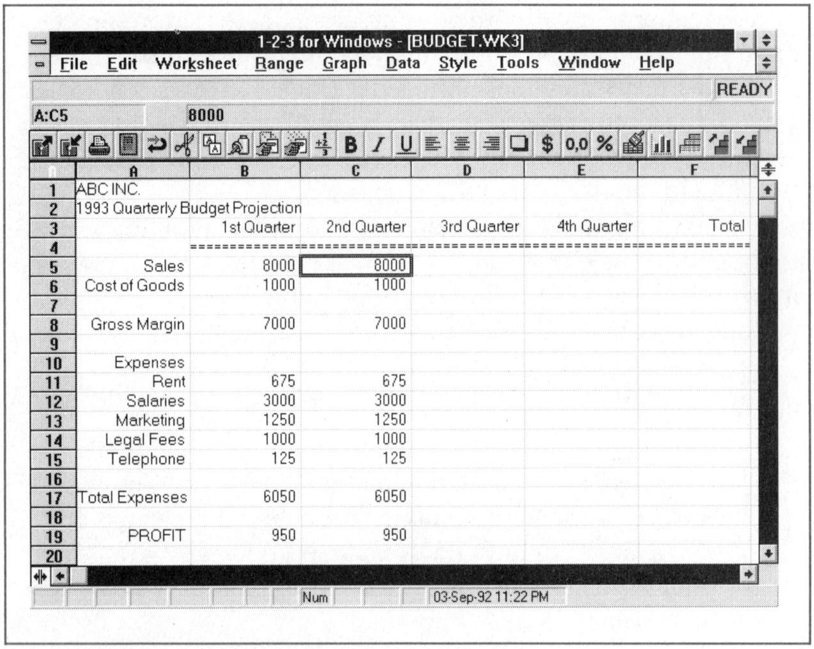

Figure 16.1: Range B5..B19 copied to C5..C19

About Relative Cell Adjustments

Copying formulas from one column to another raises an interesting question. Aren't there formulas in some of the cells we just moved that are going to have to be changed? Consider the formula that calculates the gross margin for the second quarter, which is now in C8. The formula you just copied from B8 to C8 was

+ B5 – B6

Obviously this won't reflect the gross margin for the second quarter if we change the values in C5 or C6. Or will it?

Move to cell C8 and check its formula. It reads

+ C5 – C6

How did this happen? Well, 1-2-3 assumed that when copying a range to another column that you wanted it to adjust the formulas accordingly. It adjusted the formulas by using *relative cell references.*

When a formula contains relative references, it means that the cell names in the formula refer to the positions of other cells *relative to* the cell containing the formula. Thus, when cell B8, containing the equation + B5 − B6, was copied to cell C8, the reference to cell B5 changed to C5 and the reference to B6 changed to C6.

Relative references are the most common type of references used in electronic worksheets, because, more often than not, the formulas in a row or column refer to other cells in the same row or column—not in other rows or columns. So, unless otherwise informed, 1-2-3 assumes you want relative references and adjusts the pointers in formulas it copies.

There is another type of reference, called an *absolute reference.* You use absolute references to tell 1-2-3 not to adjust the pointers in formulas when copying cells, but rather to leave them as they are. This way you can "borrow" key values from specific cells elsewhere in the worksheet. You can also mix relative and absolute references, creating what's called "mixed" references. You'll learn about using absolute cell references later. For now, let's continue copying in order to finish the other two quarters' columns.

Using the SmartIcon to Copy Cells

As you might have suspected, copying is a common operation when building worksheets. Thus, there's an icon on the icon palette that makes copying a simple process. Let's copy column D (3rd Quarter) using the icon.

1. Select C5..C19.

2. Click on the Range Copy icon, shown in Figure 16.2.

3. Now move the cursor back into the worksheet window. Notice that the cursor has changed its shape to that of a pointing finger. Point to the upper left cell of the destination range. In this case, of course, it's D5. Click on D5. The copy is completed, and the new cell data appears on the worksheet. Of course, the formulas are copied too, with relative references adjusted as necessary. Your screen should now look like Figure 16.3.

LESSON 16

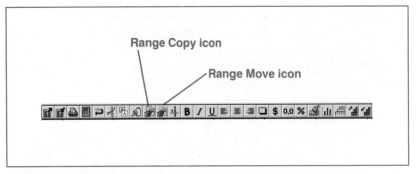

Figure 16.2: *The Range Move and Range Copy icons*

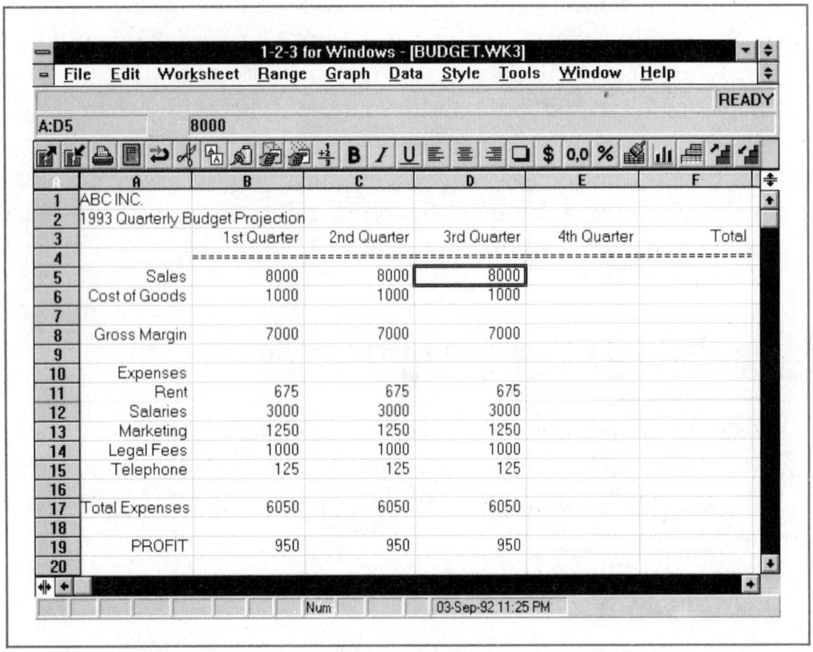

Figure 16.3: *Three of four columns are complete*

*M*oving Cells

Moving cells around is also very common, especially when you're first setting up a worksheet. I had to move cells around quite a bit when building the example worksheet, for example, in order to get everything to fit properly on the screen for the purposes of illustration. The process for moving a cell or a range is almost identical to that used for copying. Instead of copying the cells in Column D to column E, as you might expect at this point, let's move them. We'll use the icon to get the job done quickly.

① Select D5..D19.

② Click on the Range Move icon.

③ Click on cell E5. Notice that D5..D19 has now jumped to the new location.

④ Select the range again, and move it back to D5..D19 using the same technique.

Copying with the Clipboard

If you need to copy the same material more than once, you'll want to use the Edit/Copy and Edit/Paste commands. As I mentioned earlier, this technique utilizes the Windows Clipboard as a temporary storage area for data when copying between locations. Using the Clipboard has several advantages. For example, you can copy into other programs that will accept data from the Clipboard. You also have the option of copying the contents of the Clipboard more than once within 1-2-3. This is because the Clipboard hangs onto its contents until you replace it with something else by using the Edit/Cut or Edit/Copy commands.

Just so you know how to do it, now we're going to copy the range C5..C19 twice.

① First delete the range D5..D19 by selecting it and pressing Del.

② Select C5..C19.

③ Choose Edit/Copy. This puts the data into the Clipboard. It may take a few seconds for Windows to store the cells' data.

④ Click on D5 to indicate the starting point where we're going to copy in the data.

⑤   Choose Edit/Paste. The cells are "pasted" into the worksheet beginning at D5.

⑥   Move to cell E5 now. Choose Edit/Paste again. The cells
are pasted again. If you examine the contents of the calculated cells (D8, D17, D19, E8, E17, E19), you'll see that
the relative references were adjusted correctly as well.

Copying Values Only

There may be times when you don't want to copy the formulas in
a given range to the destination cells, but you still want to copy the
values that are the results of the formulas themselves. You can achieve
this with the Edit/Quick Copy command.

①   Delete the contents of cells E5..E19.

②   Select D5..D19.

③   Choose Edit/Quick Copy.

④   From the dialog box, turn on the Convert To Values check
box.

⑤   Enter **E5** (or **E5..E19** if you prefer) in the To section.

⑥   Click on OK. The cells appear to be copied, just as they were
before. However, appearances are deceptive.

⑦   Move to cell E8 and look at the edit line. It says 7000. It
used to say +E5−E6, just as D8 contains the formula
+D5−D6. As you can see, the formula was deleted from
the cell, leaving only its numeric value.

⑧   Now let's replace just the cells that have lost their formulas.
You know how to copy a range of cells already. Now use the
same technique to copy individual cells: Click on D8, then click
on the Move icon. Move the finger pointer to E8 and click.
Repeat this to copy D17 and D19 to E17 and E19, respectively.

*C*opying and Moving Tips

Here are some tips to consider when copying or moving cells.

- If you copy or move cells into an area that contains existing data, that data will be erased and overwritten. Keep this in mind especially when copying ranges. Since you can specify the destination of a copied or moved range by its upper left corner only, it's easy to forget how many cells the copied or moved range is going to overwrite. Make sure there are enough empty cells to accept the new data. You may have to move some other cells to make space. If you accidentally move or copy data into cells that already contain data, the Undo command will reverse your mistake, but you must use it before doing anything else.

- You can replicate a single cell's data over a large range of cells. To do so, select one cell and use the Edit/Quick Copy dialog box in order to stipulate a range as the destination. All the cells in the range will be stuffed with the contents of the single source cell. We could have used this feature, for example, to draw the line of equal signs (= = = =) across our budget worksheet more easily. We'd have entered \ = into B4, then used Edit/Quick Copy to copy it to the range C4..F4.

- When you use either Edit/Quick Copy or Edit/Copy followed by Edit/Paste; 1-2-3 will adjust relative cell references. However, when moving cells, things are different. References will only be adjusted by the Edit/Move Cells command. Edit/Cut followed by Edit/Paste does not adjust cell references. Therefore, it's best to use the Edit/Move Cells command when you are moving cells around the worksheet.

LESSON

Calculating Sums Horizontally

NOW YOUR FOUR QUARTERLY COLUMNS ARE COPIED and functional. Of course, many of the cell values, such as expenses and sales, are not necessarily going to be equal from quarter to quarter. But as a starting point, it was easier to replicate the cells from the first quarter than to enter them separately.

For the sake of having a more realistic model to work from, let's use the techniques you learned in Lesson 12 to edit the values of your cells, so that your worksheet looks like Figure 17.1. Remember that the formula cells in rows 8, 17, and 19 needn't be changed manually, since they can already calculate the new values you enter.

Summing Up the Totals

Having generated a more realistic worksheet, let's finish entering the data by adding formulas to column F. These formulas will reflect the total sales, costs of goods, gross incomes, and other

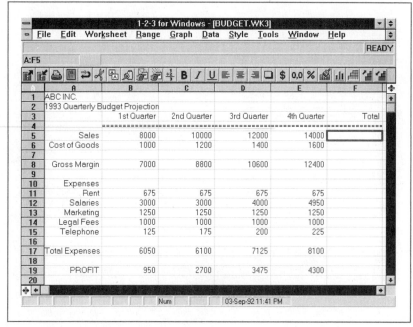

Figure 17.1: The edited worksheet

expenses for the entire year. Do the following to complete the column:

① In F5, we want the sum of B5..E5. Can you think of how to do this with no typing? The easiest way is to move to E5 and click on the Sum icon; 1-2-3 will look for the nearest cells to add up. (If you want to do it the long way, enter **@SUM(B5..E5)** into F5.)

② There are several ways to enter the summation formulas for the remaining cells. The easiest one is to use Edit/Quick Copy to copy cell F5 to cells F6 to F19. 1-2-3 will adjust the formulas appropriately. If you can't recall how to copy cells, refer back to the Lesson 15. Your worksheet should now look like Figure 17.2.

Notice that there are a few extra zeros that need cleaning up. These zeros are the result of formulas that have references to empty cells, and they are the price we paid for taking a shortcut and copying

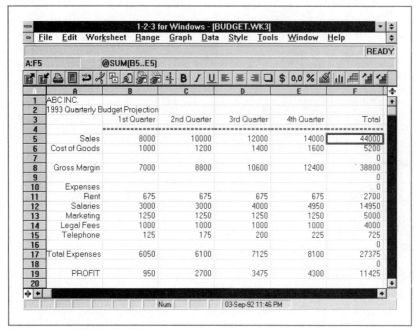

Figure 17.2: *Totals calculated*

cell F5 into the entire range from F6 to F19. Some cells that didn't need formulas got them anyway.

③ Move to each cell in column F that has a zero in it and delete it by pressing Del or choosing Edit/Clear.

LESSON

Formatting Numeric Cells

FEATURING

- Currency
- Percentages
- Decimal Places
- Exponential Notation
- Formatting a Range

YOUR NUMBERS ARE NOW ALL IN PLACE. HOWEVER, they still don't look as good as they could. The main problem with these numbers is that they don't look like what they are supposed to represent, namely, dollar figures.

Formatting Currency

It's quite easy to make an unadorned number look like dollar amounts in 1-2-3. Follow these steps:

① Press F5 (the Go To key), type in **B5**, and click on OK or press Enter to jump to B5.

② Click on the icon containing the $ sign, shown in Figure 18.1. The 8000 in B5 changes to $8000.00. Notice, however, that the value shown in the edit line has not changed. All you've changed is how 1-2-3 will display the value in the cell, and how it will print it on paper.

③ Click on the icon again. The $8000.00 changes back to 8000.

④ Click again. You're back to $8000.00. The value keeps changing because the Currency icon, like many of the other icons, is a *toggle*. Toggles are like light switches. Each click alternately turns the effect on or off.

⑤ Click on the Comma icon. This removes the $ sign, but it adds a comma after the 8.

⑥ Click on the Percentage icon (the one with the % sign in it). The 8000 amount is displayed as a percentage.

⑦ Click again on the Currency icon to format B5 as currency.

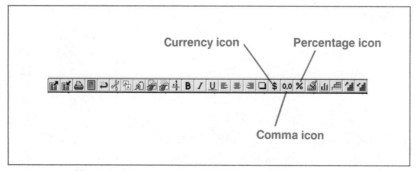

Figure 18.1: Numeric formatting icons

Changing the Format of a Range of Numbers

Now that you've got the idea of how to change the format of an individual numeric cell's content, how do you suppose you could most easily apply the dollar format to all the numeric cells in the worksheet? Obviously, you could select one cell at a time, and change its style by clicking on the Currency icon. However, it's much faster to select a larger range and then click on the desired style icon.

① Select the range B5..F19.

② Click on the Currency icon. Nothing appears to happen except that B5 reverts to General format: 8000.

③ Click again on the Currency icon. All the numeric cells are now formatted as currency, as you see in Figure 18.2.

The reason you had to click twice is because the Currency icon is a toggle. Since B5 was already formatted as currency, and it was the upper left cell in the range, the first click formatted the range back to General. A second click was required to switch them to back to currency.

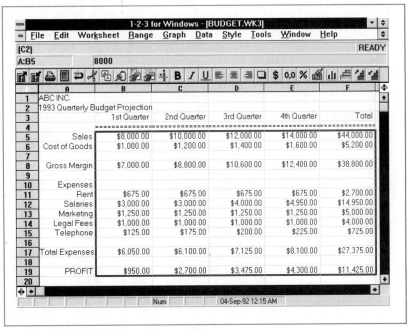

Figure 18.2: *All numeric cells formatted as currency*

Eliminating Extra Zeros

Suppose that you wanted to display the dollar amounts without the extra zeros after the decimal point. To fine-tune the format for the range, you can use the Range Format dialog box.

LESSON 18

① Select the range B5..F19 again, if it isn't still selected.

② Choose Range/Format.

③ A dialog box appears. Change the setting to Currency and the Decimal places box to 0. The results are shown in Figure 18.3.

You can choose a number of different formats from the Range Format dialog box; examples of the most common formats are shown in Figure 18.4. For each example, column C shows how the number 1629.54 is displayed by the given format and column D shows how −1629.54 is displayed. For all examples, the number of decimal places is set at 2.

If you select Parentheses format, all numbers will be displayed in parentheses, but text will not. The + / − choice may be unclear. For positive numbers, the number of + (plus) signs displayed will be equal to the rounded-off value of the number (e.g., 4 will be displayed as + + + +). For negative values, the number of − (minus) signs

	A	B	C	D	E	F
1	ABC INC.					
2	1993 Quarterly Budget Projection					
3		1st Quarter	2nd Quarter	3rd Quarter	4th Quarter	Total
4						
5	Sales	$8,000	$10,000	$12,000	$14,000	$44,000
6	Cost of Goods	$1,000	$1,200	$1,400	$1,600	$5,200
7						
8	Gross Margin	$7,000	$8,800	$10,600	$12,400	$38,800
9						
10	Expenses					
11	Rent	$675	$675	$675	$675	$2,700
12	Salaries	$3,000	$3,000	$4,000	$4,950	$14,950
13	Marketing	$1,250	$1,250	$1,250	$1,250	$5,000
14	Legal Fees	$1,000	$1,000	$1,000	$1,000	$4,000
15	Telephone	$125	$175	$200	$225	$725
16						
17	Total Expenses	$6,050	$6,100	$7,125	$8,100	$27,375
18						
19	PROFIT	$950	$2,700	$3,475	$4,300	$11,425
20						

Figure 18.3: *Decimal places (cents) are now omitted*

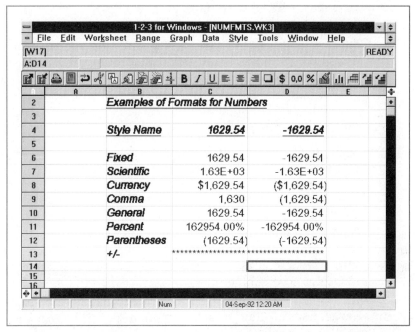

Figure 18.4: *Examples of numeric formats available from the Range Format dialog box*

displayed will be equal to the value of the number (e.g., − 4 will be displayed as − − − −). If you select any format other than General, be sure to specify the number of decimal places (0–15).

Setting Numeric Formats Globally

If you regularly work with numbers, chances are good that you prefer a particular format. If you're an engineer, researcher, or mathematician, you'll probably opt for a specific number of decimal places, or perhaps for scientific notation. If you are in business, the Currency format will more likely be your choice.

By default, 1-2-3 displays values in General format. This means commas are not used (as in 8000) and negative numbers are indicated with a minus sign. If a number has decimal places, as many as can fit into the cell will be displayed, after which they will be rounded off.

If the numbers to the left of the decimal point would exceed the width of the cell, scientific notation is used.

Though General is the default format, you can change this if you're entering lots of numbers and don't want to manually change their formatting each time. Here's how:

① Choose Worksheet/Global Settings. The Worksheet Global Settings dialog box appears.

② Click on the Format button. Another dialog box, called Worksheet Global Settings Format, appears.

③ Choose the desired format and click on OK. Then click on OK in the Global Settings box. Now all cells in the current worksheet will use the new default.

Note that global settings only affect the current file; they will not affect worksheets stored in other files.

Also, global settings do not affect cells already manually formatted with Range/Format. Ranges already set to a specific format will retain their settings even when you change the global settings. However, if you want to reset the format of a range or individual cell you have manually formatted to the format of the global settings, you can select the cell or range, choose Range/Format, and click on the Reset button in the dialog box. The cell will then take on the default format.

LESSON 19

Formatting Text Cells

FEATURING

- Fonts
- Borders
- Colors
- Removing Grid Lines

EVEN THOUGH YOU HAVE A PRETTY SPIFFY-LOOKING budget now, all the text in your cells still looks pretty much the same. The type style of the labels and values is uniform from cell to cell. None of the text is in boldface, italics, nor is it underlined, and there is nothing in your worksheet—like boxes, colors, or shading—to draw the eye to the most important cells or ranges.

In the old days before Windows, laser printers, and fancy color computer screens, you'd be left pretty much with what we have on the screen now. You might have been able to find add-on programs from other manufacturers to enhance the worksheet's appearance somewhat, but their visual effects were primitive and you couldn't easily see on the screen what you'd get when you printed things out. Now, with the rich graphic capabilities of Windows, 1-2-3 for Windows has a variety of text- and cell-formatting capabilities built in. Let's use these to visually enhance our worksheet.

Typefaces and Fonts

First, let's look at the styles of type you can use in displaying and printing your worksheets. By changing the type style, you can impart information that your numbers alone can't. You can add or decrease emphasis, or make a worksheet easier to read, or even more aesthetically attractive.

You change type styles with the Styles/Font command. With this command, you control the typeface and type size of a cell or range of cells. A *typeface* (sometimes called *type family*) refers to a general style of print. For example, the heading of this section is in the typeface called Triumvirate, and the text you're currently reading is in English Times. *Type size* refers to how big or small the letters are. The combination of a typeface and type size is called a *font*. In other words, a font is a typeface in a particular size. For example, Triumvirate 12 and Times 10 are two different fonts. The 12 and 10 are called *point sizes* because type is measured in points. (A point is $1/72$ of an inch.)

If you look back at Figure 18.4, you will see an example of some of the effects you can achieve by simply enlarging the type size. (I've also changed attributes of some of the cells there, through boldfacing and underlining, but more about that in a minute.)

Let's start by altering the font of the worksheet's title:

ABC INC.

1993 Quarterly Budget Projection

Let's center the cells on the worksheet and make the type size larger.

① Select A1..A2. Move this range to C1..C2.

② Select C1..C2.

③ Choose Style/Font. The Fonts dialog box appears.

This box lists the fonts available on your system. The fonts (typefaces and sizes) available may vary depending on whether you've changed your fonts since installing 1-2-3. You'll probably have Arial MT 14 available. I've chosen that for the title lines of the worksheet. The result is shown in Figure 19.1.

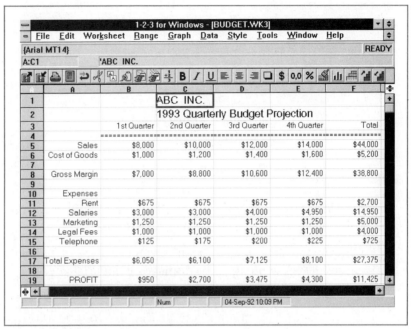

Figure 19.1: *The headings in Arial MT 14*

④ Choose a font (Arial MT 14 if it's available) from the dialog box.

⑤ Move cell C1 over a bit to the right, into D1. That centers it over the second line.

Using Boldface, Italics, and Underlining

The new font undoubtedly draws attention to the worksheet's title. Still, we could do a bit more to emphasize the title's importance.

① Click on C2. Underline *1993 Quarterly Budget Projection* by clicking on the icon shown in Figure 19.2 that looks like a big *U* with an underline below it.

② Click on D1, *ABC INC.* Click the Bold icon shown in Figure 19.2 that looks like a big *B*. This makes the selected cell

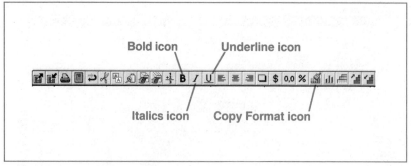

Figure 19.2: Text-formatting icons

data look bolder, or thicker. The Bold icon is another toggle. Clicking again unbolds the text. Leave it bold.

③ Click on the large slanted *I* icon shown in Figure 19.2. This causes the cell contents to be displayed in italic (slanted) lettering.

Now your worksheet should look like Figure 19.3. Notice the format line (just above the edit line). It indicates the font and style of the current cell:

{Arial MT 14 Bold Italics}

While we're at it, let's make a few cells that contain important totals stand out a little.

① Select the range B8..F8. Click on the Bold icon to boldface them.

② Do the same for B17..F17 and B19..F19.

*P*utting Borders around Important Ranges

Another way to emphasize a cell or a range is to give it a border. Let's add one around the PROFIT range.

① Select B19..F19.

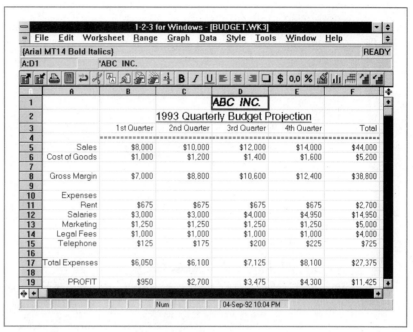

Figure 19.3: Bold and italics applied to D1

② Choose Style/Borders. A dialog box appears. This box lets you choose among the border styles shown in Figure 19.4.

③ Click on the Outline option and click on OK. Outline is the choice to use when you want to draw a box around an entire range. Note that a drop-down list box next to each border choice shows the default border style and, should you want to, lets you define the border line as single, double, or wide.

Altering Colors

You can change the color of cell data, too. This capability might be important if you are making presentations with color monitors, or if you want to facilitate the correct entry of data into spreadsheets by data entry personnel.

To change a cell's color, just select the cell (or cells) you want to alter and choose the Style/Colors command. A dialog box appears

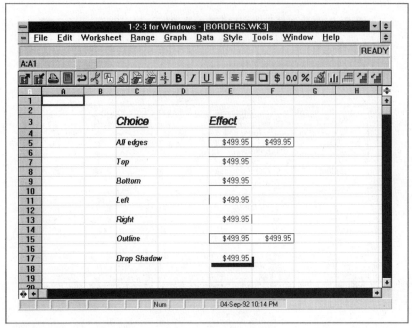

Figure 19.4: Types of borders available from the Styles/Borders box

with two drop-down list boxes: one for cell background and one for cell contents. Open the appropriate list box and click on any color to choose it.

Colors will have some effect even if you have a black and white or grayscale screen. Just choose a shade that looks good on your monitor. Typically, for a black-and-white or laptop LCD screen, you'd make the cell contents white (or gray) and the background black, for an inverse video look.

Removing Grid Lines from the Worksheet

Though they're usually helpful for finding your place in the worksheet, you may not want to see the grid lines that separate cells on the screen. Here's how to turn them off:

① Choose Window/Display Options. A dialog box appears with color choices and some other settings. The Grid Lines check box is probably turned on. Click on it to turn it off.

② Click on OK. The grid lines disappear.

③ Open the dialog box again, and set Grid Lines back on, as we will want grid lines displayed in future lessons.

Formatting Shortcuts

You now know all the common formatting options. However, if you intend to do lots of cell formatting, there are three shortcuts you might want to know about.

The first one is a form of the the Edit/Quick Copy command. This command lets you copy just the formatting of a cell or range to another cell or range. If you've done some fancy formatting on a cell, with lots of numerical or text display options, colors, and borders, it would be tedious to have to redo it for cells you add later. Instead, follow these steps:

① Select a cell with the correct formatting and choose Edit/ Quick Copy.

② Turn on the Styles Only check box.

③ Type in the range that you want to be formatted in the style of the source cell. Its format will be copied to the destination cell(s).

To save even more time, use the Copy Format icon. This icon is also shown in Figure 19.2. It copies just the formatting of a cell to another cell or range.

① Click on a cell with the formatting you want to copy.

② Click on the Copy Format icon.

③ Click on the cell or select the destination range by dragging the cursor across the range with the mouse button depressed.

Finally, if you find you are using certain formats frequently, you can set up these formats to appear on the Style menu. Eight predefined formats can be assigned to the menu. Once you set these up, all the formatting options are instantly applied to the cells you select.

① Move to a cell whose formatting you want to assign to the menu.

② Choose Style/Name. A dialog box appears with eight sections in it.

③ Click on the radio button of the number you want to assign the style to.

④ Give the style a name of your choice and an optional description. (The description is used to remind yourself about the details of the style settings.)

⑤ Click on OK. The style is added to the menu.

⑥ To use the style, move to a cell (or select a range) you want to format in the style. Then open the Style menu and choose the style from the menu.

LESSON 20

Adding and Deleting Columns and Rows

FEATURING

- The Worksheet/Insert Command
- The Worksheet/Delete Command

WORKSHEETS ALMOST NEVER COME OUT RIGHT THE first time. Even the best-laid plans... as they say. Well, in addition to editing cell contents and moving ranges around on the screen, there are a couple of other worksheet editing tricks that will help you patch up your worksheets—namely, the ability to insert and delete rows and columns.

For an example of how helpful this ability can be, take a look back at the Gross Margins and Total Expenses rows of our budget. Notice the blank rows between them and the neighboring rows. Originally, I added those to visually isolate the totals, but now that we've formatted the totals to stand out on their own, there's no longer any reason for the blank space. If we were to eliminate some blank rows, we could even use the extra space to add a line or two below the worksheet heading.

One way to remove unwanted rows or columns is to select various ranges and move them in such a way as to close the gaps. However, in large worksheets this is a lot of work, and you run the chance of copying cells on top of each other, which wipes out the data in the copied-over cell.

An easier, and safer, way to eliminate blank rows or columns is to use the Delete command. When you delete (or add) rows and columns, the actual number of them in the worksheet doesn't change; this always remains at 256 columns and 8192 rows. Your worksheet data is just moved within the matrix, and all the formulas are adjusted accordingly.

Deleting Rows

First we'll experiment with deleting some rows.

① Move the cursor to anywhere in row 7.

② Choose Worksheet/Delete. The Worksheet Delete dialog box appears. Make sure that the Row radio button is selected.

③ Click on OK. Don't worry that the Range box only indicates one cell. It doesn't matter. As long as the cursor is anywhere on the row you want to delete and the Row radio button is selected, the entire row will be deleted.

④ Save your work. (Actually, this is optional, but it's good to get into the habit.)

The row is deleted, all formulas are adjusted (this may take some time in large spreadsheets), and the cells below are pulled up one row.

⑤ Now delete row 15 in the same way.

⑥ Delete row 4 now. Notice that all the equal signs disappear. Any other data in the row would too. (If you accidentally delete a row of cells, you can use the Undo command to reverse the mistake.)

Now your worksheet looks like Figure 20.1.

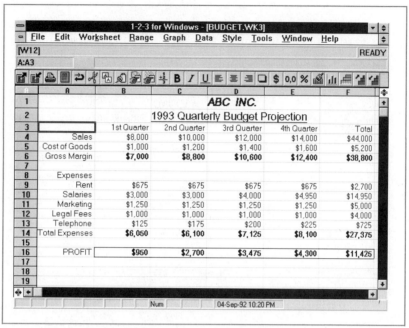

Figure 20.1:The budget worksheet after deleting blank rows

Inserting Rows

Now we'll add two rows between row 2 and row 3.

① Position the cursor on row 2.

② Choose Worksheet/Insert.

③ If the Row radio button is not already on, click on it.

④ Click on OK.

Two rows are inserted below *1993 Budget*. Your screen should look like Figure 20.2.

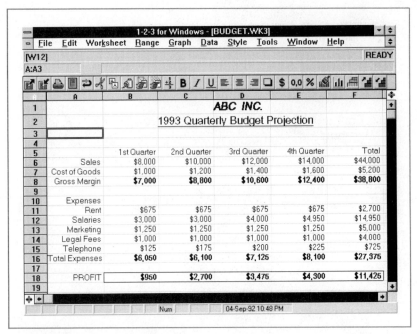

Figure 20.2: *Two rows are inserted*

Deleting and Inserting Columns

As you've probably guessed, deleting and inserting columns is just like deleting and inserting rows. Here are the steps:

1. If you're deleting columns, select a range that contains at least one call in each column you want to delete. If you're inserting columns, select a range equal to the size of the number of columns you want to insert. To insert two columns, for example, select a range straddling two columns, such as A1..B1.

2. Choose Worksheet/Insert or Worksheet/Delete. The appropriate dialog box appears.

3. Choose the Column radio button.

4. Click on OK.

The column(s) will be inserted or deleted.

Hiding Columns

FEATURING

- The Worksheet/Hide Command
- The Worksheet/Unhide Command

SOMETIMES YOU'LL WANT TO DISPLAY YOUR WORKSHEET without having to look at all the columns on screen at once. Perhaps you are working on two columns that are placed too far apart on the worksheet to appear on the screen simultaneously. Maybe you want to see two columns without the clutter of intervening columns. Or perhaps you want to print a summary report that doesn't include too many details. In any of these situations, 1-2-3 lets you temporarily hide columns of your choice.

Hiding Columns

For example, say you only want to see the annual totals for the 1993 budget and don't care about the quarterly numbers. You'd hide columns B through E. Here's how to do it:

① Select any cells in columns B through E. It doesn't matter which ones. You just have to indicate which columns to hide and this is the easiest way. Just for the experiment, select B1..E1.

② Choose Worksheet/Hide. A dialog box pops up. Choose the Column radio button (Make sure you don't select Sheet, or the entire worksheet will vanish).

③ Click on OK. Check the worksheet column headings now, and notice that they jump from A to F. Columns B, C, D, and E are temporarily hidden, as shown in Figure 21.1.

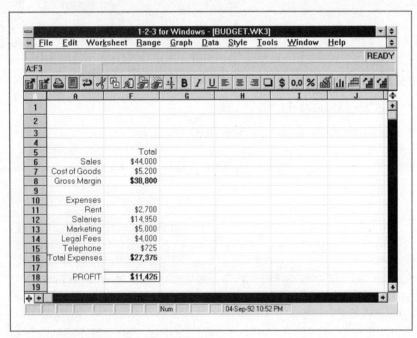

Figure 21.1: Columns B to E are hidden

Unhiding Columns

Hiding columns doesn't erase any of the data in the worksheet. To the contrary, it is all still in the file. To prove this, let's unhide the columns so they all display again.

① Choose Worksheet/Unhide.

② Click on the Columns radio button.

③ In the dialog box's Range section, you must specify a range that includes the hidden columns. Enter **B1..E1.**

④ Click on OK. The columns are returned to view.

LESSON

Preventing Titles from Scrolling off the Screen

FEATURING

- Freezing Titles

WORKSHEETS OFTEN HAVE ROW OR COLUMN TITLES that help the reader decipher the numbers in the worksheet. For example, in our budget, column A contains titles such as Rent and Telephone. If our worksheet contained more columns, scrolling to the right a few columns would cause the titles to be obscured from view, which could make viewing the worksheet or entering more data confusing.

You can prevent this by "freezing" titles in place with the Worksheet/Titles command. When you freeze rows or columns, they stay put while all other rows or columns can be scrolled. Try these steps to get the idea of freezing:

① Go to the North Pole, step outside...

Just kidding.

① Place the cursor on cell B4.

② Choose Worksheet/Titles. A dialog box appears asking whether you want to freeze a vertical row of cells (a column), a horizontal row of cells (a normal row), or both. In the case of our budget, for example, we want to freeze column A, which is vertical, so click on the Vertical button.

③ Click on OK. Now any columns to the left of the position the cursor was in when you invoked the Titles command will be locked.

④ Press the → key five or six times, or until the worksheet starts to scroll to the left. Notice that column A stays put, as you see in Figure 22.1.

⑤ Press the ← key and hold it down. The cursor moves to the left, and when it hits the second column, it will cause the scrolled columns to scroll back into view.

⑥ Unlock the frozen column now by choosing Worksheet/ Titles, choosing the Clear button, and clicking on OK.

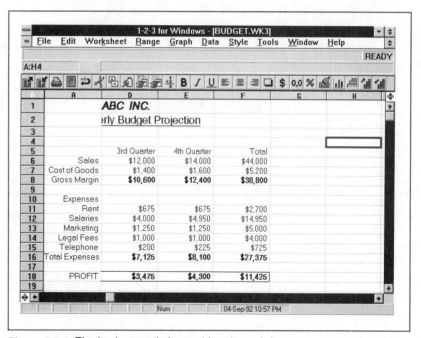

Figure 22.1: The budget worksheet with column A frozen

You can freeze row titles by following these same instructions; just remember to choose Row from the dialog box. If you want to freeze both columns and rows, choose Both from the dialog box. Regardless of the which of these three options you choose, don't forget to position the pointer on the worksheet before choosing the Worksheet/Titles command. When you OK the dialog box, columns to the left and/or rows above will be frozen.

LESSON 23

Splitting the Screen

FEATURING

- The Worksheet/Split Command
- Vertical and Horizontal Panes

WHEN WORKING ON LARGE SPREADSHEETS, IT'S OFTEN necessary to see far-flung sections of the spreadsheet at the same time. You learned in the last lesson how to freeze titles. However, freezing only works on titles that are at the top or leftmost sections of the worksheet.

The Window/Split command allows you to split the worksheet into two small windows, or *panes,* to display different parts of a worksheet. You can split the worksheet either horizontally or vertically. Once you've split the worksheet window, you can scroll each pane separately to display different sections of the same worksheet. Splitting can be done with either the mouse or the Window/Split command. Using a mouse is much easier.

Horizontal Splits

To split the screen horizontally, follow these steps:

① Place the cursor anywhere on row 9, or about halfway down the worksheet's window.

② Choose Window/Split. The Split dialog box appears. Now choose Horizontal and click on OK. The screen splits into two sections at the point where the cursor was, as you see in Figure 23.1.

③ Press F6 to move the cursor to the lower pane. Press again and the cursor jumps back to the upper pane.

④ Press Ctrl-→ to pan the worksheet one screen to the right. Notice that with each press, the two worksheet sections' columns stay synchronized. In other words, if you move two cells to the right in one pane, the other pane will automatically scroll two cells to the right. This is because the Synchronize check box in the Split dialog box is set on. If it was turned off, you could pan the windows' columns independently. Thus, you could see columns A to F in one pane, and G to L in the other.

⑤ Press Home to return the cursor to cell A1. Both panes pan back to the far left side of the worksheet.

⑥ Press the ↓ key repeatedly. The window you are in scrolls up when you reach its bottom. Release the ↓ key.

⑦ Press F6 to jump to the other pane. Use the scroll buttons and the mouse to practice scrolling. Note that each pane has its own scroll buttons, scroll bars, and scroll arrows.

⑧ Adjust each pane so that cell A22 is showing. Move to cell A22 and enter

Where does this text show up?

Notice that it appears in both panes. This is because there is really only one pane. Any changes you make in one window will be reflected in the other.

You can also copy or move data from cells displayed in one pane to cells displayed in another. Just use the same methods we used in previous lessons. Remember to press F6 to jump between panes; or if you are using a mouse, just click in the pane you want to jump to, then navigate to the desired cell.

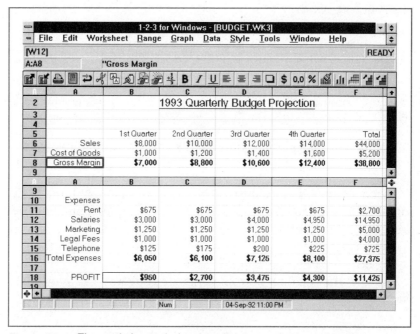

Figure 23.1: The worksheet window is split into two horizontal panes

Now turn off the split screen, returning the display to a single pane.

① Choose Window/Split.

② Choose Clear from the dialog box.

③ Click on OK. The split disappears.

Vertical Splits

Now let's try a vertical split. If you use the Split dialog box, you can split the worksheet window by following the steps above for horizontal splits. If you have a mouse, you can split the window horizontally or vertically by dragging on the appropriate Split button in the worksheet window. The Split buttons are the little two-headed arrows in the lower left and upper right corners of the worksheet window.

Here's how to use them:

① Position the mouse cursor over the Split button in the lower left corner of the worksheet window. The cursor will change shape, becoming a two-headed arrow.

② Click and drag this button along the bottom of the window to approximately the center of the worksheet window.

③ Release the button. You've divided the screen into two vertical panes, as you see in Figure 23.2.

You work with vertical panes just as you worked with the horizontal ones. You can readjust the position of the split at any time by dragging the Split button. You can unsplit the screen by choosing Window/Split/Clear or by simply dragging the bar back to the far left corner.

The horizontal Split button works the same way, only you drag the button up and down.

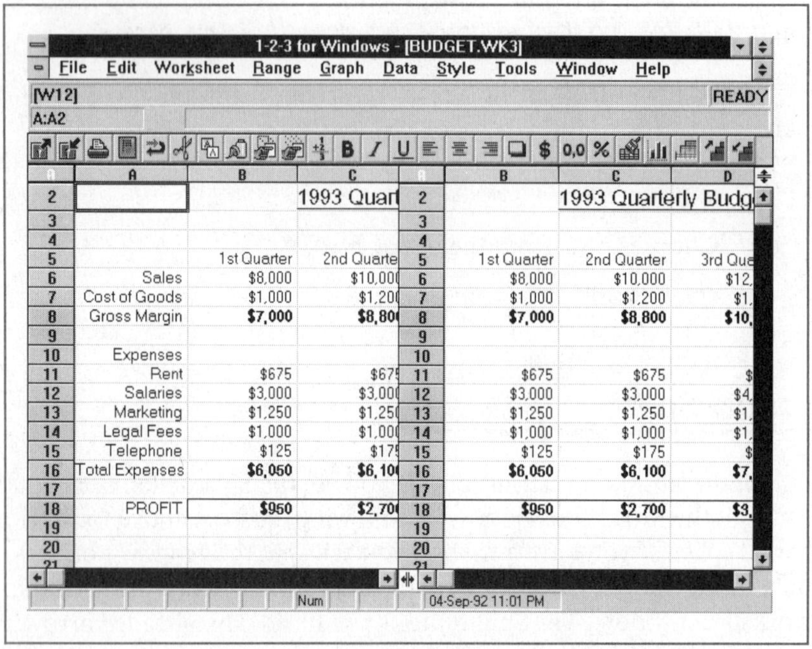

Figure 23.2: The worksheet window is split into two vertical panes

LESSON 24

Locking Cells to Protect Data

FEATURING

- Global Protection
- Worksheet/Unprotect

SOME OF YOUR WORKSHEETS MAY CONTAIN DATA AND formulas that you want to protect from alteration. For example, if you work in an office where coworkers enter data into worksheets you design, you might want to protect all the cells containing formulas, but leave the other cells unprotected so that others can enter more current data. For such situations, 1-2-3 offers a several data protection schemes. You already know about the first one: hiding columns. The second approach, called Global Protection, prevents anyone from unconsciously making changes to any cells in a worksheet.

If you want to alter a cell's or a range's contents when Global Protection is active, you to have to manually set the cell or range to an unprotected status. When you unprotect a cell or range, its color changes to let you know that you can now enter data. Since anyone can unprotect cells by turning off Global Protection, it is not a great security measure if you are worried about someone purposely tampering with your data. However, Global Protection is useful in preventing changes to cells that you or another person using the spreadsheet might accidentally make.

Using Global Protection

When you want to ensure that some cells are alterable but others (typically formulas) are not, you should first turn on Global Protection. You can then unprotect the cells you want to remain alterable with the Range/Unprotect command.

In our budget we'll want to protect the cells containing formulas—that is, all the totals cells. We'll leave the other cells unprotected. Follow these steps:

① Choose Worksheet/Global Settings. The Worksheet Global Settings dialog box appears.

② Click on the Protection check box.

③ Click on OK.

④ Try to enter data into any cell. The computer beeps and no data is accepted. You may see an error message informing you that the cell is protected.

⑤ Now you have to unprotect the cells you want to access. You can unprotect individual cells, or you can unprotect a range. Choose Range/Unprotect. A small dialog box appears. Type in the range **B6..F7**.

⑥ Click on OK. Now you can enter new data into the Sales and Cost of Goods cells.

If you decide after unprotecting some cells that you want to protect them again, choose Worksheet/Protect, and type in the range again. Protection does not prevent changes in formatting, such as font, color, and style. You can only prevent these types of changes by sealing the file as explained in the Lotus 1-2-3 manual.

If you decide you want easy access to the rest of the worksheet, you can unprotect the entire worksheet by opening the Global Settings box again and turning off Protection. To prevent future problems when we modify cell data, do turn off Protection now.

LESSON 25

Working with Ranges

FEATURING

- Naming Ranges
- Editing Range Names
- Listing Ranges

AS YOU'VE SEEN, THERE ARE MANY 1-2-3 COMMANDS that work with ranges of cells. When specifying ranges for such commands, you typically have to select the range with the mouse, or type the range's beginning and ending cells into a dialog box. This can be time-consuming, and it can lead to mistakes if you slip up a bit and type the wrong cell address.

With the Range/Name command, you don't have to remember the coordinates of ranges you frequently use. Instead, you can give ranges names that can be used in dialog boxes, in formulas, and even when printing out portions of your worksheets. For example, you could name the cells from B6 to E6 in our budget worksheet "Sales." Then, if you wanted to add up these cells, instead of having to remember and type in the formula

@SUM(B2..F2)

you could simply enter

@SUM(sales)

Naming ranges can be a real time-saver when you're devising numerous formulas, and if you give your ranges mnemonic names, the names can help remind you of that range's function. Even if the size or location of the range is changed by inserting or deleting columns or rows, all formulas that include the range's name will still be accurate, since 1-2-3 updates the range's definition.

As you create names for ranges, they are stored in a table that you can easily update and refer to. This is called a *range table*. In this lesson, you'll name a few ranges, use them in a dialog box, and see how range tables work.

Naming a Range

Let's start by naming the range of expenses for the first quarter.

① Select the range B11..B15.

② Choose Range/Name. When the cascading menu opens, choose Create. The Range Name Create dialog box opens. If you had already named some ranges, they would show up in the larger box. The smaller box labeled "Range name" is where you type in the name of the currently selected range. If you hadn't already selected the range B11..B15, you could type it into the Range box at the bottom of the dialog box.

③ We'll call this range Q1_EXP (for Quarter 1 Expenses). Type this into the Range name box.

④ Click on Create. The name is added to the range name list below.

⑤ Click on OK.

⑥ Move to cell B16. Notice that the formula has changed. Where it once read *@SUM(B11..B15),* it now reads *@SUM(Q1_EXP).* Any time you name a range, any existing formula that contains a reference to the range will be updated, replacing the cell names with the range name.

When naming a range, remember that the range name will be more useful to you if it reflects the contents of the range. You can name your ranges almost any way you want, but you do have to follow these rules:

- Range names must start with a letter.

- Always use a letter or number as the second character. Don't use a character that 1-2-3 has reserved for other purposes, such as +, −, *, /, &, >, <, @, or #.

- Don't use spaces, semicolons, or periods in range names. To separate words, you must use an underline character, as in LEGAL_EXP.

- Don't use a range name that looks like a cell address, such as B78 or A:B78.

Naming Ranges Based on Labels

Since a single cell qualifies as a range, you can name individual cells too. When naming individual cells, you'll often find yourself giving them the same names you've entered as labels. With the Range/Name/Label Create command, you can use existing labels as range names without even typing them in, as long as the labels you want to use are adjacent to the cell you want to name.

For example, in A6, A7, and A8 we have the labels *Sales, Cost of Goods,* and *Gross Margin.* We could use these labels as range names for the adjacent cells B6, B7, and B8. Here's how you would do it:

① Select the range A6..A8.

② Choose Range/Name/Label Create.

③ The Range Name Label Create dialog box appears.

④ In the Direction of Adjacent Cells box, select the button that indicates the direction from the labels to the cells you want to name. In our case, the cells are to the right of the labels, so you should click on the Right button.

⑤ Click on OK, and the range names are created from your labels.

⑥ To see the range names, choose Range/Name/Create. The new labels will be listed in the box.

Using Range Names

You can use range names in any dialog box that accepts ranges. The Go To command will use range names, too. As you may recall, pressing F5 lets you jump directly to a specific cell that you type in. It also lists the existing named ranges. Try this:

① Press F5. The Range Go To dialog box pops up, with a list of ranges.

② Double-click on the range name you want to jump to. Alternatively, press Tab to get into the box that lists the range names, then use the arrow keys to select the name you want.

③ Press Enter and the cell pointer will jump to the upper left cell of the range.

As you know, range names can be real time-savers when writing formulas, since you don't have to remember the range addresses. But if you've named a lot of ranges, trying to remember your range names can be just as difficult as trying to remember range addresses. Luckily, the F3 (Range) key makes it easy to recall your range names. Pressing F3 pops up a list of ranges that you can double-click on to drop them into a formula. Try this:

① Press F5. Type in **B21** and press Enter. This jumps you to B21.

② In cell B21 type a plus sign. This begins a formula.

③ Press F3 to display a list of range names. Double-click on Sales.

④ Type − , then press F3 again. Double-click on Cost of Goods. Finalize the formula by pressing Enter. You've just calculated the gross margin without entering any cell coordinates.

⑤ Erase the contents of this cell.

As you'll see when we cover printing, you can easily print a range rather than your whole worksheet. Using named ranges makes this a breeze, allowing you to print sections such as Income, Sales, or Expenses by name.

Listing Your Ranges

The Range/Name/Paste Table command lets you create a table listing all your named ranges. The range names are listed in the left column of the table and the addresses in the right column. Creating a range table is a good idea if you are worried about forgetting your range names. Here's an example you might want to try:

① Move to cell A20.

② Choose Range/Name/Paste Table and click on OK. Your current range names and addresses are copied into columns A and B beginning at row 20.

③ Erase these when you are finished viewing them.

Deleting Range Names

If you use range names frequently, you'll soon find you have ones you don't use or can't remember why you created in the first place. You can delete unwanted or unused range names by following these steps:

① Choose Range/Name/Delete.

② In the Range Name Delete dialog box, choose the name you want to delete.

③ Click on one of the command buttons. The Delete button deletes the name you've chosen. The other two buttons have the following effects:

- Delete All deletes all your range names. The data isn't affected, of course.

- Undefine removes the cell addresses from the name. The range name continues to exist, it just doesn't have an address.

④ Click on OK the finalize the deletion(s).

LESSON 26

Using Absolute References

FEATURING

- F4—The Absolute Key

AS YOU HAVE LEARNED, THERE ARE THREE TYPES OF cell references that can be used in 1-2-3 formulas: relative, absolute, and mixed. Up to now, you've worked exclusively with relative references. In this lesson, you'll learn how to use absolute references.

Relative references, you'll recall, will change as you copy cells or move cells around within your worksheets. For example, copying the formula

$+B1+B2+B3$

to column C will result in 1-2-3's adjusting the formula to read

$+C1+C2+C3$

If you were to insert *absolute references* into the same formula, on the other hand, 1-2-3 would not adjust the formula if you moved or copied the formula cell. Instead, 1-2-3 would simply leave the formula as it was. Using absolute references, you can "borrow" key values from specific cells elsewhere in the spreadsheet, and the formula references to these cells won't be adjusted when you copy the formula into new cells.

You indicate an absolute reference in a formula by placing a dollar sign ($) before each part of the reference cell's address. Thus to make a reference to cell B3 absolute, you would type **$B$3**. When the formula

+B1 +B2 +$B$3

is copied to cell C4, 1-2-3 adjusts the first two cell references but leaves the last one absolute, resulting in the following formula in C4:

+C1 +C2 +$B$3

The third type of reference, the *mixed reference,* incorporates both absolute and relative references into a single cell address. For example, the pointers B$3 and $B3 are both mixed references. The mixed reference B$3 means the column is relative and row is absolute; $B3 means the row is relative and the column is absolute. You enter a mixed reference just as you enter an absolute one (except, of course, that you enter only one dollar sign); however, mixed references are rarely used in worksheets and will not be covered in the exercises that follow.

Adding Absolute References

Let's add some absolute references to our spreadsheet. Since absolute references can be confusing, hold off on entering any references until we get to the numbered exercise.

Suppose you wanted to place the percentage of the total annual profit each quarter produced on the spreadsheet, as shown in Figure 26.1.

Since we know the profit for each quarter and the profit for the year, this calculation should be simple. Written as a word problem, the equation would be

(quarter profit / total profit) / 100

We can take care of the division by 100 simply by formatting the cell in Percentage format, so we're left with this simple equation:

quarter profit / total profit

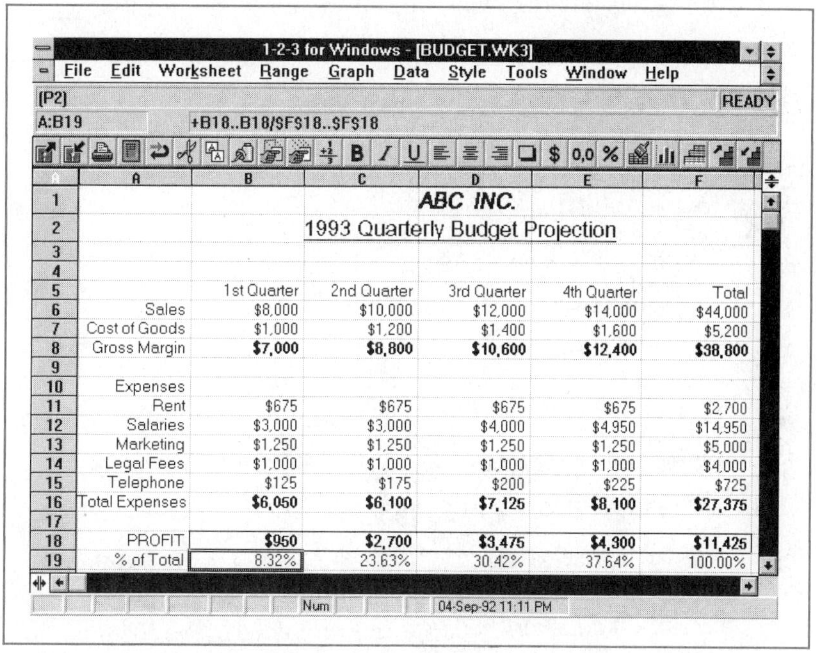

Figure 26.1: The Budget worksheet with absolute references added

Now we just have to convert the word problem into a 1-2-3 formula. For the first quarter, the formula would be

+B18/$F$18

Notice that we made cell F18, the PROFIT cell, an absolute reference. When we copy this formula across columns C, D, E, the formula will continue to refer to the PROFIT cell. However, we left each quarter's profit as a relative reference, since there are four of those (B18, C18, D18, E18), and we want 1-2-3 to adjust these references as we copy the formula to each column. Thus, when we copy the formula to columns C, D, and E, 1-2-3 will adjust the formulas like this:

In C19:	+C18/$F$18
In D19:	+D18/$F$18
In E19:	+E18/$F$18

Now, to enter the formulas we've been discussing, follow these steps:

① In cell A19, enter the label % **of Total**.

② Set the alignment for the cell to Right.

③ Move to cell B19. Type +.

④ Point to cell B18 and click. The formula now reads

+ A:B18..A:B18

⑤ Type /.

⑥ Point to F18 and click.

⑦ The formula now reads

+ A:B18..A:B18/$A:F18..$A:F18

⑧ Now for a time-saving trick. Press F4. This is the absolute key, and it speeds up entering the dollar signs. Your first press of F4 changes the latest cell reference in the formula from relative to absolute. Subsequent presses change the cell reference to mixed column (the column reference is absolute; the row reference is relative), to mixed row (the row reference is absolute; the column is relative), and back to relative. Press it several times until the formula reads

+ A:B18..A:B18/$A:$F$18..$A:$F$18

⑨ Confirm the entry by pressing Enter or clicking on the check mark. The cell should immediately calculate to 0.0831509846827133479. Actually, only 0.083150985 will show: 1-2-3 rounded it off.

⑩ Format the cell as Percentage by clicking on the Percentage icon or using the Range/Format command. Cell A19 should now show 8.32%.

⑪ Now copy the formula in cell B19 to the range C19..F19. Use either the Range Copy icon or the Edit/Quick Copy technique.

Once the cells are laid in, the formulas will calculate to look like Figure 26.1. Notice that, of course, the result in column F is 100%.

PART

4

Managing
Multiple Worksheets

27 LESSON

Using Multiple Worksheets

FEATURING

- 3D Worksheets
- Worksheet Links

THE SIMPLE FACT THAT 1-2-3 CAN ACCOMMODATE enormous worksheets does not necessarily mean that you should create them. Though most typical jobs *could* be contained on a single 1-2-3 sheet, there are good reasons for using multiple worksheets for large jobs.

For starters, it's often cumbersome to design and use worksheets that contain so much information, and it's a nuisance to have to scroll around a huge worksheet. Secondly, it's logistically advantageous to restrict the kind of data assigned to each worksheet. If you keep income on one sheet, expenses on another, and various assumptions about your business (such as inventory or salaries) on a third, this will help you keep your accounts straight and will make it easier to reuse your information in new ways later.

If 1-2-3 didn't make using multiple worksheets easy, this type of arrangement wouldn't be quite so tempting. But one of the strongest features of 1-2-3 is that it lets you work with as many as 256 worksheets within the same file. As a result, it's easy to reference cells in other worksheets in your formulas, switch between worksheets to edit them, and (as you'll see later) graph the data stored in them.

Adding a New Worksheet

Lotus lets you have up to 256 worksheets in a file. New files have only one worksheet. You add new worksheets to the file with Worksheet/Insert command. You may recall, from using this command to insert rows and columns in Lesson 20, that the dialog box you used for inserting the rows and columns also had an option for inserting a worksheet.

To add one new worksheet to the file:

① Choose Worksheet/Insert. (Open the Budget worksheet first, or switch to it.)

② In the dialog box, click on the Sheet radio button.

③ Click on OK.

A new, blank worksheet is added and covers the Budget sheet. Notice the worksheet letter (B) in the upper left corner of the worksheet window.

Cell Addressing and Navigating in 3D Worksheets

Recall that cell addresses are always preceded with a letter, such as

A:B10

The *A:* means "worksheet A." Worksheets are labeled A through Z and then start again with AA, AB, AC, and so on. Chances are good that you will only use a few worksheets per file, nowhere close to the 256 limit. Still, you'll need to know how to navigate between worksheets, how to select 3D ranges, and how to write formulas that reference other worksheets. Fortunately, moving between worksheets is easy.

① Press Ctrl-PgDn to move to the previous worksheet. If you are following the example, you moved from worksheet B to worksheet A.

② Press Ctrl-PgUp to move to the next worksheet (sheet A to sheet B).

③ There are two icons that look like several stacked worksheets containing a diagonal arrow (they are side by side on the icon palette). Click on the Next Worksheet icon shown in Figure 27.1. This moves you to sheet A.

④ Click on the Previous Worksheet icon. This moves one sheet down in the stack, to sheet B.

⑤ Press Ctrl-Home. This always moves you to worksheet A, cell A1.

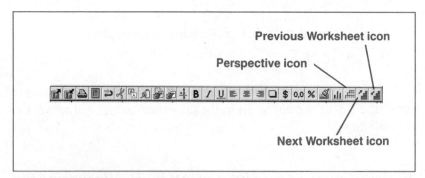

Figure 27.1: *Multiple-worksheet icons*

Viewing Multiple Worksheets

Working with multiple sheets is made easier by an option called Perspective mode. Perspective mode lets you see portions of three worksheets at one time. You can't adjust the size of the worksheet windows, but it's easy to move between them.

① Click on the Perspective icon. Or, as an alternative, choose Window/Split and set Perspective on. When multiple worksheets are displayed in perspective, they look like Figure 27.3, shown a few pages ahead. If you were to add another worksheet, it would appear in the third, empty position.

②　If you scroll one worksheet, the others will scroll too, if the Synchronize check box in the Window Split dialog box is set. Press Ctrl-→ to see both sheets scroll to the right. If they don't scroll together, open the dialog box again and set Synchronize on.

③　Press F5. The Range Go To dialog box appears. Type in **B:B25** and press Enter or click on OK. Notice that the worksheets both scroll to show cells B25.

④　Turn off Perspective mode by clicking on the Perspective icon again or by choosing Window/Split, choosing the Clear radio button, and clicking on OK.

*C*reating Worksheet Links

Now that you've added a new worksheet to the Budget file and learned to move between it and the original Budget worksheet, you may be wondering what you can do with this worksheet. The answer is that we can use formulas to *link* it to worksheet A. The second worksheet will contain a breakdown of employee salaries for the ABC company. The salary breakdown will include the number of employees and their types, their salary amounts, and the total spent on salaries for each quarter. This total will then be tied to the Salaries cells on the main Budget worksheet. Each time the totals shown in the Salaries worksheet change, the Salaries cells in the Budget worksheet will be updated to reflect the change.

*E*ntering the Data

Now let's enter the salary data on worksheet B. Enter it as shown in Figure 27.2. All the data except the totals are uncalculated (no formulas). After entering the salary amounts, enter the formulas for the totals by summing the column of numbers above them. As you may recall, the easiest way is to click on the Sum icon with the cell pointer at the bottom of each column.

It's not important for you to use the same formatting I did, but if you're curious, I've used Arial MT 14 for the headings, and the line

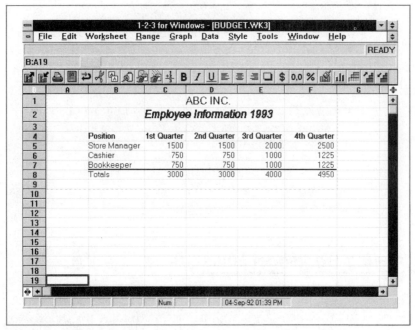

Figure 27.2: The salary data

above the totals was created with a thick border on the top of the Totals row's cells (I selected the Totals cells, chose Style/Borders/Top, and set the line style from the drop-down list box.)

Linking the Salaries to Worksheet A

Now cells B:C8, B:D8, B:E8, and B:F8 hold the salaries information for each of the four quarters, respectively. Now you have to alter the Salaries cells in the main worksheet to get their values from the calculated Totals cells on worksheet B.

① Select Window/Split and turn off Synchronize.

② Adjust your worksheets to line up like Figure 27.3. This way you can see the Salaries row in sheet A and the Totals row in sheet B. The easiest way to adjust the sheets is to move to the desired worksheet and use the ↑ and ↓ keys to scroll the sheet.

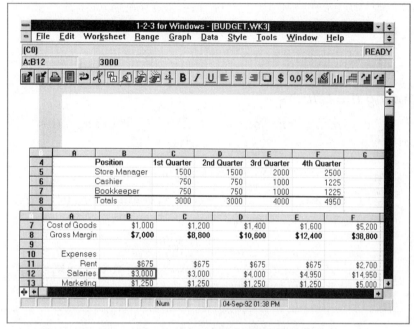

Figure 27.3: Adjust the worksheets to see these cells

We're going to use the pointing method of entering the cell references. By displaying the relevant cells of both sheets, you can easily enter the references just by pointing.

① Click on A:B12. This cell currently contains an absolute value ($3,000), but we're going to change it to contain a formula referring to the first-quarter total salaries cell from sheet B.

② Type + to begin the formula.

③ Click on B:C8 (cell C8 in sheet B). This drops the cell reference B:C8..B:C8 into the formula.

④ Accept the formula by pressing →, which moves the cursor over to cell A:C12. Type + and click on B:D8. Accept the formula.

⑤ Repeat the process for the third and fourth quarters' salaries, pointing to cells B:E8 and B:F8 for data.

⑥ Save your work, just to get in the habit.

Seeing the Effects

Now let's try changing some of the salary data and observe the effects on the bottom line of the budget.

① Adjust the display as shown in Figure 27.4.

② In cell B:F5, enter **3000**. When you confirm the entry, 1-2-3 automatically recalculates the total expenses, profit, and the percentage of profit for the fourth quarter, as well as the annual total. You can now see the fiscal impact of altering any of the salaries over the course of the year, just by plugging in new figures in sheet B.

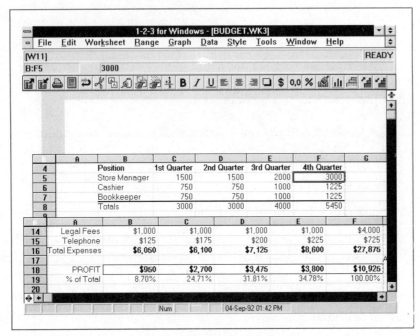

Figure 27.4: Changing values in sheet B affects sheet A

③ Try entering some other amounts in cell B:F5 to see their effects.

④ When you are through experimenting, enter **2500** into B:F5 again.

*U*sing Group Mode

Just as Synchronize lets you keep multiple worksheets' columns and rows in synch on the screen, another option, Group, ensures that other aspects of multiple worksheets are kept identical. Use Group mode when you have a series of identical worksheets, such as a series of annual budgets or weekly reports, that you'd like to format similarly. Just format your first worksheet, leave the cursor in that sheet, then turn on Group mode as explained below.

① Choose Worksheet/Global Settings.

② In the resulting dialog box, set the Group check box on.

③ Click on OK.

When Group mode is on, the current worksheet's cell formats will be applied to all sheets currently in the file or subsequently added to the file. Also, the cell pointer will be in the same location on each sheet when you jump between sheets. Finally, a number of commands will affect all worksheets in the file identically. These commands are listed below:

Range/Format

Range/Protect

Range/Unprotect

Style/Alignment

Worksheet/Column Width

Worksheet/Row Height

Worksheet/Insert Column (or row)

Worksheet/Delete Column (or row)

Worksheet/Global Settings

Worksheet/Page Break

Worksheet/Titles

To turn off Group mode:

① Choose Worksheet/Global Settings.

② In the resulting dialog box, set the Group check box off.

③ Click on OK.

LESSON 28

Using Multiple Worksheet Files

FEATURING

- Linking Files with Formulas
- Linking Files with Range Names
- Managing Multiple Files

AS YOU KNOW FROM THE LAST LESSON, IT'S POSSIBLE TO have many worksheets open at once. Since each file can store up to 256 worksheets (sheets A through IV), there's certainly more than enough room to suit most needs. However, there are still times when you should use separate files rather than separate sheets in the same file.

For example, suppose you have a business with branch offices around the country. Each branch keeps its own records locally using 1-2-3 and then sends you a disk at the end of the month. Obviously, each branch's files are separate.

Creating Linked Files

Even though data may be better off in separate worksheet files, these worksheets can still work together through links. Just as with the 3D worksheet you devised in the last lesson, linked worksheet files use cell references to other worksheet files for some of their data. The only difference is that cell references become a little more complex, since they also have to include the name of the file to which they refer. For example, a formula containing a cell reference to a linked file will look something like

    +<<BUDGET.WK3>>A:B11..AB11

or

    @SUM(<<BUDGET.WK3>>A:B11..AB11)

At first blush, this might look like too much work to be worthwhile, but with the mouse, linking files is quite easy. You can just point to the cell that links the two files and 1-2-3 does the typing. If you have both files open and in separate windows when creating the link, the process is very easy.

When a cell in one worksheet references another file, 1-2-3 looks into the file for the value. Even if the other file isn't open and active in 1-2-3, the link will still work as long as the file is stored in the same drive and directory it was in when linked to.

*C*reating a Second File to Link To

Let's create an example file that we'll link to the Budget worksheet. Assume, for this example, that the budget isn't a projection, but is an annual report instead. ABC Inc. has a separate sales department with its own worksheet that tracks sales of individual items. You plan to use this worksheet in conjunction with the annual report sheet to chronicle the year's profits.

We'll create the sales worksheet first, then we'll link the two files through a few formulas.

1. If you are in Perspective mode, turn it off since we don't need to see the Salaries worksheet.

2. Make the Budget file (worksheet A) the current file.

3. Choose File/New. A new blank worksheet called FILE001.WK3 (or something similar) covers the Budget sheet.

④ Choose File/Save As, and then name the new file
\123W\WORK\SALES.

⑤ Create the worksheet you see in Figure 28.1. I won't give
you explicit step-by-step instructions since you should be
able to do this by now using your experience creating the
Budget spreadsheet.

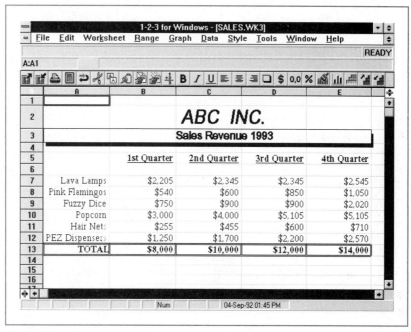

Figure 28.1: The sales statistics

All the sales statistics except for the Totals (B13, C13, D13, and
E13) are absolute values, so just type those in and format them as currency with no decimals, just as we did in the Budget sheet. The TOTAL
row does contain @SUM formulas. As you may recall, summing a
column is most easily accomplished by clicking on the cell at the bottom
of the column (in the TOTAL row), and then clicking on the Sum icon.

The headings are Arial MT 14, though it doesn't really matter
what font you use. The rest of the cell data looks different from that in
other worksheets thus far, because it's set to NewTimesRomanPS 12. I

have increased the column width with Worksheet/Global Settings a bit so the text is all readable.

Don't forget to save your work with File/Save.

*M*aking the Link

The key cells are the TOTAL cells: B13, C13, D13, and E13. Now we'll just replace the sales values in the Budget sheet with formulas that refer to the sales totals.

① Choose Window/Tile. You should now see two worksheets, BUDGET.WK3 and SALES.WK3, side by side, as in Figure 28.2. If the Budget window shows the Salaries sheet (sheet B), press Ctrl-PgDn to switch back to sheet A.

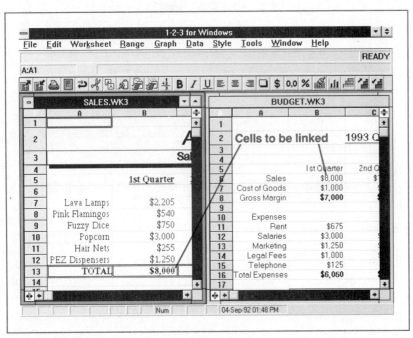

Figure 28.2: Two worksheet files open and tiled

Note that you now have two files active. Active files are open files. However, at any one time there is only one current file. The current file is the one the cell cursor is in. The current file's title bar changes to a different color or shade (darker in this book) on your screen to indicate that it is active. You can only perform operations to the current file, even though other active files can provide data or be updated by links.

In Figure 28.2 you can see the TOTAL cells for the first quarter's sales. The one on the left (in SALES.WK3) will supply the data for the one on the right (BUDGET.WK3).

② Click on the title bar of the Budget window. This makes it the current file.

③ Click on the Sales cell for the first quarter (B6).

④ Type + to indicate the beginning of a formula.

⑤ Now move the mouse pointer over to the first quarter's TOTAL cell in the Sales window (B13) and click on it. This is just like pointing to another cell in the same sheet, only in this case, it's in another sheet. Now 1-2-3 enters the complete cell reference:

+ <<123W\WORK\SALES.WK3>>A:B13..A:B13

Notice that the complete file name of the Sales worksheet becomes part of the cell's reference.

⑥ Confirm the entry. The first quarter sales figure in BUDGET recalculates. Cell B13 still displays 8,000, but the formula is now different.

⑦ Try changing the dollar amount of Pink Flamingos sales for the first quarter to see the link work, then change the value back.

⑧ Repeat the process above to link the other three totals. You will have to use the scroll buttons to scroll each window to bring the relevant cells into view. When you are through, cells B6, C6, D6, and E6 should contain the following formulas:

B6:   **+ <<123W\WORK\SALES.WK3>> A:B13..A:B13**

C6:   **+ <<123W\WORK\SALES.WK3>> A:C13..A:C13**

> D6:   + <<123W\WORK\SALES.WK3>> A:D13..A:D13
>
> E6:   + <<123W\WORK\SALES.WK3>> A:E13..A:E13

⑨ Save your work. Since the File/Save command only applies to the current file, make sure to save each file that you make changes to by clicking on its title bar first, then choosing File/Save.

Using Range Names as Links

Though in the example we spelled out cell addresses, you can also use range names as references, just as you can in single worksheets. The process is similar to what you've just done:

① Select the cell into which you're entering the formula, and press +.

② Press F3 to see a list of range names in the current file. This list also lists the names of other open files, enclosed in angle brackets.

③ Double-click on the file you want.

④ Select the range you want from the resulting list.

The range name is dropped into the formula in the other worksheet.

Managing Multiple Files

Even though only one file can be current at any time, 1-2-3 lets you have many files active (open) at a time. The actual number depends on the size of the worksheets and the amount of memory in your computer. If you have lots of files active, things can get pretty confusing. Here are a couple of file-management tricks to try:

① Double-click on the BUDGET.WK3 title bar (not the 1-2-3 title bar). This maximizes the window.

②   Click on its restore button, and it returns to its previous size.

③   Click on its minimize button now (the little down arrow on the right-hand side of the title bar).

④   Click on the minimize button for the other window. You should have two worksheet icons at the bottom of the 1-2-3 window.

⑤   Double-click on the BUDGET icon to restore it to its previous size.

⑥   Double-click on the SALES icon to restore it to its previous size.

⑦   Choose Window/Cascade. This stacks the two file's windows on top of each other. The one in the front is the current window. Clicking anywhere on the other window will bring it to the front, and make it current.

⑧   Choose Window/BUDGET.WK3. This is another way to make a file current.

⑨   Choose Window/SALES.WK3.

Troubleshooting

If you do a lot of work with linked files, you will probably make mistakes from time to time. When you open a worksheet that has invalid links, 1-2-3 will display an error message, such as ERR, in the cells that reference the second sheet. You need to find the source of the problem, so you can fix it. There are several things you can check:

- The file being linked to may not be on the right drive or in the right directory. Check the formula references by moving the cell pointer onto one of the ERR cells and looking at the edit line to read its formula. The formula will contain the path name of the linked file. Make sure it's the correct name.

- If you're working on a network, the linked file may not be available for use if it's being used by someone else on the network.

- The problem reference may be in a third file. For example, in the chain

    FILE1 → FILE2 → FILE3

    there will be a problem in FILE1 if FILE3 isn't where it's supposed to be, even if the link between FILE1 and FILE2 is correct. Open FILE2 to see if there are error messages in its cells. This may help you track down the culprit.

- If the link uses range names, check to see that the range names referenced still exist. They may have been deleted or renamed, causing an error when the destination file tried to find them in the linked file.

- If you don't see error messages, but you suspect that the values in linked cells are wrong, it may be because someone has changed values in the linked file and the current file has not yet been updated. This can easily happen on a network, where two people are independently working on linked files. The solution is to update the link by choosing File/ Administration/Update Links.

Closing Files

Remember that all 1-2-3 menus and their commands apply to the current file only—not to all active files. As mentioned above, this includes the Save command. It also applies to the Close command. To close a file:

① Make it the current file.

② Choose File/Close. As an alternative, you can double-click on the file's control box (upper left corner of its worksheet window).

Of course, if you choose File/Exit, 1-2-3 will ask you about saving each file that is active. Thus, you don't have to save each file individually if you are going to exit 1-2-3. Just choose File/Exit and answer the dialog box about saving files accordingly.

LESSON 29

Copying Data between Worksheet Files

FEATURING

- Edit/Copy
- Combining Data
- Extracting Data

THERE ARE TIMES WHEN IT'S MORE SENSIBLE TO COPY data between files rather than linking the files. For example, you may have a section of cells that you use over and over in worksheets you build. Rather than entering that section each time you build a new worksheet, you can copy it from one sheet to another.

Copying data between worksheet files can be done in three ways:

- With normal copying commands, using either the Clipboard (through Edit/Cut or Edit/Copy followed by Edit/Paste), the Edit/Quick Copy command, or the Range Copy icon. This is just like copying cells within a single worksheet except that the source and destination file names become part of the range references.

- Through the File/Combine From command, which pulls a specified range of cells into the destination file. You can then replace cells in the destination file with the source cells, or add or subtract the source cell values to or from the destination cell values as they are copied in.

- Through the File/Extract command, which creates a new worksheet file from a range in the current file.

Copying with Edit/Copy and Edit/Quick Copy

Probably the easiest way to copy material between sheets is with Edit/Copy and Edit/Quick Copy. You already know how to copy cells or ranges around on a single spreadsheet, so this should be no sweat. You just open both files, use Window/Tile to tile them, and adjust the cells so you can see the source and destination ranges. If the ranges are too big, you'll have to type the range into the Edit/Quick Copy dialog box, but that's easy enough.

As an example, let's copy the labels and 1st Quarter columns (columns A and B) from the Budget file into a new blank file.

① If the Sales file is still open, click on its minimize button to get it off the screen.

② Open the Budget window if it is closed.

③ Choose File/New to open a new worksheet file.

④ Choose Window/Tile to arrange the windows. If you've minimized the Sales file to an icon, the tiled windows will be shorter than normal. Stretch them down to the bottom of the 1-2-3 window by dragging the bottom of their frames. Position the pointer on the bottom of the file's frame. When the cursor turns into a two-headed arrow, click and drag the border down.

⑤ Scroll the Budget window so that columns A and B are showing.

⑥ Select the range A5..B19.

⑦ Choose either Edit/Copy or Edit/Quick Copy from the menus, or use the corresponding icons.

(8) Move the pointer into the destination file window, and click on the upper left corner cell of the destination range. In this case, click on cell A1. The range is copied into the new file, as you see in Figure 29.1.

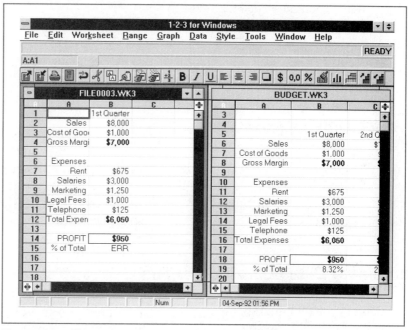

Figure 29.1: The range is copied into the destination file

Note that cell B15 has an error message in it. This is because there is an absolute reference in the formula to cell $F$19, which is back in the Budget spreadsheet. Edit/Quick Copy does not create a link between the files, so cell B15 of the new file now refers to cell F19 of the new file. An error message results since F19 in the new file contains no data (0) and the formula now constitutes a division by zero, which is illegal.

*C*opying through the Clipboard

Try copying with the Clipboard method now.

(1) From the new file, erase the range you just copied. Select it as a range, and choose Edit/Clear or press Del.

② Move back to the Budget file and select the range again.

③ Choose Edit/Copy. Nothing much appears to happen. Perhaps your hard disk drive light goes on for a few seconds. 1-2-3 is putting the range on the Windows Clipboard (which may be stored on disk temporarily).

④ Click on cell A2 in the new file to activate the cell.

⑤ Choose Edit/Paste. The range is copied in, beginning with A2 as the upper left corner of the destination.

Copying Only Values or Styles

If you use Edit/Quick Copy, you have several options that Edit/Copy doesn't give you. You can stipulate the range of the From and To locations. Also, by clicking on the check boxes in the dialog box, you can choose to copy just the values, or just the styles of the cells, rather than the whole shebang—values, formulas, and styles.

Combining Data from Another File

The File/Combine From command lets you pull a range from another file into the current one. The file containing the information you're pulling in is called the *source file*. The file receiving the data is called the *destination file*. The source file can be a 1-2-3 for Windows file or a file created with 1-2-3 Release 1A, 2, or 3.

If the destination range's cells have values in them, those cells can be updated through addition or subtraction of the incoming values. Or, if you don't want 1-2-3 to do any of this, it will simply replace the original cells with the source cells.

Combining is useful for updating one file from another. For example, you might create an inventory worksheet that could be updated from a receiving list. If you set up the two worksheets similarly, with the same order of items and relationships among cells, and combined them with the Addition option, the newly received items could be added to the existing inventory. Conversely, a shipping list that records items shipped out could be used similarly, with the Subtraction option. Combining the inventory sheet and the shipping list would decrease the inventory for each item accordingly.

When you combine data, the source file doesn't have to be open. You stipulate a range in the source file, and 1-2-3 will open the file, get the range and drop it into the destination file. This is easier if the source range is named. Then you don't have to remember the range.

Let's pull some information from the Budget file into the new file that's still on your screen, which already includes a list of items with dollar amounts that could be updated.

①　Move to the Budget file, select the range B11..B15 and name it Expenses with the Range/Name/Create command.

②　Save the Budget file with File/Save or by clicking on the File Save icon.

③　Close the Budget file by selecting File/Close or by double-clicking on its control box.

④　Maximize the new file.

⑤　Position the cell pointer in the top left corner of the range that will be the destination of the copied data. In this case, it is cell B8.

⑥　Choose File/Combine From. The File Combine From dialog box appears. Click on BUDGET.WK3 in the Files box. Note that you can pull in the whole file if you select Entire File. For example, select Range and type **EXPENSES** into the text area. Note also that you can Add, Subtract, or Copy. Make sure to choose Add for the example.

⑦　Click on OK. The data is pulled in, and the values are updated. In fact, they are doubled since we added the values to themselves. Note the PROFIT cell. There is now a negative cash flow for the quarter, as indicated by the parentheses around the ($5,100).

⑧　Perform the combination again, this time choosing Subtract. This should return the values to their previous state.

⑨ Perform the combination again, choosing Entire File, and notice that the whole file gets pulled in beginning at the active cell's position.

Remember that if you are updating existing cells, the data in the source and destination files should be organized in the same way, or your resulting values will not be accurate.

Also, be aware that cell formats are also imported with the incoming cells, though cell widths and other worksheet settings are not imported.

Extracting Data with File/Extract To

Finally, the File/Extract To command lets you copy a selected range to a disk file. In other words, it creates a separate worksheet file from a range you select.

Let's create a new file using this command. We'll extract the Sales, Cost of Goods, and Gross Margin sections of the budget.

① Close the new file by double-clicking on its control box or by choosing File/Close. Answer No to the dialog box that asks about saving it. We don't need to save it, since it was just for experimentation.

② Open the Budget worksheet again and maximize its window.

③ Select the range A1 to F8.

④ Choose File/Extract To.

⑤ The dialog box appears. Name the file MARGIN. Note that you can choose to copy Formulas (which includes values and formulas), just Values, or just Text. If you choose Text, 1-2-3 creates an ASCII text file that can be edited by programs such as PC-Write, Notepad, or any program that uses ASCII files. Select Formulas for this example. Also notice that you can stipulate a range by typing its references in or typing a range name rather than selecting first, as we did.

⑥ Click on OK, and the file is created.

⑦ Choose File/Open or click on the File Open smart icon to open the Margin file. It looks like Figure 29.2.

⑧ Close the Margin worksheet now. Leave the Budget worksheet open if you intend to go on to the next lesson. Otherwise, close them both.

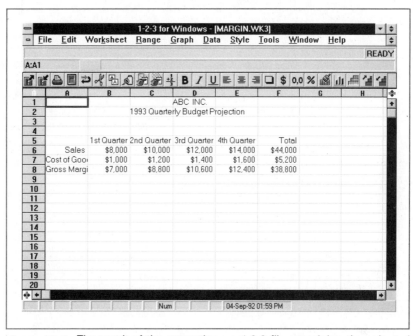

Figure 29.2: *The result of the extraction—a 1-2-3 file containing the selected range*

PART

5

Printing
Your Worksheet

30 LESSON

Preparing to Print

FEATURING

- The File/Printer Setup Command
- Selecting the Printed Range

IN THIS PART, YOU'LL LEARN HOW TO PRINT YOUR worksheets and create reports. In most of your print jobs, you'll simply be printing your data. However, you can also print your formulas for inspection, you can add headers (text that prints at the top of each page) and footers (text that prints at the bottom of each page) to your worksheets, you can print page numbers, and you can set custom margins and paper sizes. You can also include or suppress grid lines in your printouts.

The default settings for these options produce acceptable results for most jobs. However, your printouts and reports will benefit greatly from a little additional work on your part. In the next few lessons, you'll learn how to use of 1-2-3's print options to best suit your needs.

The procedures in these next few lessons also apply to printing graphs. Once you learn how to create graphs in Part Six, you can refer back to this section if you need help printing them.

Even if you don't have a printer, you still may want to work through these lessons so that you'll know what to do when you do have a printer. Most of the steps in the lessons on printing will still work even if you don't have a printer plugged in and working.

Checking to See If You Have a Printer Installed

Just as most other Windows programs do, 1-2-3 for Windows uses the Windows Print Manager. This means that Windows takes care of the details of printing your document. The Print Manager relies on information you (or someone else) provided when installing the Windows software on your computer.

It's possible that you don't even have a printer driver installed, in which case you're not going to get very far if you try to print. (A printer driver is the software that translates your worksheet data into commands your printer can understand.) To find out whether you have a printer installed, do the following:

① Choose File/Printer Setup. The Printer Setup dialog box appears. A printer name should appear in the list box. If it doesn't, then you have to install a printer. You do this with the Windows Control Panel. You should refer to the *Microsoft Windows User's Guide,* or another book on the topic of Windows, such as *Mastering Windows 3.0* (SYBEX), for information on installing printers.

② If the box has more than one name, choose the one you plan to print to.

③ Click on OK.

Note that the type of printer you have installed will affect how closely your printouts will resemble what you see on your screen. Your printouts may not actually include all the fonts, styles, and attributes that appear on screen. A Preview option in 1-2-3 lets you see how a print job is actually going to look, though, before you print. This saves you both time and paper.

Choosing a Range

The next step in the process of printing a worksheet is to select the portion of the worksheet you want to print. This is important, because if you print the whole worksheet, the result will be a monstrous report about 130 feet long and about 20 feet wide! Most of this would be empty cells, of course—and wasted paper.

Usually you'll want to print out only the cells containing your data, or a specific subset of those cells. On a single worksheet, this is called a 2D range. If you are using a file containing more than one worksheet, then you may want to print only a portion of one of the worksheets in the file, or perhaps a section containing cells from parts of each worksheet (a 3D range).

You can tell 1-2-3 to print any number of ranges. The ranges will be printed one after another on the same page. They will be broken between pages if they are too large to fit on a single sheet.

The easiest way to print a range is to select it with the mouse and choose the File/Print command. If you want to print multiple ranges, you can print them one a time using this technique, or you can separate the ranges by a comma in the Range section of the Print dialog box. As you might suspect, you can also use range names in such a list. For example,

A:A1..F22

will print the range A1 to F22 in spreadsheet A;

A:A1..F22,B:A15..G30

will print the range A1 to F22 in spreadsheet A, then print A15 to G30 in spreadsheet B;

A:A1..B:F22

will print the range A1 to F22 in spreadsheet A, then print A1 to F22 in spreadsheet B. This is a 3D range. The range

A:A1..F10,EXPENSES

will print A1 to F10, then the EXPENSES range.

Suppose we want to print the entire budget projection contained on worksheet A of the Budget file. Here are the steps you'd take for selecting the range:

① Open the Budget worksheet file.

② Adjust the screen so you can see the whole budget.

③ Press Home to move to cell A1. Now select the range A1..F19. Use the F4-key approach this time. Press F4, then use the → and ↓ keys to select the range. Press Enter when the range is enlarged to the correct size. Your screen should look like Figure 30.1.

④ Now go on to the next lesson where you'll preview your printout on the screen.

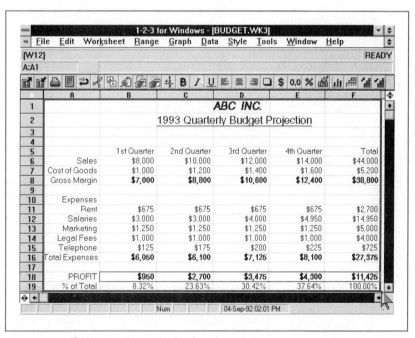

Figure 30.1: Selecting the entire budget for printing

31 LESSON

Previewing Your Printout

FEATURING

- Previewing Single Ranges
- Previewing Multiple Ranges

BEFORE PRINTING, IT'S ALWAYS A GOOD IDEA TO preview your report's layout. You can do this quickly with 1-2-3's File/Preview command. After selecting the print range, choosing File/Preview displays on your screen a miniature page that closely resembles the appearance of the printed document. Preview lets you quickly fine-tune your printouts, avoiding the need to print them, correct what's wrong, and print them again.

The File/Preview Dialog Box

In the last lesson, you opened the Budget worksheet and selected the range A1..F19. Let's preview it.

① After selecting the range to be printed, choose File/Preview. The Preview dialog box pops up.

The selected range is already entered in the Range text area. You can change this if you wish by typing in a range name or range address. Recall from the last lesson that you can enter more than one range if you separate them with a comma.

In the From Pages section of the box, you can specify which pages of the printout you want to preview. The default is 1 to 9999. You don't have to alter this unless you are working with a large worksheet and know exactly which page you want to look at, or unless you have entered several ranges to print, separated by commas. If you're previewing a large spreadsheet, you won't know the page number, though, unless you've printed or previewed it once already.

The Starting Page setting determines what page number is printed on the first page. The Page Setup button is used for altering headers, footers, and other options. These options are discussed in Lesson 32.

② Click on OK. In a couple of seconds you'll see the previewed page, as shown in Figure 31.1.

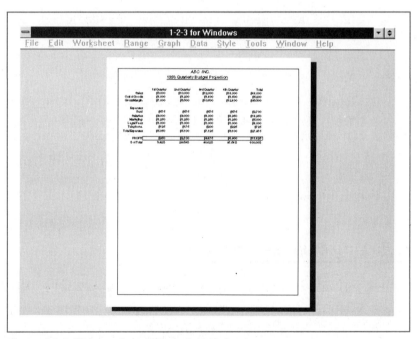

Figure 31.1: The previewed Budget worksheet

Obviously the text is a bit small to read unless you are eagle-eyed. But you get an idea of the data's placement on the page. The black lines around the edge will not print. These lines represent the margin settings, which can be changed, as I'll explain in the next lesson.

③ Press Esc to return to the spreadsheet. Notice that the selected range now has a dotted gray line around it. This line indicates the active print range and will stay in effect until you preview or print a new range.

Previewing Multiple Ranges

Let's preview two ranges this time. The first range will be the one you just previewed. The second range will be the employee salary information from sheet B of the Budget file. You created this range several lessons ago.

① Choose File/Preview again. The dialog box should still have the Range section filled in with A1..F19. Move into that section of the box, and edit the section to read as follows:

A:A1..F19,B:A1..F9

(Remember when editing text box contents to press one of the arrow keys or click the I-beam cursor once on the highlighted text to deselect it. If you don't, the current contents of the box will be replaced by the first character you type.)

② Click on OK. The preview screen appears again, with two ranges printed this time, as you see in Figure 31.2.

Previewing Multiple Pages

As you can see, 1-2-3 dumps one range on the page just after the first one. Suppose you wanted each of the ranges to print on a separate page. How would you do this? You could just fill the selected range with blank cells or add a range of blank cells from somewhere else in the worksheet, until the print range was large enough to display across two pages. Since all the rows below the selected range in worksheet A are blank, you can just increase the range area in this case.

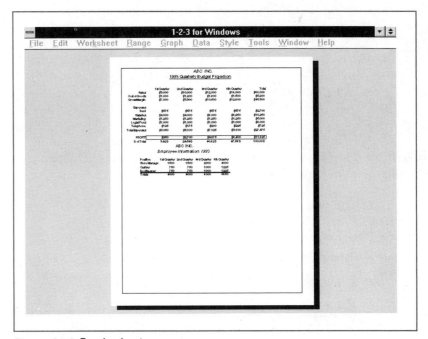

Figure 31.2:Previewing two ranges

① Press Esc to return to the worksheet.

② Choose File/Preview again. This time make the ranges read

   A:A1..F60,B:A1..F9

③ Click on OK. The first page now shows only the budget.

④ Press Enter to see the second page, which should show only the salaries.

　　If you're previewing a large number of pages, you can press Enter to see the next page, and Esc to return to the worksheet.

　　Note also that the column width settings and font size can greatly affect the placement of text on the printed page. If you were to return to the worksheet and reset the global column width to 13 in the Worksheet/Global Settings dialog box, the budget would be centered better on the page.

32 LESSON

Setting Printing Options

FEATURING

- Headers and Footers
- Saving Page Setups
- Scaling Printouts

AS YOU MAY HAVE NOTICED IN THE PREVIEWS WE JUST did, the printout contained no frills such as page numbers, headers, or footers. Unless you request these options, your printouts will be fairly plain in appearance.

The default printing settings will produce printouts that are adequate for most purposes. However, if you want to spice up your printouts for presentation purposes, it's a relatively painless task: You just select your options from the Page Setup dialog box. Once you're happy with the settings, you can save them on disk and recall them for later use. These settings control the appearance of both your screen previews and your actual printouts.

Using the File/Page Setup Dialog Box

To use the Page Setup dialog box, follow these steps:

① Make sure the Budget file is still open. Select range A1..F19 if it is not already selected.

② Choose File/Preview. The Preview dialog box appears.

③ Click on the Page Setup button. A large dialog box appears, as you see in Figure 32.1. This is the same dialog box you get if you choose File/Page Setup, but for your convenience, it's available for setting up a preview.

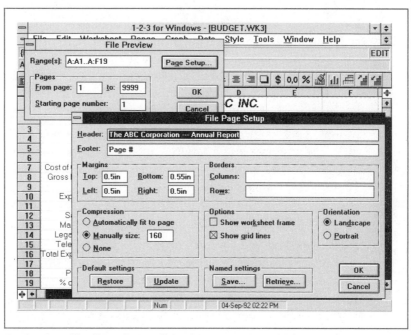

Figure 32.1: The Page Setup dialog box

From the Page Setup dialog box, you can set the following options:

- Header: Adds headers that you want to print at the top of each page.

- Footer: Adds footers that you want to print at the bottom of each page.

- Margins: Sets the top, bottom, left, and right margins for the page.

- Compression: The Automatically Fit to Page option compresses a print range so printed data is smaller and more data fits on a printed page, or it expands a print range so your data fills the page. The Manually Size option lets you decide the percentage by which to increase or decrease print size instead of letting 1-2-3 do it automatically. The default is 100 percent.

- Borders: Lets you choose which columns of data to print at the left of every page and rows of worksheet data to print at the top of every page. This is similar to freezing titles while using a worksheet as an aid to identifying the meaning of cells. This option is particularly useful when printing a range that doesn't include your row or column labels.

- Options: Lets you print the worksheet frame and/or the worksheet grid lines along with the data. Adding grid lines can make reading across rows easier. The Show Worksheet Frame option prints the column letters and row numbers across the top and down the left side, just as you see them in the worksheet frame.

- Orientation: Lets you choose whether the printout is in Portrait mode or Landscape mode. Portrait mode prints the "short way," across the page. Landscape mode prints the "long way." (Landscape mode may not be available for your printer.) If you have wide spreadsheets, you may want to use Landscape mode.

- Default Settings: The Update option makes the current Header, Footer, Margins, Borders, Options, and Orientation settings the default page settings for all pages printed from the file. The Restore option replaces the currently selected settings with the default page settings for the file.

- Named Settings: The Save option lets you save the current page settings in a file that you can later load. The Retrieve option reloads a previously saved file of settings from disk and makes them the page settings for the current file.

Using Page Setup Options

Using the above information, you should be able to try out most of the settings. There's absolutely no harm done by experimenting, since nothing is stored to disk—just don't click on Update. If you choose an option that looks terrible, just press Esc, reopen the dialog box (the shortcut is to press Alt-F-V to open the Preview menu, then Alt-G to get to the Page Setup dialog box), change a setting or two, then select OK in both boxes to preview.

Once you have made some settings, you can select any range and click on the Preview icon, shown in Figure 32.2, to quickly preview the range without having any dialog boxes slowing you down.

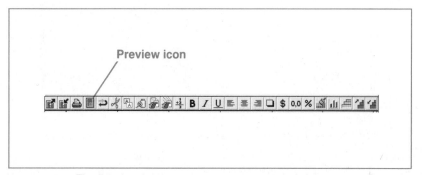

Preview icon

Figure 32.2: The Preview icon

Try some of the options to see their effects:

① Keep the same range selection you had from the previous exercise: A1..F19.

② Choose File/Preview, then Page Setup. Fill in the dialog box according to the settings shown back in Figure 32.1. Notice the # symbol after Page, in the Footer box. This symbol causes the page number to be printed. It will advance with each new page printed if your print job will produce more than a single page. Through experimentation, I arrived at the 160 percent sizing shown in the Compression box, which filled the page just right.

LESSON 32

Click on OK in the Page Setup dialog box, and then click on OK in the Preview box. The result is what you see in Figure 32.3.

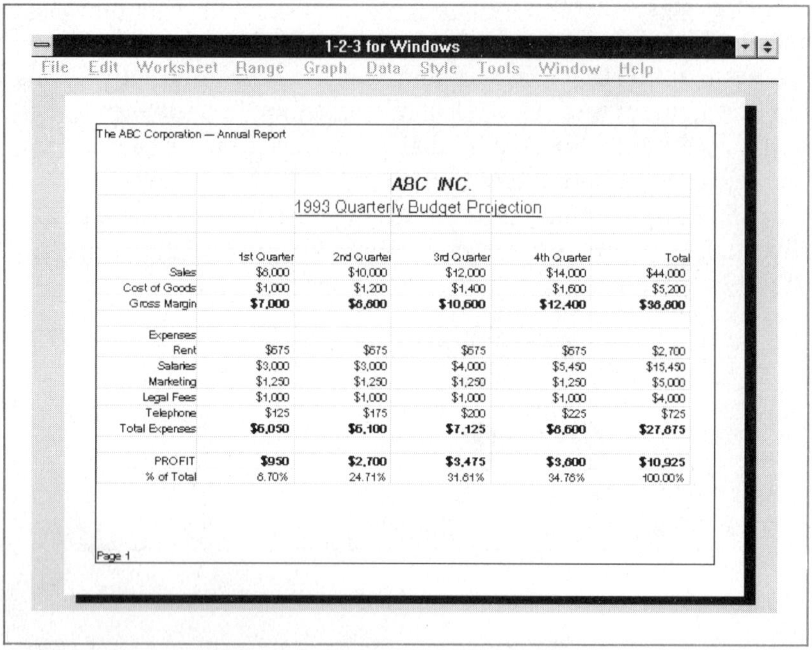

Figure 32.3: The enhanced screen preview

Saving and Reloading Preview Settings from Disk

Now we'll save the settings you just made, so you can load them up later.

① Reopen the Page Setup dialog box.

② In the Named Settings section, click on Save. A typical file box appears. Name the file LESSON32.AL3 (note that 1-2-3 uses the file extension AL3), and click on OK. Don't change the extension. File names must comply with DOS filename standards: a maximum of eight characters, no spaces, and no asterisks or question marks.

③ Now return all the settings to their previous defaults by clicking on Restore in the Default Settings section.

④ To bring up your saved settings, choose the Retrieve button. A file box comes up; it should list LESSON32.AL3. Double-click on it, and watch as your previous settings are reinstated. Remember this for saving your print settings.

⑤ Once again, return the box to the default settings by clicking on Restore.

33 LESSON

Printing the Worksheet

FEATURING

- The File/Print Command

ONCE YOU'VE SET THE RANGE YOU WANT TO PRINT, previewed it, and made a few modifications with the Page Setup dialog box, you are ready to print out your work on paper.

Preparing to Print

Before you print your worksheet, make the following preparations:

① First, turn on your printer.

② Then, make sure it has paper and is online and hooked up properly to your computer. Most printers have an online switch that controls whether the printer is ready to print or not.

③ If you have more than one printer, Choose File/Printer Setup to ensure the correct printer is selected.

As mentioned earlier, Windows should have previously been informed about your brand and model of printer and to which computer port it's connected. If you're in doubt about this, assume everything is OK; 1-2-3 will tell you if it's not.

Printing

Finally, after all those previews and preparations, you're ready to produce some hard copy. Follow these steps:

① Choose File/Print. The Print dialog box pops up.

Notice that you can choose to preview the printout from this dialog box. The effect is identical to choosing the command from the File menu. You can also get to the Page Setup dialog box from here. The route through which you access the dialog boxes is up to you and doesn't affect the choices you make in them. For example, the Page Setup settings you make from the Preview dialog box will still be active when you open the same box from the Print menu.

② Enter or amend the range(s) you want to print in the Range section. Note that if you want to print a long label that covers adjacent cells, you should extend the print area to include all the cells the label covers.

③ If you want to, preview the printout again by clicking on Preview. You will be returned to the worksheet after previewing your printout, though, so you'll have to choose File/Print again.

④ If you want to make any adjustments, click on Page Setup to bring up the Page Setup dialog box. Make the changes and click on OK.

⑤ When you're ready to print, click on OK. A message will appear on your screen stating that the file is being printed.

The file is sent to the Windows Print Manager, which in turn takes care of sending your worksheet data to the printer. This all happens automatically. The Print Manager icon will appear on the Windows desktop. If you were to arrange the windows on your screen to reveal the bottom edge of the desktop, you'd see it. By double-clicking on the icon, you can open the Print Manager window, from which you can pause or cancel the print job. If your computer encounters some difficulty with the printing process, the Print Manager will alert you in a dialog box. Refer to the Windows manual or another reference source on Windows for details on using the Print Manager.

PART

6

Graphing
Your Worksheet

34 LESSON

Types of Graphs

FEATURING

- Bar Charts
- Pie Charts
- Line Charts

ONE OF THE BEST THINGS ABOUT THE WINDOWS version of 1-2-3 is its ability to produce high-quality graphs. With almost no effort or expertise, you can create impressive color graphs.

You can graph almost any spreadsheet data in 1-2-3. A well-designed chart (or graph—the two terms are interchangeable) will convey the meaning of your numbers visually rather than numerically. By plotting your numbers in a chart, you can more easily spot trends and relationships in and among your data, and more clearly communicate your findings to others.

Without computers, chart-making can be an expensive and tedious job, often requiring special skills, tools, and personnel. Worse yet, any alteration of the charted data sends the art staff back to their drawing boards to start again—from scratch.

With 1-2-3, you can jump between viewing the chart and altering the data in the worksheet and see the effects immediately reflected in your charts. You can even have the chart and the data on the screen at the same time in separate windows, eliminating the need to jump between screens.

You can create seven basic types of charts with 1-2-3. Each type is shown in Figure 34.1.

- Bar: The bar chart, sometimes referred to as the histogram, consists of vertical boxes or bars arranged side by side. The height of each bar corresponds to the value it represents. Variations on the bar chart include the stacked bar chart, which creates a single vertical bar for a set of related values, and the 3D bar chart, which adds visual impact.

- Line: The line chart shows related information as a series of horizontal lines drawn in a "connect-the-dots" fashion. Typically, line charts are used to display changes over a period of time. Variations include the 3D line.

- Area Line: Much like the stacked bar, the area line chart uses the line below it (rather than the X-axis) as its starting point. This illustrates the contribution of each section of data to the whole.

- High-Low-Close-Open (HLCO): HLCO charts are modeled on the stock market charts you see in the newspaper that show you the fluctuations of a stock's value over a period of time. Each item being tracked is represented by a vertical line, with recognizable tick marks indicating the highest and lowest values the item reached and the opening and closing values of the item (such as the start of the day and the end of the day).

- Mixed: This type of chart combines the line chart and bar chart into a single graph. Mixed charts can be useful for charting dissimilar types of data.

- Pie: The old, familiar pie chart is simply a circle sliced into wedges. Each wedge represents a value in a single list of numbers. An attractive 3D version of the pie chart is also an option.

- XY: Sometimes called a scatter chart, this type of chart plots points against an X- and Y-axis to display the relationships between pairs of numbers.

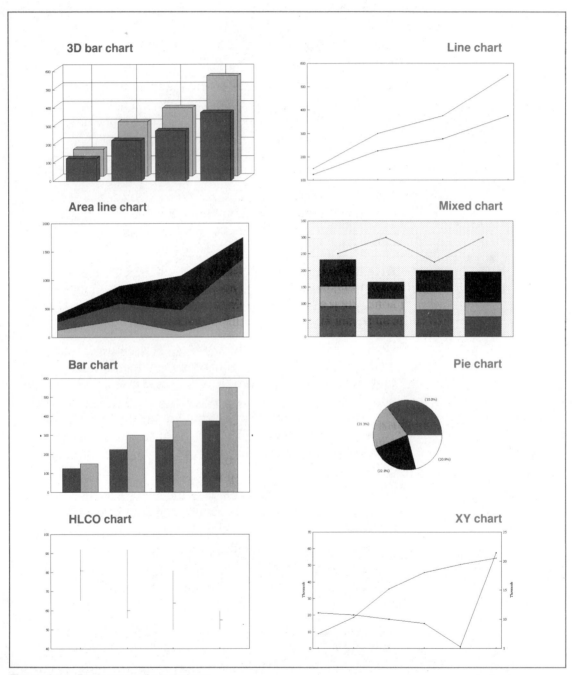

Figure 34.1: *Basic types of 1-2-3 charts*

LESSON 35

Planning Your Chart

WITH SO MANY TYPES OF CHARTS TO CHOOSE FROM, you may be wondering how you'll even begin to graph your worksheet. That's why it's a good idea to plan your charts before you create them. In this lesson, we'll discuss the mental steps you should take before creating a chart, and then in the next lesson we'll implement them at the keyboard as you create your first chart.

Design Considerations

Designing a chart takes some forethought, just as creating a worksheet does. You'll need to consider in advance just what message you want your chart to convey to the observer. Generally speaking, it's a good idea to make charts as simple as possible. Don't try to include too much data or other information in a single chart. It's better to use several charts instead, since after all, the idea of a chart is to make your data easily understood.

The best way to design a chart is with a piece of paper and a pencil in hand. What type of chart should it be? Should I use a pie chart, bar chart, or one of the other choices? What data will be displayed?

Who will be using the chart? What should the increments, or units, of the chart be? Finally, what should the labels, titles, or other explanatory markings be and where should they be placed?

Once you have a sense of how you'd like your graphs to look, go back to the computer, load the worksheet containing the data, and start creating it. All the data you want to chart must be in the worksheet. Also, to be graphed, the data has to be organized into ranges that can easily be selected into groups. Since 1-2-3 cannot jump around the worksheet to find data for the chart, each group of numbers you want to chart must be contiguous.

LESSON 36

Creating a Chart

FEATURING

- The Graph/New Command
- Arranging Your Data

SUPPOSE SOME CHARTS OF THE PROJECTED BUDGET for ABC Inc. are needed before the company goes public. Potential stockholders will be anxious to see such things as the expected expenses and earnings for the 1993 fiscal year.

We'll be using the Budget file to create some graphs, so you should find that file and load it, if it isn't loaded already.

Creating a Bar Chart

Let's start by charting estimated expenses over four quarters. You could show this type of growth using a line chart, or you could use a bar chart with time plotted from left to right and costs charted vertically, as in Figure 36.1.

Here's how to create the new chart:

① Select the range A11:E15, since this is the range we want to chart.

② Choose Graph/New.

LESSON 36

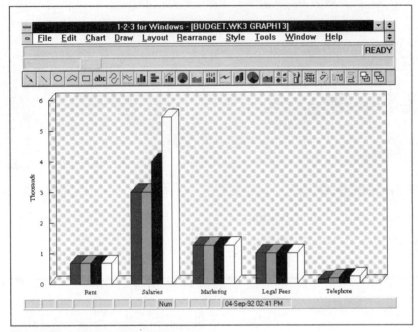

Figure 36.1: 3D bar chart of A11 to E15

③ A small dialog box pops up with the default name of the graph in it: GRAPH1. Click on OK.

④ A fairly spartan line graph comes up. This is the default graph type, so it comes up first. Notice that the menu bar and icons change when you are graphing.

⑤ Change the graph type by choosing Chart/Type. A dialog box appears listing type of graphs you can choose.

⑥ Click on each button. Notice how you get an example of each type. If there are variations available for one of the graph types, two or more little pictures will be displayed to the right.

⑦ Click on 3D Bar.

⑧ Three different styles of bar charts will appear. Click on the upper left one. Now click on each of the others. Notice that when you click, the selected style's picture is depressed like a control button or a like a key on a touch-tone phone. This indicates which of the chart variations is selected.

⑨ Click again on the upper left style.

⑩ Click on OK, and 1-2-3 draws the graph instantly. The graph should look like that in Figure 36.1.

Notice that the default chart has no legends to indicate which quarter is which. We will add these manually later. However, 1-2-3 is smart enough to scale the chart reasonably, from the lowest value to the highest value in the range, so that the chart looks good. On the Y-axis (the vertical line on the left), tick marks are computed and labeled automatically by 1-2-3 in whatever it considers to be the most logical manner. You can adjust the tick marks later if you want.

Finally, note that the labels in the first column of the selected range were automatically placed below each set of four bars. This makes it easy to create an instant graph, if the data is arranged properly.

If your data is arranged poorly, your graphs will turn out poorly. Thus, you will make things easy on yourself by laying out your data in a manner similar to the range we just selected. The labels for the chart sections should be in the column furthest to the left, followed by a column or columns of values to be charted. If you don't have labels included in the range, 1-2-3 will chart the numbers, and you'll have to add the labels manually.

LESSON

Adding Legends
and Titles

FEATURING

- The Chart/Legend Command
- The Chart/Headings Command

YOU CAN SEE JUST FROM GLANCING AT YOUR NEW BAR chart that salaries make up most of the expenses of ABC Inc. However, you are familiar with the chart and know its purpose without even looking at it. The casual observer might find the chart vague without some more textual information to clarify the significance of the bars.

*A*dding Legends

A *legend,* sometimes called a key, is a series of little patterned or colored boxes at the bottom of a chart used to clarify what the various sections of a graph mean. Each colored section represents a bar, a slice of a pie, or whatever is appropriate to the type of graph. Let's add a legend to our chart.

1. Choose Chart/Legend. A dialog box appears.

2. There are six text areas in the dialog box, labeled A through F. Each letter corresponds to one set of data in the graph.

For example, notice that on the chart, there are four bars above Rent. As you know, each bar represents the rent for one quarter of the year. The bar farthest to the left shows the first quarter's rent. The second bar in the group shows the second quarter's rent, and so on. Now, for applying a legend, the leftmost bar in a group is referred to as A, the second bar is B, and so on, for each group. Thus, you would fill in the box as you see in Figure 37.1.

③ Click on OK.

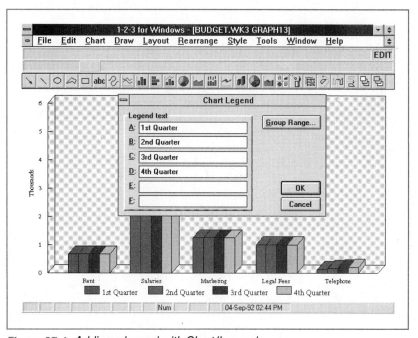

Figure 37.1: *Adding a legend with Chart/Legend*

*A*dding Titles

You can also add a title and subtitle to a chart to indicate what it's about. Follow these steps:

① Choose Chart/Headings.

②   A dialog box pops up. Type

   ABC INC.

   into the Title text area, and type

   1993 Budget Projection - Expenses

   into the Subtitle text area.

③   Click on OK, and the titles appear at the top of the chart. By
   default, 1-2-3 assumes you want the main title larger than the
   subtitle.

Changing Graph Types

FEATURING

- Switching Windows
- Tiling Windows
- Automatic Updating

ONCE YOU HAVE SET UP A GRAPH AND ADDED A LEGEND and titles, you can easily change the appearance of the graph. Perhaps the graph type you originally chose didn't present the data as you thought it would. No problem; you can just change graph types. Or maybe you want to change some of the worksheet data the graph is based on. Again, this is easy; you can move between your worksheet and graph with just a simple command.

Choosing a Different Graph Type

Let's suppose you decided that a 3D bar graph isn't exactly what you wanted, and you'd prefer a regular bar graph.

1. Select Chart/Type.
2. From the dialog box, choose Bar.

LESSON 38

③ The normal bar type (not stacked bar) is probably already selected, as is Vertical. If these options are not selected, select them.

④ Click on OK. The graph is automatically redrawn to appear as a plain bar graph.

This graph doesn't look all that exciting, so how about another version of the 3D bar?

① Bring up the Chart Type dialog box again.

② This time choose 3D Bar, but click on the variation in the right side of the dialog box that stacks the bars from front to back.

③ Click on OK, and the results look like Figure 38.1.

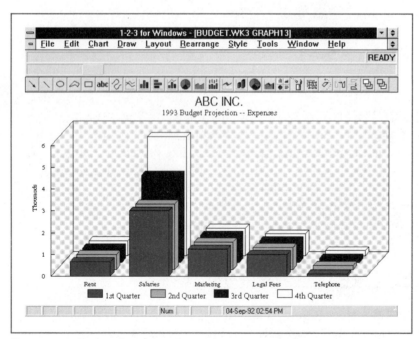

Figure 38.1: Budget Expenses chart redrawn in a variation of the 3D bar

Getting Back to Your Data

Often you'll want to get back to your worksheet, twiddle some numbers, and then see the graph again. There are a number of ways to do this.

Switching Windows

The first technique provides the greatest visible workspace for both the graph and the worksheet. Each graph you create is listed on the Window menu along with any open worksheets. You can switch between worksheets and graphs by selecting any graph or sheet from this list. Try this now:

① Choose Window/BUDGET.WK3. In a few seconds, the worksheet reappears.

② Now you can examine your data, alter it if you wish, and see the results when you return to the graph.

③ Choose Window/BUDGET.WK3 GRAPH1. This returns you to the graph.

Tiling Windows

The second approach is to tile the graph and worksheet windows. Tiling windows can be handy if you are working with a small section of data on the worksheet and won't feel too hampered using a smallish window. It can also speed up your work, since 1-2-3 won't have to redraw the entire screen each time you make a change to the graph.

① Choose Window/Tile, and 1-2-3 puts up the spreadsheet and the graph in windows, side by side, as shown in Figure 38.2. It scales the graph window nicely to make it visible in its entirety. (Your windows may be reversed.)

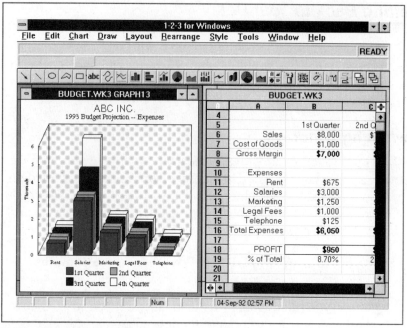

Figure 38.2: Tiling the graph and worksheet window

② Click on the worksheet window, then on the graph window. Notice that the icon palette changes depending on which window is active.

Now let's change some of the spreadsheet data, so we can see how 1-2-3 automatically updates charts.

① Click on the Budget window again.

② Use F5 (the Go To key) to go to cell E14 (Legal Fees, 4th Quarter).

③ Type **3000** into the cell and press Enter. (Your legal fees are expected to skyrocket that quarter due to patents you hope to apply for.) As soon as you press Enter, 1-2-3 recalculates the worksheet and redraws the chart.

④ Your engineer just called. Those patents won't be necessary after all. Return cell E14 to its previous value of 1000. The graph is redrawn.

LESSON 39

Managing Your Graphs

YOUR GRAPHS ARE STORED ON DISK WHENEVER YOU save your spreadsheet with File/Save or the File Save icon. When you reload the worksheet, all the graphs you've created are available for you to use again.

As you experiment with graphs and create a number of them for a given worksheet, you may find it frustrating to move among all your graphs. Here are a few tricks that will help you manage your graphs more effectively.

Viewing Existing Graphs

When you open a worksheet file, none of the graphs stored in it will appear on the Window menu. You have to open the graph first. To open an existing graph in a window:

① Choose Graph/View from the worksheet menu.

② Choose the graph to view.

③ Click on OK.

The graph is opened in a window. Once you add a graph to a range in your worksheet, this process isn't necessary, as you'll see in Lesson 42.

Switching from One Graph to Another

If you have several graphs open in windows, you'll need to move among them if you intend to work with them. One way to switch to another graph is to open the Window menu and choose the one you want. Naming the graph something descriptive (as explained below) makes choosing the right one even easier. When you select a graph, you will immediately be moved to its window.

Or, just as you tiled your graph and worksheet into two windows last lesson, you can have several graph windows on the screen at the same time. Then you can switch from one graph to another by clicking on the desired graph's window. Once a window is active, you can use its minimize, maximize, and restore buttons to alter its size, or you can drag its frame from the side or corner. The disadvantage of having lots of graphs tiled is that they become difficult to see, since 1-2-3 scales them down to fit on the screen.

Another approach to choosing graphs is to cascade your graph windows by choosing Window/Cascade. Once cascaded, you just click on the title bar or a corner of a particular graph's window to bring it the foreground. Figure 39.1 shows several graphs cascaded.

Naming Your Graphs

Notice that some of the graphs in Figure 39.1 have names other than GRAPH1 or GRAPH2. These are names I assigned to the graphs. You don't have to name a graph if you don't mind the default

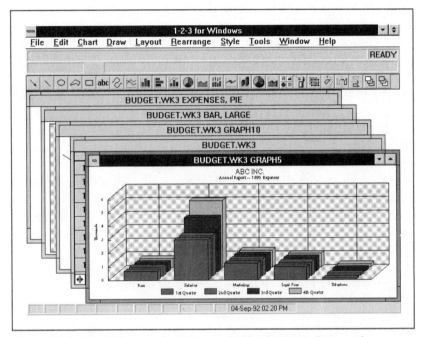

Figure 39.1: Cascading graphs makes switching between them easier

names, since 1-2-3 assigns a default name like GRAPH1 to each graph you create. But if you use the default names, you'll have to view each graph to know what's on it (unless you have a remarkable memory). To avoid that inconvenience, name your graphs descriptively.

You have the opportunity to name a graph only when you first create it. When you choose Graph/New from the worksheet's menu bar, you see a dialog box asking for the name of the graph. If you don't want to use the default name, type in a name of your choice. It can be up to 15 characters long and can include punctuation marks and spaces.

*C*learing Unwanted Graph Data

Each time you go back to the worksheet window to select a new range and then graph it, 1-2-3 creates a new graph rather than adding the new range to the old graph. In short order, you will notice lots of graph names on the Window menu.

Creating graph after graph rather than modifying the first one results in a stockpile of graphs you don't want to keep. You shouldn't keep them either, since they tie up disk space and computer memory. Keeping old graphs slows 1-2-3 down, since each graph is redrawn whenever you change data that is plotted on it.

If you intend to go back to the worksheet to try using a new range for the graph, or if you don't like some of the settings in the graph and want to start over, you can do this with the Clear command.

You can use the Clear command to erase certain elements of the graph, but leave others intact. This way you can work with the graph again, instead of starting from scratch. The Chart/Clear command lets you clear the entire chart, individual ranges, all the ranges, or just the settings. Here are the steps for clearing a graph:

①　Select the graph window you want to clear.

②　Choose Chart/Clear.

③　The Chart Clear dialog box appears. The check box options in this dialog box have the following meanings:

- X is the list of labels across the X-axis. In this case, it's the labels in column A—Rent, Salaries, Marketing, etc.

- A through F are the Y-ranges. These are the data you've selected in the worksheet to chart. For example, in our budget worksheet, the A range (first range) was the column of labels in row A: A11..A15. The B Range was B11..B15, and so on.

- All (X, A–F) deletes all ranges and labels from the graph.

- Entire chart clears all settings for the graph.

- Chart settings clears the label, heading, legend, axis, color, hatch (the cross-hatch pattern assigned to parts of a graph), font, and line settings for the graph.

Fill in the check boxes appropriately and click on OK.

Note that you can also change the ranges by choosing Chart/Ranges from the Graph window.

Deleting Unwanted Graphs from the Worksheet

Once you have a graph you like, you should delete any graphs that you don't want. This will eliminate confusion when selecting which graphs to view. You use Graph/Name/Delete from the worksheet menu to delete a graph. Here are the steps, even though we're not going to delete any graphs now:

① Choose Graph/Name/Delete.

② In the list box, select the graph name you want to delete.

③ Click on Delete.

40 LESSON

Adding a Grid and a Data Table

FEATURING

- X-Axis Grids
- Y-Axis Grids

ON SOME CHARTS, PARTICULARLY ON THE 3D ONES, judging the values of the bars or lines may be difficult without some aid. Two simple options come to the rescue here—Grids and Data Table. The Grids option adds lines as a backdrop to the graph. The Data Table option adds a small explanatory table to the graph.

Adding a Grid

Let's add a grid to the 3D bar chart.

1. If you don't have the 3D bar chart on screen, activate its window now and maximize it. If your worksheet was closed, you may have to use the Graph/View command to open it first.

2. Pull down the Chart menu and choose Borders/Grids. The dialog box you see in Figure 40.1 appears. Turn on the X-axis and Y-axis grids, as you see in the figure.

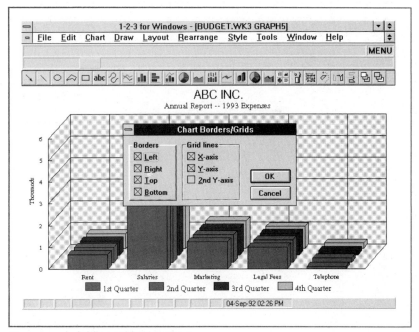

Figure 40.1: *Adding grids to a chart*

The result is also shown in Figure 40.1. Note that you can select to have only X-axis (horizontal) or Y-axis (vertical) grids turned on, even though we did both.

The Borders options turn on and off borders around the periphery of the chart.

*A*dding a Data Table

Now we'll add a table below the chart to indicate the exact figures for each quarter's itemized expenses.

① Choose Chart/Type. The Chart Type dialog box appears.

② At the bottom of the box is an option box called Include Table of Values. Turn this option on.

③ Click on OK. The results are shown in Figure 40.2.

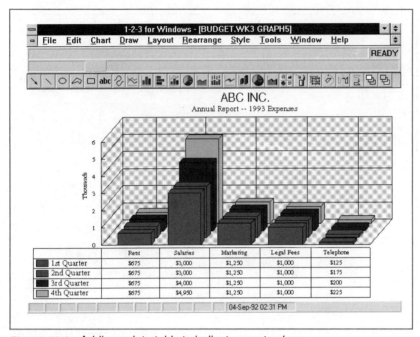

Figure 40.2: *Adding a data table to indicate exact values*

LESSON 41

Making a Pie Chart

FEATURING

- A Single Y-Series

NEXT TO BAR GRAPHS, PIE GRAPHS ARE PROBABLY THE most popular charts. Pie graphs are particularly useful when you want to portray part of something as a percentage of the whole. Pie graphs can only display a single set of data (called a Y-series), however, so there are certain limitations to this type. For example, we could only plot one quarter's expenses, not all four, as we did with the bar graph. In that chart, we had four sets of data, or Y-series—one set of expenses for each quarter.

Let's try graphing out the company's first quarter expenses to get an idea of the relative proportions of each category.

1. In the worksheet, select range A11..B15.

2. Choose Graph/New.

3. Name the graph "Expenses, Pie," and click on OK. The default line chart appears.

4. Click on the 3D Pie Chart icon shown in Figure 41.1, or choose Chart Type/3D Pie. Figure 41.2 shows the resulting pie chart, tiled with the data that produced it.

LESSON 41

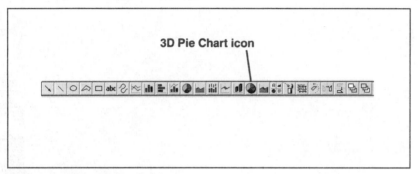

Figure 41.1: The 3D Pie Chart icon

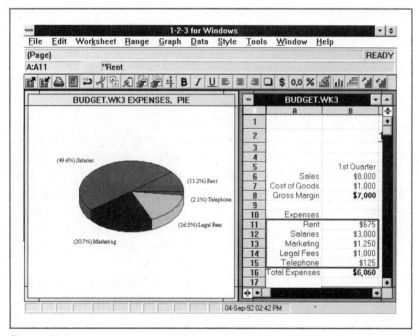

Figure 41.2: The pie chart

Notice that 1-2-3 thoughtfully includes percentages next to each piece of the pie, followed by the labels (Rent, Salaries, etc.) included in the worksheet range. Since pie graphs show a Y-series as portions (percentages) of a whole (100 percent), these markings will always display whenever you create a pie graph. The text on the chart is rather small, however. You will learn how to increase the size of graph text in Lesson 43.

LESSON 42

Placing a Graph in a Worksheet

FEATURING

- Inserting a Graph
- Repositioning a Graph
- Deleting a Graph from the Worksheet

GRAPHS DON'T HAVE TO RESIDE ONLY IN THEIR OWN windows. You can actually place them in worksheets. When you print or display the worksheet, the graph will print out next to your data. You can size the chart to the proportions you choose and place it wherever you want.

The process of placing a graph in a worksheet is just like moving a range of data cells. You select a destination range for the graph, choose the correct command, and it's pasted into place. When you save the worksheet, the graph's location and size are saved as part of it.

Inserting the Graph

As an example, let's place the Budget Expenses graph (the 3D bar graph) just below the worksheet data.

① Maximize the Budget worksheet window.

② Select the range B21..F34.

③ Choose Graph/Add to Sheet. The Graph Add to Sheet dialog box appears.

④ Choose the graph you want to add to the sheet. In my case, it was GRAPH5. Your graph's name may be different. Notice that you can alter the destination range from the box should you desire to.

⑤ Click on OK.

The graph is dropped into the range, as you see in Figure 42.1.

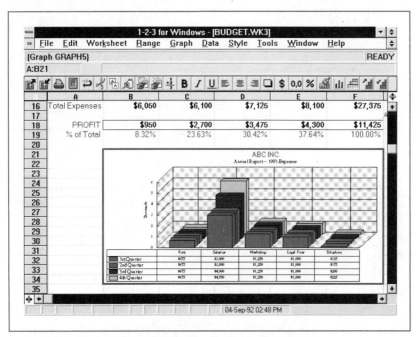

Figure 42.1: The graph is added to the worksheet matrix

The range size you select before choosing the Graph/Add to Sheet command determines the amount of space the graph will occupy when you paste it in. If you want the graph to be small on the worksheet, select a smaller range. If you want it larger, select a larger range.

The graph you have pasted into the worksheet is not just an image. It's actually a live graph. Changing data in the range from which the graph is derived will alter the graph. Try changing a cell, such as Rent, for one of the quarters, and watch the effect as the graph redraws. (Return the cell to its original value after experimenting.)

Repositioning or Resizing a Graph

If you later decide you want to reposition or resize the graph, do the following:

① Click anywhere on the graph to select it.

② Choose Graph/Size. A dialog box appears.

③ Ensure the correct graph name is highlighted.

④ Specify the new range.

⑤ Click on OK.

Removing the Graph

If you later decide you want to remove the graph from the worksheet, do the following:

① Position the cell pointer anywhere on the graph.

② Press the Del key. The graph is removed from the worksheet range it previously occupied. It is not removed from the graph list, however, and can still be viewed, modified, printed, or re-added to the worksheet, just as any other graph can.

43 LESSON

Altering the Size and Style of Text

FEATURING

- Selecting Fonts

IN THIS LESSON, YOU'LL LEARN HOW TO ENHANCE YOUR graphs by changing the size and style of type that 1-2-3 uses in the graph's headings, labels, and legends.

Changing Fonts

The sizes and styles of the text 1-2-3 has chosen for the graphs we've made thus far are certainly acceptable. The main titles have been large, subtitles and legends smaller. The type style has been fairly pleasing.

However, for certain applications, you may discover you need to change the type size and style. For example, the labels for the pie chart we created seemed too small. And when we inserted the bar chart in the worksheet, the labels and the data table became too small to read easily.

Luckily, you can alter the font settings for a graph, affecting both the screen display and your printouts. Let's increase the size of the labels on the pie chart.

① View the Expenses,Pie chart by one means or another. The easiest way is to open the Window menu and choose it. If the graph isn't open (and its name is thus not on the Window menu), choose Graph/View from the Budget worksheet window and choose the graph from the list.

② Choose Chart/Options/Fonts. The font dialog box you see in Figure 43.1 appears.

③ From the drop-down list boxes, you can choose the fonts for the indicated titles, legends, or labels. Open the third section in the box and choose Arial MT 14.

④ Click on OK. In a few seconds the graph is redrawn with the new font size, as shown in Figure 43.1. Now you can certainly read the categories of expenses on the pie chart.

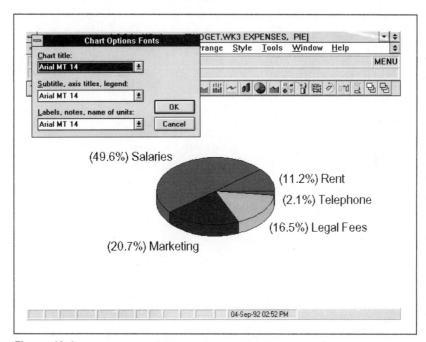

Figure 43.1: *Changing the fonts of the heading, labels, and legends*

The font changes will only affect the current graph, not other graphs that might be open or stored with the worksheet. However, changes you make to a graph will be reflected in any copy of the graph inserted into a worksheet. Since graphs in worksheets tend to be reduced in size, increasing the font size increases their legibility.

You will probably have to experiment a bit to determine which fonts you like best. Unfortunately, there's no substitute for printing out lots of graphs, since the proportions and resolutions of fonts on your screen will most likely differ from the final printed appearance. In general, you'll do well to use large sizes (24 or 14) for titles, and something a little smaller for other text.

For business graphs, you should stick with simple fonts such as Arial or NewTimesRoman. Script fonts are generally less effective, since they're less readable. The size you choose for the remainder of a graph's text depends on the type of graph and the size of the labels and legends. Too large a font size can cause larger labels, legends, and numbers to overrun one another.

LESSON 44

Adding Graphics and Explanatory Text

FEATURING

- Selecting Objects
- Moving Objects
- Drawing Lines

ALTHOUGH THE BASIC GRAPHS 1-2-3 CREATES CAN LOOK fairly impressive, you can enhance them with additional graphics and text. Graphics can include lines, arrows, freehand drawings, polygons, rectangles, and circles. You can also add text in various sizes and type styles.

Each item you add to a graph, including text, is called an *object*. Once an object is added to the chart, that object can be manipulated in a variety of ways. You can rotate, skew, turn, flip, and resize objects. Since the graph itself is also considered an object, it too can be bent, sized, flipped or rotated. As you might imagine, with a little effort you can spice up your graphs considerably.

Adding Text

Since explanatory text is the addition you'll most likely want to make to a graph, let's start with that. We'll give the Expenses,Pie graph slightly less cryptic labels.

① Bring up the Expenses,Pie graph in a maximized window.

② Choose Chart/Ranges and clear out the X data range. This is the range containing the labels used for the horizontal axis in a bar chart; in a pie chart it is the range used to label the slices of the pie. For our chart, the X data range is A11..A15. Eliminating this range wipes out the labels on the chart, but that's OK, since we're going to add our own text.

③ Click on OK.

④ The percentages are still displayed, since 1-2-3 adds those all by itself. Let's make them smaller in font size. Choose Chart/Options/Fonts and change the Labels font to something around 10 points in size. It doesn't matter which typeface.

⑤ Choose Draw/Text, or click on the ABC icon. A dialog box appears, asking what you want to type in. Type

1st Quarter Salaries

and press Enter. The text appears on the screen in smallish type. Now as you move the mouse, the text moves with it. Move it into the upper left quadrant of the window, and click. When you click, the text is pasted into position. Notice that the text has several little dots around it. These are called _handles,_ and they mean that the text object is selected. Just as with cells, you can edit, copy, move, or format an object only when it is selected.

⑥ Click on an empty, blank spot anywhere else in the graph window. The handles around the text disappear. The text is now deselected.

⑦ Click on the text again, and it becomes selected once more.

⑧ Now drag the text around a bit more. The cursor turns into a little hand while you are dragging. Objects such as added text and graphics can always be repositioned.

⑨ With the text selected, choose Style/Font. Switch to a larger font, such as Arial MT 14, and click on OK. The graph is redrawn to show the larger font.

⑩ Now add the following text items for the other slices, moving counterclockwise around the pie. Leave some space between the text and the pie for the arrows we're going to add next.

1st Quarter Marketing Costs
1st Quarter Legal Fees
1st Quarter Phone
1st Quarter Rent

Drawing Lines

Now we'll add arrows to point from the added text to the various slices in the pie.

① Choose Draw/Arrow, or click on the Arrow icon shown in Figure 44.1.

② Move the cursor to the area just below the word *Quarter* in 1st Quarter Salaries.

③ Click once. This sets the beginning position (anchor point) of the line.

④ Move the mouse toward the circle's largest slice and when you get fairly near it, to the point where you want the arrow, then double-click. This terminates the line.

⑤ Repeat the arrow drawing process for each of the labels, making your graph look something like Figure 44.2.

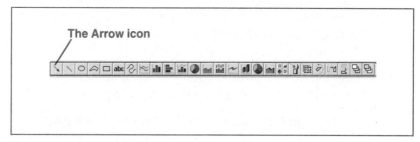

Figure 44.1: *The Arrow icon*

LESSON 44

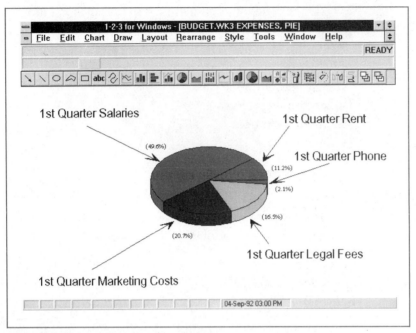

Figure 44.2: Lines added to the graph

Drawing Other Types of Objects

You've now experimented with the Text and Arrow drawing tools. As you can see from the icon palette and the Draw menu, there are other types of objects you can draw. The general instructions for drawing any of the object types (except text, which was explained above) are as follows:

① Choose the type of object you want to draw, either by clicking on the appropriate icon or by choosing from the Draw menu.

② Move the cursor to the position where you want to place the object, and click once. This sets the anchor point.

③ Move the mouse to draw the line, box, circle, or whatever.

④ When the size is correct, click twice. This finishes the
drawing process. The object is now selected and can be
moved, copied, deleted, or modified (see Lesson 45 for
an explanation of possible modifications).

Note that if you are drawing a ellipse or rectangle, you have to
hold the mouse button down while drawing. When you release the
mouse button, the object is finished. You don't have to click twice. If
you want to create a perfect circle or square, hold down the Shift key
while drawing.

Figure 44.3 displays some examples of graphic objects. Some of
the effects shown in that figure are explained further in Lesson 45.

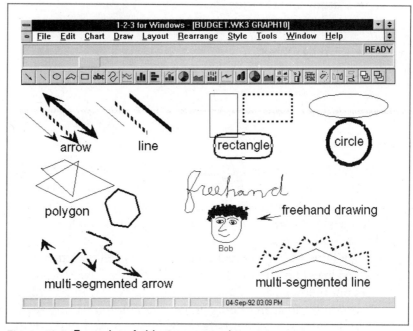

Figure 44.3: Examples of objects you can draw

Manipulating Your Graphics

FEATURING

- Cutting and Copying
- Selecting Multiple Objects
- Resizing Objects
- Zooming In

AS YOU MAY HAVE GUESSED, THE DRAWING CAPABILITIES of 1-2-3 for windows are quite extensive considering that the program's primary purpose is for designing worksheets. Not only can you draw a wide variety of objects, you can enhance and manipulate them in numerous ways.

Figure 44.3 illustrated several of these enhancements, such as dashed lines and arrows of varying thicknesses, and "smoothed" corners on multisegmented lines and rectangles. If you had the inclination, you could spend hours enhancing a graph with these drawing tools. In this lesson, I'll briefly outline how to use 1-2-3's editing tools to modify the objects you've drawn.

Selecting Multiple Objects

Selecting an object is a prerequisite to moving, copying, deleting, or otherwise altering it. As I mentioned last lesson, you can select an object by clicking on it. However, clicking doesn't work for multiple objects or for graphics consisting of many objects. For instance, the Freehand Bob face in Figure 44.3 consists of of many separately drawn freehand lines. I could not simply click on the face to select it and move it. Only one line, such as one portion of an eye, might move, leaving the other parts stationary and disassembling poor Bob. Fortunately, there are several ways to select multiple objects in 1-2-3.

*L*assoing Multiple Objects

You can select a number of objects at once by lassoing them.

① With the normal arrow pointer, position the mouse in the upper left corner of the area containing the items you want to select.

② Click and hold the mouse button. The cursor changes to a pointing hand.

③ Drag the mouse. A box with a dotted line (called a bounding box) appears as you do so. Keep dragging the corner of the box to extend the selection, until it surrounds the objects in question. If you don't get them all the first time, repeat the process.

*S*hift-Clicking

Another way to select objects is by using the Shift key and mouse together. This is useful when things are so tightly packed that the lassoing technique forces you to select neighboring items you don't want to select.

① Click on the first object.

② Hold the Shift key down, and click on the second object.

③ Repeat for each item you want to select.

*R*eplicating Objects

Rather than repeatedly drawing the same item, you can replicate objects you've drawn, including text. This can be a great time-saver.

① Select the object(s).

② Choose Edit/Replicate. A copy of the object appears slightly to the right of the original. It is already selected and can be dragged around.

If you want to copy an item from one graph to another, use the Copy command to put it on the Windows Clipboard. Then it can be pasted into another type of document, or into another chart's window.

Deleting Objects

To cut an object out of your graph:

① Select it.

② Press Del or choose Edit/Delete.

To recall the deleted item, choose Edit/Undelete. You can undelete an item until you delete another item.

Sizing an Object

Another useful object-editing feature is the Rearrange/Adjust Size command, which lets you resize an object. This beats redrawing it, especially if it's a complex item.

① Select the object to be resized.

② Choose Rearrange/Adjust Size. A bounding box appears around the object. Drag the box until the size roughly approximates the size you want the object to be.

③ Click the mouse to finalize the resizing process.

*R*earranging Objects

Here are a few other commands you can use to jazz up your graphs. These are available from the Rearrange menu. There are also icons for some of these commands; refer to the inside front cover of the book to see these.

- Rearrange/Flip: Flips the selected object(s) vertically or horizontally.

- Rearrange/Quarter Turn: Turns the selected object(s).

- Rearrange/Turn: Turns the selected object(s) any number of degrees around a center axis.

- Rearrange/Skew: Slants the selected object(s) horizontally or vertically.

To use one of these:

① Select the object to be altered.

② Choose the desired command from the Rearrange menu.

③ Use the mouse to adjust the object by moving its bounding box, unless the command does it without mouse intervention (as with the Flip and Quarter Turn commands).

④ Click when you are through adjusting.

Figure 45.1 shows examples of the effects you can achieve with these commands.

*R*everting to the Original Form

When you alter an object, 1-2-3 always remembers the original version of the object. You can thus return the object to its original state.

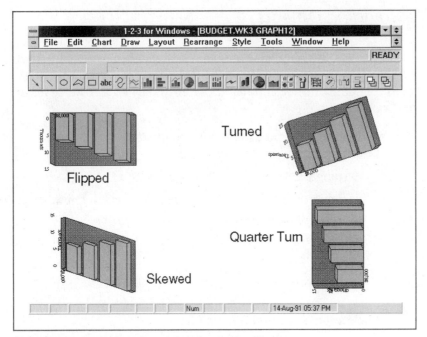

Figure 45.1: Examples of rearranged graphic objects

① Select the object(s) to return to original state.

② Choose Rearrange/Clear.

*C*hanging Line Width and Types

As you saw in Figure 44.3, lines need not be skinny and solid, with arrowheads at one or both ends. You can draw lines in a variety of styles. Any time after you draw a line, its settings can be altered.

① Select the line or lines in question.

② Choose Style/Lines. From the dialog box, choose the width and style. You have to open the drop-down list boxes to make the choices.

③ You can also elect to add arrowheads on either end of the lines by clicking on the appropriate check boxes.

④ Finally, you can choose an amount of smoothing. I used smoothing to round the corners of the multisegmented arrow in Figure 44.3. Try each setting (Medium, None, and Tight) to see the effects. They vary depending on the object.

Changing Fonts

You already know how to change the font and type size of the headings, legends, and notes you add to graphs with the Chart/ Headings dialog box. Changing the font of text you add as a graphic object is a little different:

① Select the text item whose font you want to change.

② Choose Style/Font. From the dialog box, choose the type size and style. If you want, click on the Bold, Italics, or Underline settings. You can also alter the width of the underline from the drop-down list box.

Changing Colors

You can change the colors of the text 1-2-3 places for you (labels, notes, and headings), and of the objects and text you add with the drawing tools. The colors shown up only on a color screen, or when you print your worksheet on a color printer.

To change the color of 1-2-3's text:

① Choose Chart/Options/Color.

② From the dialog box, choose the colors for each category of text you want to alter, and click on OK.

To change the color of objects and text you added to a graph:

① Select the object.

② Choose Style/Color. A dialog box appears. This contains four drop-down list boxes, two of which (Interior Fill and

Background) present color palettes containing many colors. The other two (Text and Line) only offer a few color choices. They both work the same, however. Just click on the color you want. The four boxes having the following meanings:

- Text: Alters the color for text you added to the graph.

- Line: Alters the color for the selected line or arrow, or for the perimeter of a selected polygon, ellipse, freehand drawing, or rectangle.

- Interior fill: Alters the color for the interior of the selected object. If you've selected a graph itself as the object, this setting determines the color inside the graph's frame.

- Background: Sets the color for the background of the graph.

Zooming In to Work on Details

Drawing small objects is difficult. It requires fairly good coordination and a lot of patience. It's even more difficult if you've got a smallish computer screen. Fortunately, there are several commands that will help you draw and adjust small objects. With these commands, you can enlarge the objects in the graph so that the drawing tools are easier to use. All of these commands are accessed through the Window menu. Their functions are listed below.

- Enlarge: Each time you choose Enlarge, the graph is enlarged. Since some of the graph will be off-screen after enlarging, you may have to use the scroll bars to reach the part of the graph you're working on. Pressing the + key has the same effect as choosing Enlarge. There are four possible sizes, so after four presses of +, that's it.

- Reduce: Has the reverse effect of Enlarge. If the graph is displayed in normal (Full) size, this command isn't available. It's only available when the graph is enlarged one or more sizes.

- Full: Returns the graph display to normal size.

- Zoom: Lets you define an area to enlarge dramatically so that you can work very carefully on it, or select small components of it. After choosing Zoom, define the area to zoom into by drawing a boundary box around it. When you release the mouse, the bounded area is enlarged, filling the entire graph window. When you are through working on the zoomed area, choose Window/Full to return to normal size. Figure 45.2 shows a section of Figure 44.3 enlarged with the Zoom command.

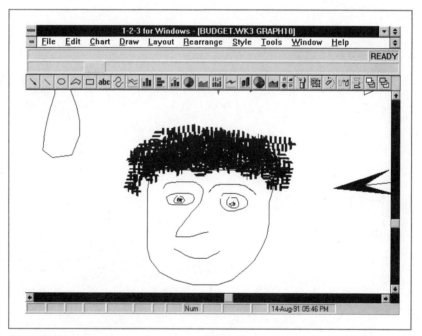

Figure 45.2: Use the Zoom command to draw or work on small objects

PART
7

Using the
Database Manager

46 LESSON

Database Basics

IN THIS PART OF THE BOOK, YOU'LL LEARN HOW TO create a 1-2-3 database, enter data into it, retrieve desired information from it, and modify and update the database in a variety of ways. This lesson discusses 1-2-3 databases, how they work, and what they can do for you.

A *database* is really nothing more than a list of things—people, addresses, amounts, or anything else that can be put into a list. In other words, it's just a collection of information that has something in common, a bit like an electronic filing cabinet.

A 1-2-3 database can consist of a list of information stored in a single worksheet, or it can consist of information stored in multiple worksheets. Each worksheet contributing to the database's information is called a *database table*.

If you have multiple tables in a database, they can be on separate worksheets. Each table, however, must be stored in a single worksheet, not broken up over several worksheets.

Advantages of an Electronic Database

Like any filing system, a database isn't very useful unless you have a way of quickly retrieving the information you want and of getting new data into it and old data out of it. You will also want to rearrange the database. A 1-2-3 database can arrange your information in chronological order, in alphabetical order, or in other ways.

Although 1-2-3's is not the most powerful database program in town, it does have lots of features and is relatively easy to use. The 1-2-3 database is very similar in appearance and operation to the spreadsheet tool, so many of the operations you're already learned—such as entering, editing moving, and copying data—will apply to database operations as well.

Fields and Records

Like the spreadsheets you've experimented with thus far, databases consist of a series of rows and columns. A database also stores its data in cells. However, in a database the columns are called *fields* and the rows are called *records*. To illustrate this, let's consider one of the more common databases we regularly use: a telephone book. A typical entry (record) in a phone book might look something like this:

	Name	**Address**	**Phone**
Record 1	Fred Flintstone	32 Hudson Rock Hwy.	324-4665

As you may suspect, the fields in this database would be Name, Address, and Phone. All of Fred's information (data) is listed in a single record of the database (in this case, Record 1). Other people would be listed in subsequent records, one for each person in the phone book.

Each entry in Fred's record is stored in a cell, just as you stored values, labels, and formulas in the spreadsheet. Just as with a worksheet, you can copy, move, format, edit, calculate, and print out data stored in the cells.

The major difference between a 1-2-3 database and a worksheet is that with a database table you can create and maintain lists of things in the same way you would use a filing cabinet or Rolodex file. You can find what you want in a hurry because 1-2-3 can keep the items sorted and organized, and can search through heaps of data very quickly to locate just the information you want. A worksheet, on the other hand, specializes in performing calculations on a constant number of interrelated values.

LESSON 47

Designing a Database

FEATURING

- Entering Fields
- Entering Data
- Rearranging Fields

THE TELEPHONE BOOK EXAMPLE IS A RELATIVELY simple and practical one, therefore it's a good example to start working with. Once you create the phone book database, you can probably use it later to keep track of business or personal contacts.

Making a Phone Book Database

There are two steps to creating a database. The first step is to think about the number and arrangement, or order, of the fields you'll want in it. The second step is to enter the data.

Design Considerations

Unlike a new worksheet, which has cells already created and waiting to be filled in, a database has to be designed by you before you enter any data. The layout of a database is called its *structure*. Setting up the structure amounts to laying out a single sample record, with the fields arranged in a row, just like the headings (1st Quarter, 2nd Quarter, etc.) that we had at the tops of the columns in the Budget worksheet. Each record in the database must conform to the structure you create at the outset.

It pays to put a little advance thought into just how many fields you want in a new database. If you don't break down your data into enough fields, you may run up against limitations in rearranging or retrieving records later. For example, you could store each person's street address, city, and state in one field. But should you want to look people up or print them out according to their home city later, this could be a problem. So, it's best to separate the street, city, and state data into three distinct fields.

Here are some other considerations when designing databases:

- Do you intend to group records together in some way? If you do, enter them in a single table rather than across several. This makes seeing them easier.

- Are there fields that you'll want to see more often than others? If so, put them next to each other, preferably at the beginning of the table (columns A, B, C, D, etc.). You won't have to scroll the screen to see these fields when you open the worksheet. Put other fields further out to the right. Another approach is to separate the less frequently used data, putting it in another table.

- If you intend to combine data from two tables into a report or a combined table, you need a link, or common field, in both tables. For example, having a part-number field in a shipping table and in an inventory table will help coordinate the two tables later. Make sure the data that will go into a field shared by two tables is unique, so that there isn't any confusion between records that might otherwise be identical. This is particularly important with databases containing people's names, since more than one John Smith or Jane Anderson is likely.

*F*ield Rules

The first row in a 1-2-3 database table is automatically reserved for the field names. In order for certain procedures to work correctly, you must observe the rules for creating field names:

- Don't put blank cells (columns) between field names.
- Enter the first record immediately below the row of field names. (Don't enter a row of dashes or = signs below the field names.)
- Field names must be text labels, not values or formulas.
- Don't name fields something that looks like a formula or a cell address (such as RX70).
- Don't include semicolons, periods, hyphens, spaces, commas, or number signs (#) in field names.

*C*reating the Database

For our personal telephone book, we'll use the following fields, at least to start:

First_Name   Last_Name   Phone   Street   City   State   Zip

To create the structure:

① Open a new worksheet by choosing File/New. A new, blank worksheet appears.

② Save the file as PHONEBK.WK3 in the 123W\WORK directory.

③ Maximize the worksheet window, if it isn't already maximized. Type in the field names and adjust the column widths to match what you see in Figure 47.1.

*E*ntering the Data

Now enter the ten records of address-book data that you see in Figure 47.2.

LESSON 47

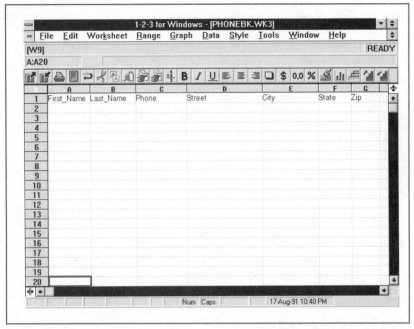

Figure 47.1: *The structure and column widths for the PHONEBK database*

Note that you'll have to enter single quotes before the phone numbers, street addresses and zip codes. Without the quote mark, 1-2-3 will consider these to be numerical values and will act strangely. It will try to perform subtractions with the phone numbers; it will beep when you try to enter the addresses since it will think you're trying to enter formulas that start with number but which have unacceptable syntax; and it will chop off leading zeros at the beginning of the zip codes (05333 will become 5333), assuming—ignorantly—that these leading zeros are not necessary. As a general rule, you should always use the quotation mark for any integers that are not going to be used as numerical values.

Don't puzzle over the order of the entries here. As we'll see in Lesson 48, sorting the records in a database is easy and one of the joys of working with databases.

Of course, you can format fields as you like. All the formatting options covered in lessons about worksheets will apply to database tables. Notice that in Figure 47.2 I've boldfaced and underlined the field names.

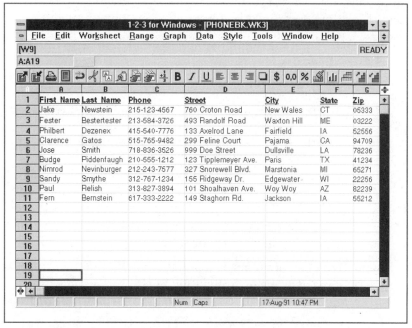

Figure 47.2:The data for the PHONEBK database

How to Navigate and Rearrange Fields

Since a database is really nothing more than a worksheet with cells set up in a special way, navigating, editing, copying, and moving data all work the same as they do with a normal worksheet.

It's not uncommon after laying out a database that you'll decide to add another field or rearrange your fields for easier scanning or simpler data entry. For example, you may be working with paper forms that list information in a specific order. If you're entering that data into a worksheet, arranging your fields in an order identical to the forms will simplify the task. Then you can type in the first field, press → to enter it and move the cell pointer to the next field, enter the next field's data, and so on.

If you decide that a field column isn't where you want it, simply insert a blank column where you want it to go, select the column you want to move, and choose the appropriate Move command. With a large database, moving a field could pose a problem if you don't know how to select such a long column of cells. (Remember, this is like selecting a range of cells in a worksheet.) Here's how to do it:

① First use Worksheet/Insert to insert a blank column where you want the field moved to.

② Then select the column to move. This can be done two ways.

- The first is to drag with the mouse, starting at the top of the column, and moving down to the bottom of the window, to the border. Then keep the button down and don't move the mouse. The window will be begin to scroll automatically, selecting cells as it goes. Just wait until the last record appears, then release the mouse button. The whole field (column) will then be selected.

- The other approach is to use the Edit/Move Cells command. The dialog brought up by this command lets you stipulate the range you want to move, which is a little easier than waiting for the screen to scroll a mile.

③ After the range is selected, use the appropriate Move command. If you selected using the mouse, you can use the Range Move icon, then point to the top cell in the destination column. If you used the dialog box approach, enter the starting destination cell, or the entire range of the destination.

Of course, these techniques apply to selecting and moving large ranges of cells in worksheets too, so keep them in mind.

LESSON 48

Sorting Your Database

FEATURING

- Key Fields
- The Data/Fill Command
- Reordering a Database

IT OFTEN HAPPENS THAT THE ORDER OF RECORDS IN A database is rather haphazard. Records are usually entered in the order they are acquired (chronological order), yet you'll more frequently want them to be in alphabetical or numerical order.

For example, the phone book database was entered in no particular order, so finding a given record might take you a while. With an unsorted database of several thousand names and addresses, finding a given record without any sorting aids would be difficult, to say the least.

One of the greatest conveniences of computerized databases is their ability to quickly sort or rearrange their data records according to your needs. The database included in 1-2-3 is no exception here. You can sort your database in many ways, and fairly rapidly, since 1-2-3 keeps your entire database in RAM rather than shuffling it off to disk as some programs do.

Once the database is sorted to your liking, you can, of course, save it on disk in the new order for future use. For that matter, you could store several copies of a database (assuming you had the disk space for it) sorted in different orders. Once the database is sorted, all subsequent commands, reports, screen listings, printouts and form viewing you do will occur in the new, sorted order.

About Sorting Keys

The field that the database is sorted on is called the *key field*. You can choose up to 255 key fields to sort by if you wish. Normally, you will use only one or two, but you may want to use more. The key fields operate in order of precedence. The first key, called the *primary key*, determines the first piece of information the database sorts by. For example, a city's phone book is sorted, in the first instance, by last name.

The second key field is called the *secondary key*. It and any additional key fields (called *subordinate keys*) determine the order of records that appear identical under the primary key. For example, in a phone book John Smith should appear after Bob Smith, not before. If you sorted only by last name, this would not be assured. You would have to sort by last name, followed by first name as the secondary key.

Sorting Order

Additionally, 1-2-3 gives you the option of sorting in ascending (A to Z and 0 to *n*) or descending (Z to A and *n* to 0) order. It's rare that you'll want to list the Z's before the A's, but descending order is often useful for numerical sorting. For example, you might want to see your expenses or sales with the largest figures appearing first.

Doing a Sort

Let's sort our phone book list by the Last_Name field. Sorting is easiest if you work with named ranges, so first, name a couple of ranges—the area you're going to sort and the field you want to sort by (the key field).

① Select the entire set of records, from A2 through G11.

② Choose Range/Name/Create and name the range "People."

③ Select just the Last_Name column (B2..B11), choose Range/ Name/Create and call the range "Last."

Now that the ranges are named, we can sort the data easily.

① Choose Data/Sort.

② The Data/Sort dialog box appears. Notice that there are several spaces you can fill in, indicating the first and second key fields as well as the area to sort. Type **PEOPLE** in the Data range box and **LAST** in the Primary key box. As a shortcut to typing the range names, you can use the F3 (Name) key to choose the ranges.

③ Choose the Ascending button, since we want A's before Z's.

④ Click on OK.

⑤ Almost instantly, the database reorders itself with last names in alphabetical order as you see in Figure 48.1.

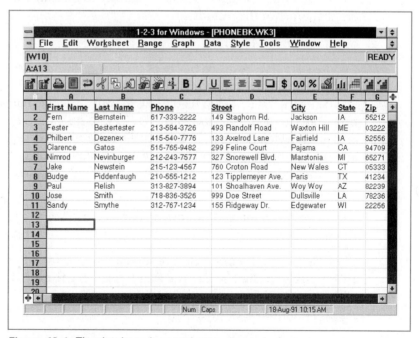

Figure 48.1: The database is sorted according to last name

Resorting the Database

What if you wanted to reorder the database in its original sequence again? You couldn't, because there isn't any logical order to it, other than the chronological order in which it was entered. Here's a trick you should consider with any database you're going to reorder. Before sorting, you can use the Data/Fill command to fill a new field with a sequence of ascending numbers. Then you do your sorting. After you're through with the task you sorted for, sort again, this time using the column of numbers. Here's how it works:

① First, undo what you just did by selecting Edit/Undo. The records will jump back to their original order. As you can see, sorting is undo-able if you don't use any other commands in the meantime.

② Now create a new field in column H called "Resort." Just enter **Resort** in H1. You can boldface it if you want. This is the column that's going to hold the numbers to indicate the original order of the records.

③ Select the range H2..H11.

④ Choose Data/Fill. A dialog box pops up. Figure 48.2 shows how to fill it in, and what the effects are when you click on OK. Since we want 1-2-3 to fill the cells in with ascending numbers from 0 to n in 1-step increments (1, 2, 3, 4, etc.), the Step area in the dialog box is set to 1. (Actually these are the default settings, so assuming the correct range was already selected when you chose the Data/Fill command, you don't have to type anything. Just click on OK.)

⑤ Adjust your column widths now, so that you can see all the fields at once.

⑥ Since we've added a new field, we should redefine the PEOPLE range to include it. Choose Range/Name/Create and click on PEOPLE. Then edit the Range box to read A2..H11, and click on OK.

⑦ Choose Data/Sort again. Enter **PEOPLE** in the data range and **LAST** as the primary key. This time choose Descending from the dialog box. Names are now listed in reverse alphabetical order.

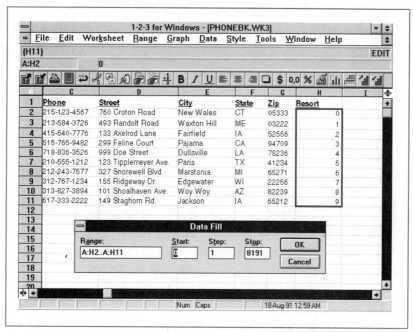

Figure 48.2: *Using Data/Fill to fill a field with consecutive numbers*

Now, just to get things back into proper order, resort using the Resort field.

① First, name the resort range. Here's a tip, though. When defining a sort key, you only have to refer to one cell in the key's column, not the whole column. So, rather than selecting the range H2..H11, just move the cell pointer to H2 and choose Range/Name/Create. Name the range "Resort" and click on OK.

② Choose Data/Sort. Enter **PEOPLE** as the data range and **RESORT** as the primary key. Choose Ascending sort order.

The database is reordered to its original state.

Sorting Tips

If you wanted to sort your list so that Bill Smith came before John Smith, you would stipulate First_Name as the secondary field, and choose Ascending as the sort order for both key fields.

Be aware that the sorting order that 1-2-3 uses is determined by the *collating sequence* as set during installation of 1-2-3. The collating sequence determines the order in which letters, numbers, blank cells, and symbols will be ordered in a sorted list. The default setting for this is called "Numbers first," which uses the following order of precedence:

① Blank cells

② Labels beginning with a space

③ Cells beginning with a number (e.g., 760 Croton Rd. or 4,000)

④ Cells beginning with letters (a before A, b before B)

You can change the collating sequence only by reinstalling 1-2-3.

LESSON 49

Finding Data

FEATURING

- Searching the Database
- Limiting a Search

IN LARGE DATABASES, MOVING FROM ONE RECORD TO another sequentially can take a lot of time, especially if you are jumping long distances. But since each record in a database has a number (the row number), you can use the Go To command (or F5) to jump directly to a specific record very quickly.

For example, say you want to edit the Phone cell of record 403. Press F5 (or choose Range/Go To). The Range Go To dialog box appears. Just type in a cell address that's part of the record you want to jump to, such as A405.

However, using Go To is only useful if you have printed the database and included the column and row numbers in the printout, so that you know the row number associated with each record. Typically, you'll know only the name of the person or item whose information you want to retrieve or edit. In such cases, you can use the Edit/Find command to find a given record.

Finding a Record

Suppose, for example, you want to find Philbert Dezenex's phone number (assuming your database has become much larger and you can't just see it). You can spell his name correctly, but don't know his record number.

① Choose Edit/Find. The Edit Find dialog box appears.

② Type in the range or range name in the database that you want to search. In this case, we can use PEOPLE since we've already named the entire range of the database.

③ Enter **Philbert** as the text to search for and click on Find Next. The cell pointer jumps immediately to Philbert's cell.

④ Cancel the dialog box, and you can now read the rest of Philbert's record.

When searching in this way, if the text or value you're looking for isn't found, you'll be alerted in a dialog box that says *String Not Found*. In English, this message translates to "Couldn't find what you wanted." Try typing it in again, checking the spelling, range, and so on.

Incidentally, Edit/Find works for finding cells in a worksheet too. You might make a note of this. Also, note that you can use this dialog box for replacing existing data with new data. Just fill in the Replace With text area, and using the Replace or Replace All buttons.

Repeating a Search

The Search command finds only one record at a time. That is, 1-2-3 finds the first cell containing letters you specify, and stops. But what if there are several cells that meet the search condition? Try these steps to see how you can quickly repeat a search.

① Move to cell A2.

② Choose Edit/Find. The range should still be filled in by 1-2-3, which remembers the last search range. Pull the dialog box down to the bottom of the window, so that you can see all the records. Some of the box will be off the screen, but that's OK so long as you can enter the search criteria and see the Find Next button.

③ Type in **ne**, click on Find Next, and 1-2-3 will find the next cell with an *ne* in it.

④ Click on Find Next again, and 1-2-3 jumps to the next cell with an *ne* in it.

⑤ Keep pressing Alt-N and notice that 1-2-3 jumps through all the cells with *ne*. There should be six cells that have *ne* in them. Selecting Find Next after the last *ne* is found brings up a dialog box that reads *No more matching strings.*

Case Matching

Note that 1-2-3 found *New Wales*, even though you didn't type in *Ne* as the search criteria. You don't have to be careful about lowercase and uppercase letters when searching for data. 1-2-3's search command is case-insensitive, meaning that it doesn't care what case you type in. PAUL will find Paul, and even cLaReNcE will find Clarence.

Limiting the Search to a Selected Area

Sometimes you may want to limit a search to a portion of the database, particularly if the database is large and would take a great deal of time to search. Or perhaps you want to search through only one field rather than letting 1-2-3 lead you through a trail of matching text in other fields that are irrelevant to your search.

Here's an example of how to limit a search:

① Choose Edit/Find. Move the dialog box so you can see the data.

② Type in **C2..C11** as the search range.

③ Enter **222** in the Search For area, and click on Find Next.

Notice that the phone number 617-333-2222 on row 11 was found, but the 222 in the Zip field wasn't. That's because we limited the search to the Phone field. Even if you try the search again, the 222 in the Zip field of records 2 and 8 will not be found.

LESSON 50

Creating Queries

FEATURING

- Data/Query
- AND Criteria
- OR Criteria

THE SEARCH AND SORT COMMANDS ARE USEFUL FOR finding a particular record in a database; however, there may be times when you want 1-2-3 to display a *group* of records in a database that meet certain criteria. Consider your Phone Book database. Say you wanted to see

- All people with zip codes falling between 50000 and 90000.
- People whose last names fall between A and D or Abrahms and Davis
- People who live in Iowa

Neither the Search nor the Sort command would be much help in these instances. Instead, you need to make a request that would isolate certain types of records.

This type of a request is called a *query* in database lingo. The real and practical power of any database lies in its ability to use queries to extract only the information you want.

Creating a Query

In 1-2-3, a query is created using a series of simple, logical rules, or *criteria*. Query criteria can be based on words, numbers, or formulas. They can be simple (for example, list all the Joneses) or complex (for example, list all the Joneses who live in Seattle and whose zip codes are between *x* and *y*).

Once a query is created, you tell 1-2-3 to go into Query mode with Data/Query. In this mode, pressing ↑ or ↓ jumps between records that meet your criteria, skipping over the others.

Another command, Extract, lets you create a new table consisting of only the matching records, eliminating the non-matching ones. This table can be created in a separate file or in an empty range in the source file.

Setting Up a Query

A query requires at least two things: an *input range* and some criteria. The input range tells 1-2-3 which records to look through. An input range contains one or more data tables, including the field names. (Using multiple tables in a query gets quite complicated, so we're not going to cover it here. You should consult the 1-2-3 manuals for information on that.)

The criteria tells 1-2-3 what information it should use to compare the records to. You can optionally stipulate an *output range,* into which 1-2-3 will copy matching records.

A Simple Query

First we'll create a simple query. Let's say you want to be able to quickly jump to the records of all the people who live in Iowa. Here's how to set up the query.

① With the PHONEBK database selected, enter the data as you see it in Figure 50.1. I've copied the names of all the fields down into an empty part of the worksheet. You don't have to copy them all if you're not going to use them in the

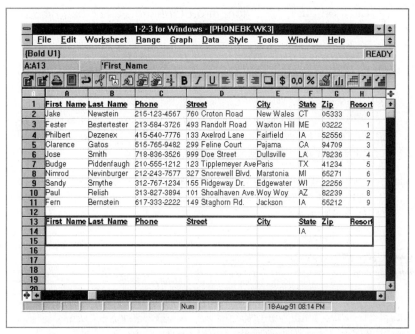

Figure 50.1: Setting up the query to select people from Iowa

query, but it doesn't hurt, and then they are there if you want them. Notice that the letters *IA* are in the cell immediately below *State*.

② Now, just to make things easier, we're going to name the range containing the criteria, since 1-2-3 is going to ask for its range when we do the query. It's easier to remember the range name than the cell addresses. So, select A13..H15 and name the range QUERY1 using Range/Name/Create. While you're at it, redefine the PEOPLE range to be A1..H19 to include the field names.

③ Choose Data/Query. The Data Query dialog box appears. Since you want to search all the records, enter **PEOPLE** as the Input range. You have to stipulate the Criteria range, so enter **QUERY1** there since that's the range containing the field names and the criteria. You can leave the Output range box as is.

LESSON 50

④ Click on Find. 1-2-3 goes into FIND mode. The first record meeting the criteria (records with IA in the State field) is highlighted, as shown in Figure 50.2.

⑤ Press ↓ to see the next matching record.

⑥ Press ↓ again. You hear a beep indicating there are no more matching records. As you can see, there are only two matching records. Note that all other records are skipped over, since they don't meet the criteria.

⑦ Press F7 to bring up the Query dialog box. Then, click on Cancel. This terminates FIND mode and returns 1-2-3 to READY mode.

Complex Queries

By using AND and OR criteria, you can create much more complex queries than what we just created. AND criteria let you specify multiple criteria for a query, thus making the query more selective. OR criteria, by contrast, make a query more flexible.

AND Criteria

Suppose you wanted to see people in Iowa whose last names are Dezenex. If you had a big enough phone book, there might be more than one. By creating a query that uses AND criteria, you can instruct 1-2-3 to find all the people who live in Iowa AND whose last name is Dezenex.

① Type **Dezenex** into the Last_Name criteria field. Now 1-2-3 has two criteria: states that are Iowa (IA) and last names that are Dezenex.

② Choose Data/Query again, and fill in the ranges just as you did before.

③ Choose Find. The result of the search is just one record. Pressing ↑ or ↓ produces only beeps, indicating there are no other matching records.

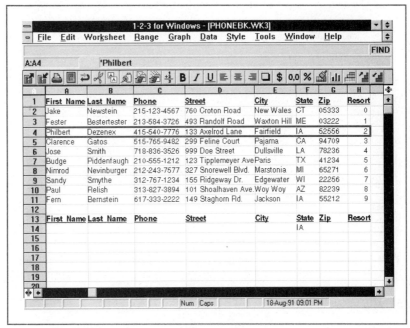

Figure 50.2: *The first matching record is highlighted*

OR *Criteria*

In contrast to AND criteria, OR criteria allow you to broaden, rather than narrow, your requests. For example, you could create a query that would find all the people who live in Iowa OR whose last name is Gatos. This would produce three records.

① If 1-2-3 is still in FIND mode, exit it with F7 followed by Cancel.

② Add Gatos to the second row in the Last_Name criteria field, as you see in Figure 50.3.

③ Run the query again, using the same ranges as before (PEOPLE and QUERY1).

1-2-3 finds three records this time: the two Iowa residents, and Clarence Gatos. As you can see, if criteria are entered on separate lines, 1-2-3 interprets them as OR criteria.

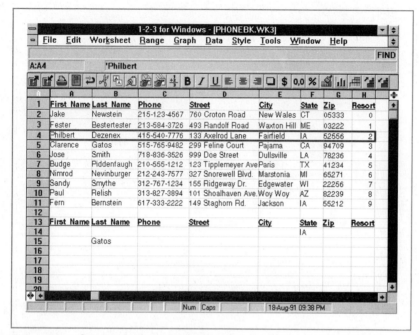

Figure 50.3: Combining multiple criteria on separate lines creates OR criteria

LESSON 51

Using Wildcards in Queries

FEATURING

- * and ?

THERE MAY BE TIMES WHEN YOU WANT TO BROADEN A query by using *wildcards*. Wildcards are symbols that will match any text during a query. You use them in conjunction with normal characters. Say you wanted to find all Bernsteins, regardless of whether the name is spelled with *e* before *i* or *i* before *e*. Using the wildcard character ? for the *e* and the *i,* as in Bernst??n, you could find Bernstein or Bernstien. In fact, a query using Bernst??n would even find Bernstzzn.

1-2-3 recognizes two wildcards: the question mark (?) and the asterisk (*). The ? represents a single character of any value. The * represents any number of characters of any value.

The ? works fine when you know exactly how many letters are in the word you're looking for. If the number of letters might vary, then use the * sign. For example, say you had a database of words. You want to find all words that begin with the letter *W* and end with the letter *Y,* regardless of how long they are. You would use this formula as the criterion:

W*Y

This would find Woy, Wally, or Wy.

Here's another example. Say you wanted to find all the people in our database whose last names begin with *S*. Under Last_Name, you'd enter

S*

as you see in Figure 51.1. The result will be two records, Smyth and Smith.

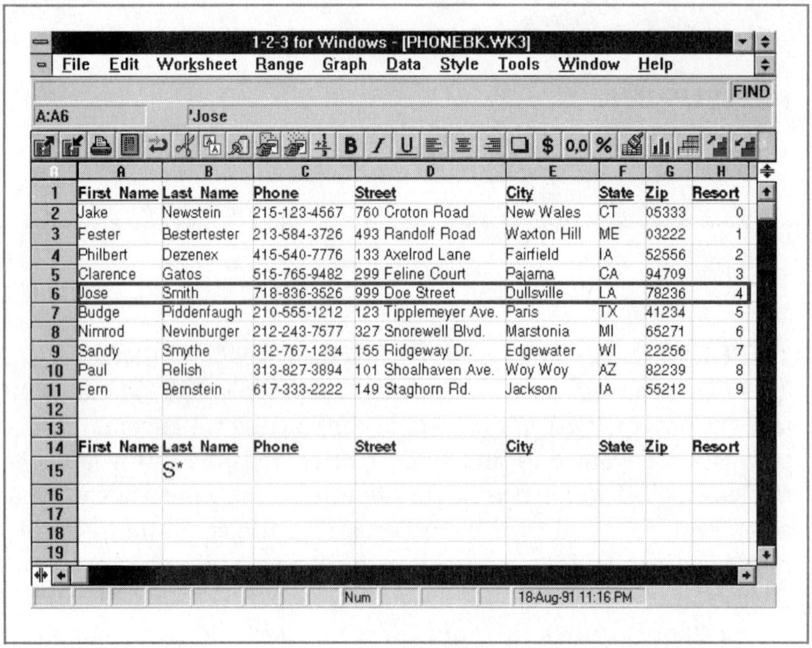

Figure 51.1: Using the * wildcard to find all last names beginning with S

LESSON 52

Extracting Data

FEATURING

- Creating an Output Range
- Coloring Ranges
- The Data/Query/Extract Command

SO FAR IN OUR EXAMPLES, YOU'VE HAD TO USE THE arrow keys to see which records in the input range match the criteria. While using the arrow keys to view matching records is fine if there are only a few, it can be tedious when you have numerous matching records. If you want to use database queries to generate something like a printed list of potential property sales to pass around at a meeting, or a list of out-of-stock inventory items to fax to your supplier, using the arrow keys to view matching records is quite impractical.

Fortunately, you can have 1-2-3 create a new table of items that meet your criteria by specifying an *output range* for matching records. You may have noticed that the Data/Query dialog box has a third section for specifying the output range. If you specify a range there, you can use the Extract button in the box to create a table of selected records and fields elsewhere in your data table or in another file. Then you can save or print the output range as you would any other range of 1-2-3 data.

Setting Up an Output Range

Let's set up an output range in the section below the criteria area of the worksheet.

1. Copy the field names from row 1 (A1..G1) to row 17 (A17...G17). (We can leave the Resort field off. Fields that aren't named in the output range will be omitted.)

This creates the output range that 1-2-3 will use to copy matching records to. You only need one row in the range—the row containing the field names. When it extracts the matching records, 1-2-3 figures out how many rows to add below the field names.

2. Select the output range A17..G17. Use Range/Name/Create to name it OUTPUT. Now you should have at least three ranges named: PEOPLE, QUERY1, and OUTPUT.

3. Move the QUERY1 criteria range up a row—either by deleting a row (Worksheet/Delete) or by moving the range. It should now occupy the range A13..H15.

You now have an output range. If you want to ensure that you've accurately defined all the ranges we'll be working with, you can create a list of the defined ranges to see what each named range's address is. Choose Range/Name/Paste Table. In the Range section of the dialog box that pops up, enter A21 and click on OK. Scroll down to A21 to see the list of your named ranges and their cell addresses. It should read as follows:

OUTPUT	**A17..G17**
PEOPLE	**A1..H11**
QUERY1	**A13..H15**
RESORT	**H1..H1**

RESORT isn't relevant to us at this point, so if you don't have it, don't worry. If the other addresses or names are different, use Range/Name/Create to correct them before moving on.

When you're working with ranges, especially ones that might overlap and cause confusion, it's good practice to give each range some distinguishing characteristic on your screen, such as borders, colors, or shading. Let's assign a color to each of the three ranges we'll be using.

① Choose Style/Color. In the Style Color dialog box, double-click on the Range section. Then press F3 to bring up the Range Names list. Double-click on PEOPLE, which drops the name into the Color dialog box. (Remember this as a quick way to use range names in dialog boxes.)

② Choose a new background color (or shade, if you're using a monochrome monitor or laptop LCD screen) for the PEOPLE range, and click on OK.

③ Repeat the process for the two other ranges, giving them colors that will visually differentiate them from one another. Your screen should now look something like Figure 52.1.

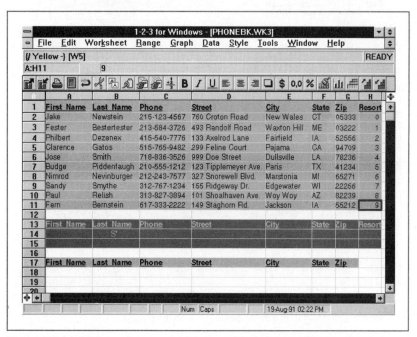

Figure 52.1.: Giving colors or shades to ranges helps you interpret your data

*E*xtracting Some Data

Now that we're all set up, let's extract some data records based
on query information.

① Type **S*** in the Last_Name field in the criteria section, if it
isn't still there from last time. (I've centered it for better
visibility in the figure.)

② In the Data Query dialog box, type **PEOPLE** in the
Input range box, **QUERY1** in the Criteria range box, and
OUTPUT in the Output range box. Choose Data/Query.

③ Click on Extract. Now 1-2-3 compares the records against
the criteria and copies matching records into the output
range. There should be two records in the output range, as
shown in Figure 52.2.

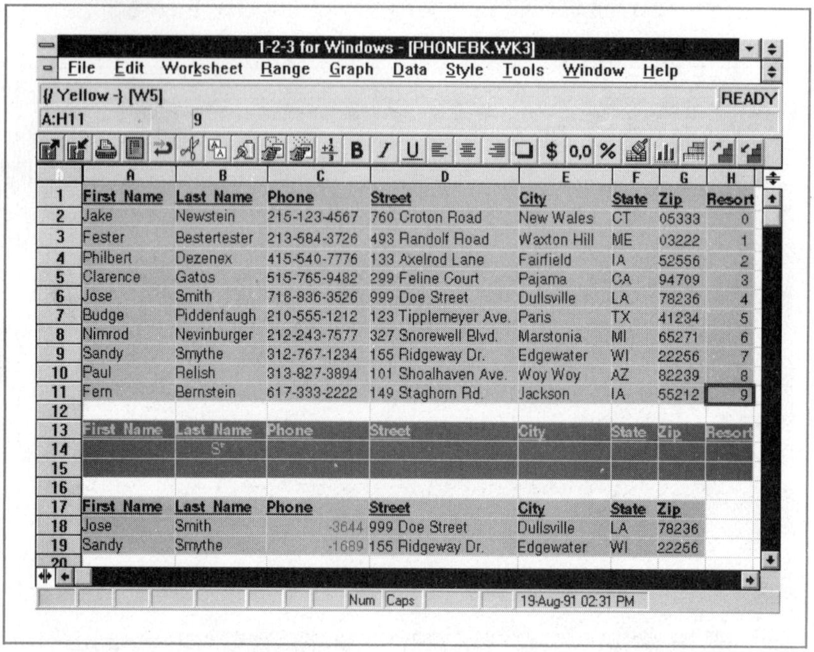

Figure 52.2: The extracted data

④ Notice that the Resort field data is missing in the output range. Only the fields named in the output range will be included when you do an extraction. Notice also that the phone number data looks wrong. This is because 1-2-3 didn't copy the formatting for the phone field into the corresponding output range. Thus, it subtracted the number elements from each other. Reformat the phone field with Range/Format/Text. The data will now appear correctly.

⑤ Try another extraction. Move to the S* cell (B14) and enter **D*** in place of the S*. This should extract all records with last names beginning with *D*.

⑥ Choose Data/Query again. All the correct ranges are left from the last time (though they may be named by cell addresses). Just click on Extract.

Only one record meets the criteria: Philip Dezenex's. Notice how the previous two records were both eliminated, with the new one taking their place. You can do as many extractions as you want without piling data records on top of one another.

⑦ Try another extraction, only this time, don't set any criteria. This will result in all the records being copied to the output range.

⑧ Rearrange the State and Zip field names in the output range by typing **Zip** into F17 and **State** in G17. Do the extraction again, noticing that the 1-2-3 reverses the field data. By rearranging field names in an output range, then extracting the whole table, you can create a new table from an old one.

53 LESSON

Using Formulas as Search Criteria

FEATURING

- @VALUE
- Formula Rules
- Operators
- Protecting Data

OVER THE LAST FEW LESSONS, YOU'VE CREATED SOME relatively simple queries that didn't require formulas. More often than not, simple queries will perform day-to-day tasks such as showing you everyone whose names fall between D and M, or who lives in certain zip code ranges. There will be times, though, when you'll want to list such things as

- Inventory items that cost more than $200 each *and* whose quantity exceeds 20

- Houses within a certain zip code range whose price falls between $150,000 and $200,000 *and* that have termite reports below $500.

You can generate such lists by using complex queries that combine various criteria. You can apply more than one criteria to a single field, or you can apply criteria to multiple fields. You can also use formulas in your queries. With all these possibilities, you can make your queries as complex as you want.

Using Operators and Formulas in Queries

In your queries, you can use several logical and mathematical operators to create formulas that compare the data in the database fields to your criteria. These operators can be combined with cell references, with values you specify, or with @functions. The operators and their effects are listed below. Don't worry if you don't understand the meaning of all the operators. Their uses will become clearer with some experimentation.

Operator	Effect
=	Equal to
< >	Not equal to
<	Less than
>	Greater than
< =	Less than or equal to
> =	Greater than or equal to
#OR#	Or
#AND#	And

Once you start throwing in lots of operators and @functions, your formulas can get pretty complicated, just as they can with worksheets. As you know from the lessons on worksheet formulas, formulas are processed by 1-2-3 using standard algebraic methods. Thus, they are interpreted from left to right, with innermost parentheses evaluated first. Multiplication and division are calculated before addition and subtraction.

You enter formulas for finding or extracting records much the same way as entering other criteria, except that you have to include the name of the field in the formula. For example, suppose you had an inventory database and wanted to extract all records whose COST field contained values greater than $500. Under the COST field in the criteria range you'd enter

> **+COST>500**

With that in mind, consider again this inventory database. Suppose you wanted to extract records with costs of over $500 and under $1000. You'd combine the two criteria using #AND#, like this:

> **+COST>500#AND#COST<1000**

Notice how you have to include the field name twice—once for each part of the formula.

Here's another example, using OR criteria. For costs *over* $1000 OR *under* $500, you'd enter

> **+COST>1000#OR#COST<500**

The @VALUE Function in a Formula

Enough theory. Let's use a formula in a query with the Phone Book database. Suppose you wanted to see the records with zip codes 20000 and 80000. This should be easy. You'd think you'd just use the formula

> **+ZIP>20000#AND#ZIP<80000**

Unfortunately, if you tried this, it wouldn't work. Recall that you entered the zip codes as labels (with ' as the first character) to prevent the leading zeros from disappearing in the display. The idea of the formula is correct, but we need to use one of 1-2-3's built-in formulas, called *@functions,* to compensate for the zip codes being entered as labels.

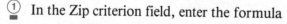 In the Zip criterion field, enter the formula

> **@VALUE(ZIP)>20000#AND#@VALUE(ZIP)<80000**

When you press Enter, the cell's contents will say ERR. This is OK. It's common when entering formulas into query criteria ranges. It doesn't mean the formula won't work. It will, but it will just say ERR. If you like, you can reformat the cell with Range/Format/Text to see the formula displayed correctly in the cell.

② Perform the data extraction with Data/Query/Extract. The results are shown in Figure 53.1.

The @VALUE function was needed to convert the zip codes which are entered as labels to values that 1-2-3 can numerically evaluate. This is a good trick to remember, since you'll have to use the @VALUE function whenever you use a label within a numerical formula. You'll learn more about @functions in Part Eight.

Multiple Field Criteria with Formulas

Before we can experiment further, you will need some new material to work with. Even though you could use the Phone Book database for most of the following exercises, a database with additional numbers is more apropos.

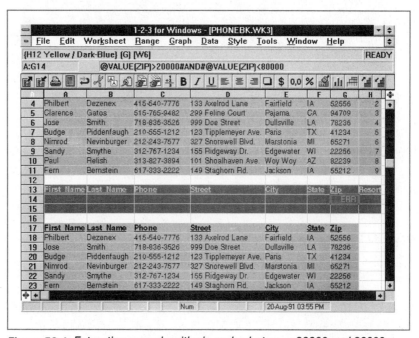

Figure 53.1: Extracting records with zip codes between 20000 and 80000

LESSON 53

① Add another worksheet to the file with Worksheet/Insert, and enter the field names and records shown in Figure 53.2. Notice there's nothing in the last field. Don't worry about that yet. It's going to be a calculated field.

② Now copy the field names down to add a criteria area and an output area. Look ahead to Figure 53.2 to see how I've done it.

③ Give the ranges a color if you like.

④ Name the three ranges. Call the input range INVENTORY, the criteria range QUERY2, and the output range OUT-PUT2. Refer to Figure 53.2 for the ranges. Remember you only have to select one row for the output range.

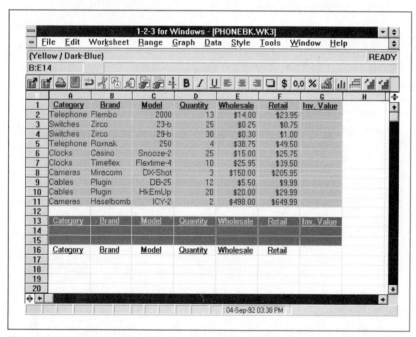

Figure 53.2: The Inventory database

Now let's try some practical examples using the inventory database. Each exercise entails running Data/Query/Extract. Since you already have some experience in extracting data, these instructions will be abbreviated: I'll show the formula(s) you have to enter in the criteria range, and which field name to put it under. If you can't remember precisely how to extract data, refer back to Lesson 50 for more detail.

① To display all items with more than 5 and fewer than 15 units in stock, enter the following formula in the Quantity field of the criteria range:

+quantity>5#AND#quantity<15

② Now choose Data/Query, fill in the dialog box with the appropriate ranges, and click on Extract. If all goes well, 1-2-3 will extract the records for the Flembo telephone, the Timeflex clocks, and the Plugin DB-25 cables.

③ To see all items with more than 5 and less than 15 units in stock *and* that have a retail price of over $15.00, enter

+quantity>5#AND#quantity<15

in the Quantity field of the criteria range. (Note that you don't enter the dollar sign in the retail entry, nor do you have to format the criteria range as currency for the query to work properly. Formatting never affects the real value in a cell.)

④ In the Retail field, enter

>15

⑤ Again, choose Data Query, fill in the dialog box, and click on Extract. Now only the Flembo telephone and the Timeflex clocks records will be extracted.

*A*dditional Rules of Querying

Here are a few other querying rules and examples for your reference:

- For a simple condition, no quotation marks are necessary in the query fields. You can enter values exactly the way they appear in the input range if you're looking for an exact match. For example, if you are looking for an item with a quantity of 13, just type **13** under the Quantity field. This rule holds true for labels (text) as well.

■ You don't have to worry about the formatting of numbers. As mentioned above, whether a value is represented as currency, is in scientific notation, or is shown as a percentage doesn't matter—100 will still match $100, and .10 will match 10%.

■ You can enter *'DEZENEX* or *'dezenex* to look for Dezenex—1-2-3 doesn't distinguish between upper and lowercase.

■ To list all records *except* Dezenex, use the Not Equal To operator (<>) before the criteria. For example, entering <>*Dezenex* in the Last_Name field will list everyone except Dezenex.

■ You can protect certain critical fields so that during the process of using a database you don't accidentally erase or modify their data. These techniques are identical to protection of a worksheet range, since a database is really nothing more than a worksheet. Please refer to Lesson 24 to learn how to protect records and fields in your database.

LESSON 54

Adding a Calculated Field

FEATURING

- Calculating the Inventory Value Per Item

THE LAST FIELD OF OUR INVENTORY DATABASE, INV. value (Inventory Value), was left blank because that is going to be a *calculated field*. A calculated field is a database field whose data is derived from calculations performed on data in other database fields. Thus a calculated field is like a spreadsheet cell with a formula in it that references other cells.

A typical field formula for a calculated field might be

+ Retail * .07

which would calculate a seven percent sales tax. Of course, calculated field formulas can be complex too. For example,

+ ((Gross income)-(Cost of Sales))/4

would calculate a company's gross margin for a quarter year.

When creating a calculated field, you enter its formula in the cell holding the field name in output range. Then you extract the data as usual. As 1-2-3 copies the data records in, it calculates the new field and adds it to each record.

Let's add a calculated field to all the records of the Inventory database. This field will report the amount of money tied up in a given inventory item; in other words, it will report the inventory value. We can calculate this amount by multiplying the quantity of each item in stock by the wholesale price of that item. Follow these steps:

1. In cell G16, enter **+quantity*wholesale**. ERR will appear in the cell.
2. Delete any entries in the criteria cells by selecting them and choosing Edit/Clear Special. In the Edit Clear Special dialog box, check only Cell Contents. This will leave any formatting such as background and foreground colors intact.
3. Now do the extraction with Data/Query/Extract. (Check that the ranges are still set properly, of course.) With no criteria set, all records will be copied to the output range.

Figure 54.1 shows the results. I've scrolled the screen up a bit to show all the copied records, and I've formatted cell G16 as text so you can see the formula.

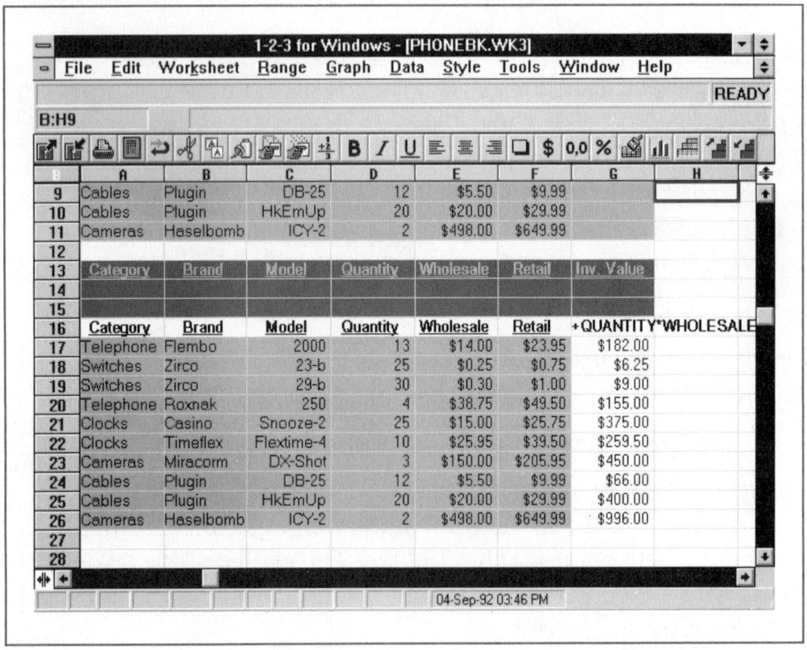

	A	B	C	D	E	F	G	H
9	Cables	Plugin	DB-25	12	$5.50	$9.99		
10	Cables	Plugin	HkEmUp	20	$20.00	$29.99		
11	Cameras	Haselbomb	ICY-2	2	$498.00	$649.99		
12								
13	Category	Brand	Model	Quantity	Wholesale	Retail	Inv. Value	
14								
15								
16	Category	Brand	Model	Quantity	Wholesale	Retail	+QUANTITY*WHOLESALE	
17	Telephone	Flembo	2000	13	$14.00	$23.95	$182.00	
18	Switches	Zirco	23-b	25	$0.25	$0.75	$6.25	
19	Switches	Zirco	29-b	30	$0.30	$1.00	$9.00	
20	Telephone	Roxnak	250	4	$38.75	$49.50	$155.00	
21	Clocks	Casino	Snooze-2	25	$15.00	$25.75	$375.00	
22	Clocks	Timeflex	Flextime-4	10	$25.95	$39.50	$259.50	
23	Cameras	Miracorm	DX-Shot	3	$150.00	$205.95	$450.00	
24	Cables	Plugin	DB-25	12	$5.50	$9.99	$66.00	
25	Cables	Plugin	HkEmUp	20	$20.00	$29.99	$400.00	
26	Cameras	Haselbomb	ICY-2	2	$498.00	$649.99	$996.00	
27								
28								

Figure 54.1.: A calculated field

As you've probably guessed, the calculated field will work much like a spreadsheet's formula field does, and any new data in the Quantity or Wholesale field will change the results in the calculated field. For instance, you can now move to the Quantity field, change some values, and see the effects immediately in the Inv. Value field.

LESSON

Managing Your Database

FEATURING

- Modifying Records
- Replacing Records
- Deleting Records
- Extracting to a File

THIS LESSON EXPLAINS A FEW MORE COMMANDS THAT you'll want to use to maintain your databases. Most of them use the Data/Query dialog box. The last one, for creating a new file from an existing one, relies on the File/Extract To command.

Modifying Records

Database information is often in flux. There will probably be times when you'll want to make changes either to individual records or to groups of records. Finding individual records for updating can be done using a simple query or the Edit/Find command. (Edit/Find searches all the cells in a selected range for text, values, or formulas you specify.)

For updating a group of records that have something in common, however, you'll want to use the Data/Query/Modify command. This command will pull out records you specify in the criteria range, placing them in an output range, just as Extract does. After you edit the group of records you can use the Data/Query/Modify/Replace command to return the modified records to their original homes.

Here are the steps to take to modify some records and replace them:

① Create a query that will extract the records you want to modify. They have to be from a single input range in a single table. Specify the input, criteria, and output ranges just as you do for a normal extraction.

② Choose Modify/Extract from the dialog box.

③ Cancel the Query dialog box.

④ Edit your records.

⑤ Choose Data/Query/Modify/Replace. The edited records are returned to their original locations.

As you can see, modifying records is a fairly easy task. However, if used improperly, the Modify and Replace commands can cause massive data loss. Make sure to read the rest of this section to prevent any such loss of data when using these commands.

There are two ways to define the output area when extracting data. The first is to select an output range of cells that includes the field names as well as a certain number of rows below the field names as the destination for the copied records. If there isn't room for all the extracted records, the ones that don't fit get chopped off.

By contrast, the approach we've been using (specifying only the field names as the output range), tells 1-2-3 to use as many rows as it needs for the output range. This is fine as long as you know you have room in your worksheet for the records. It can be dangerous, though, since 1-2-3 doesn't check the contents of the output area before writing on top of it. It just dumps extracted records into the output area, starting with the first row below the field names, and continuing down the end of the worksheet (row 8192). This means that 1-2-3 will overwrite existing rows, erasing their data.

Therefore, when using this approach, make sure you have room in your worksheet for the output records. If you have a limited amount of space to work with, add another worksheet and use that as the output range. Then, just add the worksheet letter before the destination range (e.g., B:A1..A19) to have 1-2-3 dump the extracted records there. This caveat applies for normal extractions as well as extractions that will be following by the Replace command.

Also, don't include fields that have formulas in them when specifying the output range. If you do, the formulas will be lost when you replace the records back in the database with the Replace command. This happens because 1-2-3 copies only values to the output range, not formulas. Thus, when it writes those cells back into the input range, values are copied on top of the original formulas, wiping them out.

Finally, take care not to change the input, criteria, or output ranges in the Query dialog box between the time you extract and time you replace the records. If you do (by using another query command, for example), 1-2-3 won't properly replace the records when you choose Data/Query/Extract/Replace. So, extract, edit, and replace your records in that order, without using any other query commands in between.

Inserting Records

Databases are known not only to change, but to grow. As you need to add records to yours, you'll have to consider how best to do it. There are several basic approaches you can take:

- Add the new record to the bottom of the database, on an empty row. If the database was sorted, then you'll probably have to resort it if the new record is now out of order.

- Scroll through the database, use Edit/Find, or use Data/ Query/Find to find the correct position. Then insert a row using Worksheet/Insert/Row, and add the data.

- If you have a number of records to add, you can use Query/ Modify/Insert to move a group of records from one location (such as another file, table, or range) to the destination table. (See "Extracting Records to a File" below for a discussion of how to reference a range in another file.)

Deleting Unwanted Records

Naturally, there will be times when records will become outdated and you'll want to purge them from a database. Deleting a record from a database erases it permanently. There is no way of reversing the erasure unless you use Undo immediately after the deletion.

There are several ways to delete unwanted records in 1-2-3. Data/Query/Delete lets you delete records meeting certain criteria. If you want to delete a bunch of records with a common characteristic, this is the easiest way. Of course, you can also delete individual records scrolling by around, using Edit/Find, or creating a query that will get you to the record you want to delete. Once you've found your record, choose Worksheet/Delete/Row to erase it.

Here's how to delete a series of records with Data/Query/Delete:

① Choose Data/Query/Delete.

② Specify the input range and the criteria range. No output range is required. Note that if you don't have any criteria in the criteria range, *all the records will be deleted!*

③ Click on Delete in the dialog box. You'll be given a chance to back out if you want, via a message box.

④ Click on OK to go through with the deletion process.

Deleting Duplicate Records

Duplicate records often pop up in databases. This is usually due to an error made by someone entering records, particularly if several people have been adding records. Sometimes, duplicates may not be mistakes. For example, if customer information is entered into the database each time the customer purchases a product or makes an order, duplicate records will result. In any case, there will probably be times when you'll want to clean house.

You delete duplicate records with the Data/Query/Extract/ Unique command. Here's how:

① Choose Data/Query.

② Specify the input, criteria, and output ranges. Be careful that the output range doesn't overwrite any rows you want to keep.

③ Set the Extract Unique Only check box to on.

④ Choose Extract. All the records except duplicates are copied to the output range.

Now you can move the new table back to the old table's location with Edit/Quick Copy, or by cutting and pasting. If you copy the new table to another new worksheet (say B) in the same file, you can eliminate the original worksheet (A) with Worksheet/Delete/Worksheet.

Extracting Records to a File

You may want to extract data to another file that you can put on disk and give to a colleague, use as the basis for another worksheet, or send to a branch office via modem. Here's how to extract data records to such a file:

① Select and name the range you want to copy.

② Choose File/Extract To.

③ Fill in the range or range name in the Range section of the dialog box.

④ Fill in the destination file name and the drive. You can omit the WK3 extension if you want, since 1-2-3 will fill it in automatically.

⑤ Select one of the options in the Save As box. Normally, you'll just leave the setting at Formula, the default. However, if you want to change it, here are meanings of the settings:

- Formulas: Copies formulas, values, labels, and work-sheet settings. This is the default.

- Values: Same as above, but converts formulas to values in the new file.

- Text: Creates an ASCII text file readable by any program that reads standard ASCII files, such as Windows Note-pad, PC-Write, or Microsoft Word for Windows.

⑥ Click on OK.

Data is copied into the destination file beginning at cell A1. Of course, this will copy all the fields from the database range you've selected. If you want to filter out specific records and fields using a query, you can use this two-step process: First, create an output table using Data/Query/Extract. Then use File/Extract To to send the output range to a new file.

Joining Tables Together

The explanations in this book regarding databases have described single rather than multiple-table databases. As mentioned in Lesson 46, you can combine tables to create larger databases. This requires the use of special range names for your input and criteria ranges and compliance with more complex rules for field naming between the tables. For more information about joining tables, refer to the *Lotus 1-2-3 for Windows User's Guide*.

PART

8

Functions

56 LESSON

Using 1-2-3 Functions

FEATURING

- The @AVG Function
- Averaging a List of Cells

IN 1-2-3, YOU USE FUNCTIONS TO ANALYZE AND MAKE calculations on the information in a worksheet. You've already experimented with @SUM, the function that adds the values in a range of cells. Using @SUM, you've seen how a function can do the work of a much longer formula, making your work a lot easier, and reducing the chance of error. Other functions let you carry out special calculations, perform statistical analysis, extract information from a database, and make decisions within a formula.

Some functions, like @SUM, are nothing more than quick, shorthand substitutes for ordinary formulas. On the other hand, many functions perform special operations that you couldn't do otherwise. For example, the @NOW function finds the current date and time from your computer's built-in clock. The @IF function chooses between two different courses of action in a formula based on whether a condition you want to test is true or false.

In this lesson, you'll practice using some of the most common functions in your Budget worksheet. In the other lessons in this part, you'll learn to use particular functions to solve some common problems.

Calculating an Average

When random variations in your data obscure the real trend, you can calculate an average using 1-2-3's @AVG function. Technically, @AVG generates the arithmetic mean of a range of values—it's the equivalent of adding them up and dividing by the number of values in the range. Like @SUM, @AVG belongs to 1-2-3's group of statistical functions—there are eight groups in all, summarized for you in Lesson 63.

Let's obtain the average profit per quarter for the year shown on our Budget worksheet. There's no icon for @AVG as there is for @SUM, so you'll have to enter the function into the cell where you want the average displayed. In 1-2-3, functions are entered in formulas within cells, just as you would enter a formula for subtracting one cell from another. But many times, as in this case, a function constitutes the entire formula.

① Open BUDGET.WK3.

② Move the cell pointer to cell G17 and enter **Avg. Profit per Quarter**. Widen the column to properly contain the label.

③ Type **@AVG(** into cell G18.

④ Notice that we typed an open parenthesis. This allows you to point to a range of cells to use with the function. (Like most functions, @AVG must be supplied with values or cell references, called *arguments,* with which it makes its calculations.) In this case, use the ← key to move the highlight to B18, the first cell in the range to be averaged. Notice that 1-2-3 places the cell address B18 in the edit line for you.

⑤ Press . (period) to anchor B18 as the first cell in the range. Two periods (..) appear in the edit line, indicating that you're specifying a range. Now move the cell pointer to the last cell in the range, E18. Again, you'll see the address in the edit line, which should read *A:B18..A:E18.*

⑥ Press Enter. A close parenthesis appears in the contents box, completing the @AVG function. ABC Inc.'s average quarterly profit appears in cell G18, as shown in Figure 56.1.

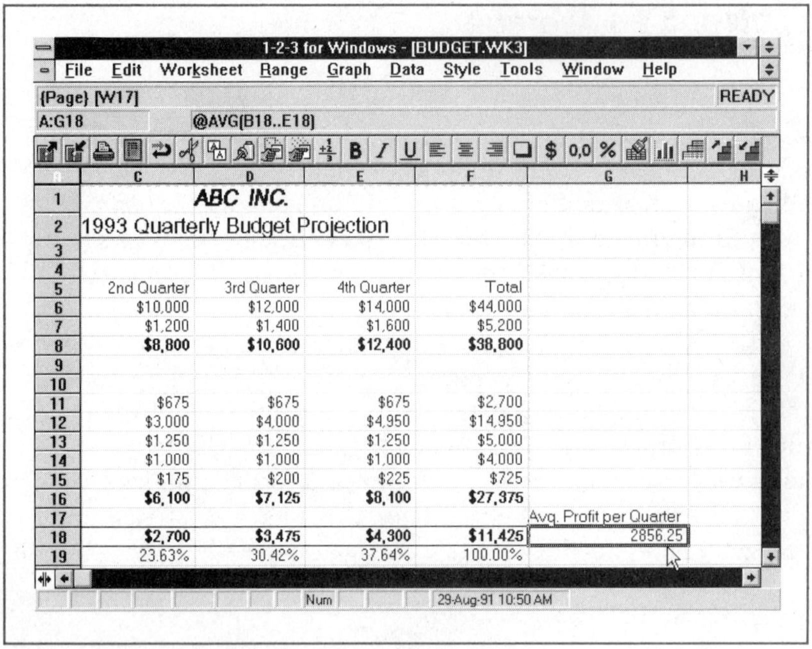

LESSON 56

Figure 56.1: ABC Inc.'s average quarterly profit

Of course, you can also specify the range of cells to be averaged with the mouse. After you type in **@AVG(**, you would click on the first cell in the range, B18. Then, without letting up on the mouse button, drag across to the E18, highlighting the range. When you release the mouse button, type a close parenthesis to complete the function. The result appears in G18.

*A*veraging a List of Specific Cells

So far, you've used the @SUM and @AVG functions on ranges of cells. Functions such as these can also be used on a list of specific cells. Let's say you want to know how much your firm's salary expenses are on average, but there is a one-time blip in salaries in the second quarter that doesn't reflect your ongoing operations. To calculate the average of salary expenses over the first, third, and fourth quarters, find a blank cell, say G12.

① Type **@AVG(** into the cell.

② Press ← to move the cell pointer to cell B12, which contains the salary expense for the first quarter.

③ Type a comma, and 1-2-3 enters the B12 address into your function. (Within a function, you can use a comma or a semicolon to separate values in a list of arguments.)

④ Note that the cell pointer has jumped back to cell G12. Press ← to move to cell D12 for the third quarter salary, then type another comma.

⑤ Finally, move to cell E12. Press Enter to complete the function and display the average value.

57 LESSON

Looking Up Data in a Table

FEATURING

- The @HLOOKUP Function

OFTEN, YOU'LL WANT A WAY TO EXTRACT A SPECIFIC piece of information from a database table. For instance, let's say that ABC Inc. pays each employee a base salary corresponding to that employee's "step" on the payroll ladder (the step might be based on both job description and seniority). With 1-2-3, you don't have to enter the salary for each employee one at a time, or type in a new base salary for every employee each time there's a cost-of-living pay increase. Instead, you can have 1-2-3 look up the base salary that matches each employee's step.

To see how this works:

1. Move to worksheet B.

2. Choose Worksheet/Insert/Sheet to insert a new worksheet (C).

3. Now fill in the worksheet with the data shown in Figure 57.1. Don't bother with formatting unless you want to.

4. Set column widths to adequately display the data.

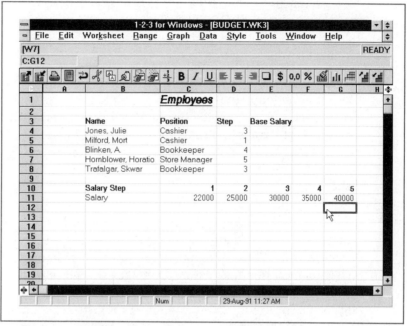

Figure 57.1: The Employees database

You're now ready to use 1-2-3's @HLOOKUP function to automatically enter each employee's base salary. Like many functions, @HLOOKUP requires a list of specific arguments. In this case, the function's format looks like this:

@HLOOKUP(search value,table range,row offset)

As in all functions, you separate the arguments with commas or semicolons. You must not leave spaces between the arguments. In addition, each function recognizes only certain types of arguments—it won't work if you give it the wrong number of values or invalid values to work with.

Here's how to proceed with @HLOOKUP:

① Move the cell pointer to E4 for Julie Jones' base salary.

② Type @.

③ This time, instead of typing the rest of the function yourself, use 1-2-3's Name command by pressing F3. Normally, pressing F3 brings up a list of range names, but when you are ending a function, it lists all available functions. Scroll down the list and choose HLOOKUP. When you click on OK, 1-2-3 inserts the function and an open parenthesis into the edit line for you.

④ The first argument for @HLOOKUP is the search value, which is what you're looking for in the table. In this case, we want to locate the salary step for this employee. If Ms. Jones was forever stuck at step 2, say, you could enter **2** here. But since she may get promoted or get a "step up" for experience, type **D4** to have @HLOOKUP read her step from that cell.

⑤ Type a comma.

⑥ Next, enter the second argument, the range of cells that constitute the table. Since you'll be using the table repeatedly for each employee, you must define the range using absolute cell addresses. For this reason, you must type in the address range yourself, followed by a comma. Type **C10..G11**. Then press F4 once to change the references to absolute. The edit line will read

@HLOOKUP(D4,$C:$C$10..$C:$G$11,

Notice that the worksheet letter (C) also gets a dollar sign in front of it.

⑦ The third argument, the row offset, tells @HLOOKUP which row of the table contains the information you want to retrieve. In this case we want to extract the base salary amounts. Enter the number of rows that @HLOOKUP should drop down from the table's top row (the first row in the range you entered in step 6). Since the salary data is 1 row below the top, type **1** followed by a close parenthesis.

As soon as you press Enter to finish the function, @HLOOKUP scans the first row of the table looking for the value listed in cell D4, which is 3. Finding a match in the third column of the table, @HLOOKUP obediently drops down 1 row and extracts the value recorded in that cell, placing it in cell E4 for you, as shown in Figure 57.2.

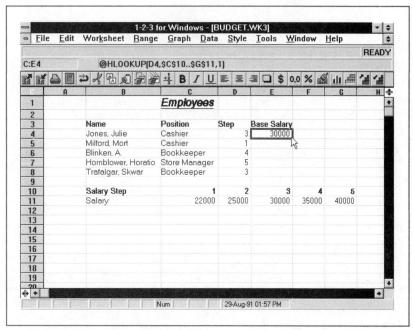

Figure 57.2: Using @HLOOKUP to look up the base salary

Now use the Range Copy icon to reproduce your @HLOOKUP formula from cell E4 to the other four cells in column E of your employee worksheet. Voila—instant base salaries for all.

By the way, the *H* in @HLOOKUP stands for "horizontal." This is a horizontal table, since the top row contains the values that are matched to the search value, the first argument in the function. There's a comparable @VLOOKUP function for vertical tables—it works the same way, except that the values to be matched are in the first column, and the third argument is a column offset.

58 LESSON

Keeping Track of Dates

FEATURING

- The @NOW Function
- The @DATE Function

TIME IS AS IMPORTANT AS MONEY IN EVERY AREA OF business or personal finance. Fortunately, 1-2-3 makes it easy to answer questions such as "How much did we spend on supplies during July?" or, more pleasantly, "How many sales did I make this month?"

If all you want to do is record the date that a sale was transacted or an employee was hired, you can enter the date as a label. But in that case, 1-2-3 won't know it's a date, and will treat the entry like any other text. If you want to perform calculations with the date—perhaps to find out how long that employee has been on the job—you must record the date in 1-2-3's special date format.

Internally, 1-2-3 keeps track of dates as five-digit numbers, representing the number of days since the turn of the century. Like any other number, a date can be added to, subtracted from, or even—though I can't think of a reason to do it—multiplied. Times are stored as the decimal portion of the date number. Fortunately, you can have 1-2-3 display a date number in a date or time format you're used to.

Using the @NOW Function

Let's see how this works with the @NOW function. The @NOW function reads the date and time stored in your computer's own clock and inserts it into the formula for the current cell. Since @NOW takes no arguments, you can use it by itself to show today's date and the current time whenever you print your worksheet. But since @NOW represents the date in 1-2-3's numeric system, you must format the cell to display this number as a readable date or time. Here's how:

① In worksheet C of BUDGET.WK3, select cell A2.

② Type **@NOW** and press Enter. A long number with a couple decimal places appears in the cell. This is 1-2-3's internal representation of the current date and time.

③ Choose Range/Format. Scroll down the list of formatting options to the 31-Dec-90 choice and select it. Click on OK.

④ Today's date should now appear in cell A2. If you don't see the correct date, don't blame 1-2-3—almost certainly, your computer's clock is set to the wrong date.

Now, for a cell to display the current time:

① Move to cell A3.

② Again, type **@NOW** followed by Enter.

③ Choose Range/Format once more. Press **7**. Immediately you're moved to the 11:59 AM option in the list. Click OK and the correct time in hours and minutes will appear in the cell.

Watch the time entry in cell A3 for a minute or two. You'll soon realize that it doesn't change. You must recalculate the worksheet whenever you want to update the date or time—before printing, for instance. Do so by pressing F9.

Using the @DATE function

The @DATE function calculates the five-digit date number for a year, month, and day that you enter yourself, or that comes from cells in the worksheet. This date number is then available for calculations.

Returning to the example we've already discussed, let's say you want to know how long employee Jones has been on your staff, perhaps to see whether she's passed her probationary period. You'll start with the new Employees worksheet prepared in the last lesson.

① In row 3, add two new labels in columns F and G:

Hire Date   Days Employed

② Now enter the hire date for Ms. Jones, choosing a date about a month prior to today. To use the @DATE function, you must supply it with the year, month, and day, in that order. So, if Ms. Jones was hired on March 19, 1991, you would type **@DATE(91,3,19)** in cell F4.

③ Format the cell with Range/Format so that the date appears in readable form.

④ Now move to cell G4, for Days Employed. Here, you'll use a function as part of a larger formula for the first time. To calculate the number of days since Ms. Jones was hired, type in the formula **@NOW − F4**, and press Enter.

⑤ Immediately, 1-2-3 calculates and displays the number of days since the hire date until today. This result is more precise by a good many decimal places than you probably want it to be. To display it as an even number of days, click on the 0,0 icon or use Range/Format to select the Fixed format and 0 decimal places.

Your worksheet should now look like Figure 58.1.

Using the @INT Function

One final trick will make the Days Employed value more meaningful, and will also introduce one of 1-2-3's mathematical functions,

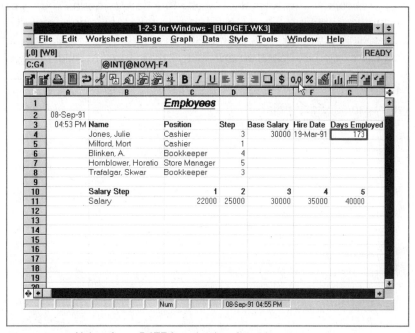

Figure 58.1: Using the @DATE function in a formula

@INT. The @INT function removes the decimal portion of a number. For example, it would change 1.6 to 1.

Now, recall from the previous exercise that there was fractional part of the calculated value for Days Employed. That part of the number represented the fraction of the current day that had elapsed from 12:00 midnight until the moment you calculated the cell.

Here's the problem: If you calculate the cell after 12:00 noon, the fractional part is larger than .5. When you format the result with Range/Format, the value in the cell gets rounded up to the next larger number of days. While mathematically proper, this isn't what you want—generally, in situations like this, only full days of employment are counted.

To calculate the number of full days employed correctly, simply enter the following formula into cell G4:

@INT(@NOW) – F4

Notice how this formula uses one function to modify the result of another function. The @INT function takes the value from cell B2—today's date and time, generated by @NOW—and strips off the part following the decimal point. The hire date stored in cell F4 is then subtracted from this number to give the even number of full days since Ms. Jones was hired. You don't even need to use Range/Format to remove the decimal points.

LESSON 59

Making Financial Calculations

FEATURING

- The @PMT Function
- Setting Up a Loan Payment Table

FINANCIAL FUNCTIONS MAKE UP ANOTHER IMPORTANT group of 1-2-3's functions. Among the most useful of these is @PMT, which lets you calculate the payments you must make on a loan or annuity. To experiment with @PMT:

① Insert another new worksheet (D) with Worksheet/Insert/Sheet. Title it "Loans and Investments" by entering that label into cell A1.

The @PMT function takes three arguments, in the following pattern:

@PMT(principal,interest,term)

Let's say you want to borrow $150,000 over a 15-year period at an annual percentage rate of 9.65%. You'll be making monthly payments. To simplest way to find the amount of your payment is to enter the specific numeric values for your loan as arguments directly into @PMT.

② Move to cell B3 and type

  @PMT(

③ Since the loan amount or principal is $150,000, type in **150000** as the first argument in the function, then type a comma.

④ The next argument is for the interest rate. You must express this as the rate for one payment period. In this case, a payment period is a month, so type **.0965/12** followed by a comma (.0965 is the same as 9.65%).

⑤ Finally, enter the term—actually, the number of payments you'll be making. Since your loan will be amortized over 15 years, type **15*12** followed by a close parenthesis to finish the function.

⑥ Press Enter. Your monthly payment is calculated and displayed.

⑦ Click on the Currency icon to format the result in dollars and cents.

Creating a Loan Payment Table

A more flexible way to use @PMT is to set up a table in your worksheet, entering the values for principal, interest rate, and term in separate cells. Since the function can read cell values as arguments, you can easily see how changing the interest rate, loan amount, or term changes your monthly payment. In addition, you can set up the worksheet to display the interest rate as an APR, instead of a monthly interest rate, and the term in years, rather than months.

① Move to B3 and press Del to clear it. Then, enter the following labels, starting with row 5:

  In cell B5:   Principal amount

  In cell B6:   Interest rate (APR)

In cell B7:   Term in years

In cell B8:   Monthly payment amount

② Widen column B to accomodate the labels.

③ Type **150000** in cell C5, **.0965** in cell C6, and **15** in cell C7.

④ Format C5 as a dollar amount and C6 as a percentage. (Widen column C if the principal amount displays as asterisks.)

⑤ In cell C8, type the following formula

@PMT(C5,C6/12,C7*12)

⑥ Press Enter to complete the formula and calculate the monthly payment amount. Format the cell as a dollar value. Your worksheet should now look like Figure 59.1.

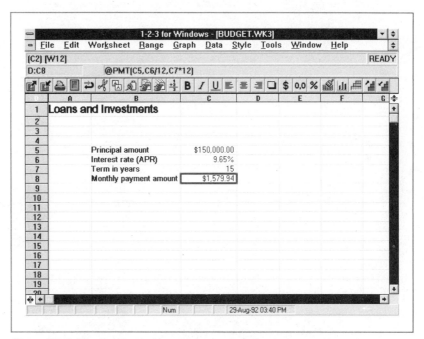

Figure 59.1: The Loans and Investments worksheet

⑦ Experiment with the effects of a changing interest rate
on your monthly payment by typing new values into cell
C6. Remember to express percentages in decimal form
(enter 10% as .10, for example).

If you want to compare several loan scenarios, just use the
Range Copy icon to copy the range from C5 through C8 into one or
more adjacent columns, then change the values as appropriate.

LESSON 60

Using Other Functions

FEATURING

- Using Help
- Function Categories

AS YOU'VE BEGUN TO SEE, 1-2-3 OFFERS A RICH SET OF functions that let you accomplish a wide variety of tasks that would otherwise be more cumbersome or impossible. In this lesson, you'll learn about the range of available functions and the kinds of data analysis and manipulation you can perform with them. First, though, let's practice getting help with functions while you're working in 1-2-3.

Getting Online Help for Functions

Of course, there's no way I can cover all of 1-2-3's functions in detail in this brief book. Fortunately, you can get specific instructions on how to use any function from 1-2-3's online Help system.

When you open the Help menu, notice that there's an entire menu choice devoted to functions—@Functions. Click on it to open a Help window that gives basic information about functions. As always, you can get further information about any underlined topic by clicking on it.

To get help on any specific function, scroll through the text to the underlined entry called @Function Index. You're presented with a alphabetized list of individual functions. Click on the function you're interested in to display relevant detailed help.

Of course, even these details won't be all that helpful if you don't know which function you want to use in the first place. The remainder of this lesson will introduce you to the main groups of functions in order to help get you started when you need to choose a function for a particular task. Beyond that, you'll have to consult the *Lotus 1-2-3 for Windows User's Guide* that came with your copy of 1-2-3.

Understanding Function Categories

As you know, 1-2-3 functions are grouped into eight categories. Let's look at each category in brief to get a sense of the range of tasks you can accomplish with functions.

Statistical Functions

The statistical functions perform calculations on simple lists of numbers. The @SUM and @AVG functions, both of which you've used earlier, are good examples. Other statistical functions let you count the number of cells within a range, find the highest or lowest value within a range, or calculate the standard deviation or variance of a range.

Mathematical Functions

Instead of looking up trigonometric values such as sines and cosines in tables, or calculating square roots the longhand way, you can use 1-2-3's mathematical functions to compute results like these in a single step. You can even generate a random number.

Database Functions

The database functions carry out statistical calculations on information in 1-2-3 database tables. You can optionally specify criteria that data must meet to be included in the calculations. For example, you might use the @DSUM function to add a set of values that meet your criteria, perhaps to add the number of orders for a specific part.

Financial Functions

With 1-2-3's financial functions you can analyze the rate of return of investments, compute cash flows and present and future values, and calculate depreciation. You can also make loan and annuity calculations—as you've already seen, you can determine the monthly payments for loans and annuities, but you can also figure out payment periods when other factors are set in advance.

Date and Time Functions

You used @NOW and @DATE back in Lesson 58. Other similar functions let you extract the year, month, or day from a date, or determine the time (in minutes, hours, and seconds), or just the hour, minute, or second.

Logical Functions

Logical functions evaluate whether a given condition is true or false. For example, you can determine whether or not a cell contains text or a numeric value. The @IF function, one of the most common logical functions, automatically selects one of two options in a formula based on whether a condition you specify is true or false.

String Functions

This group contains functions that specialize in text, or strings, within cells. You can search for a cell that contains a given string, extract a specific number of characters from a specific section of a string, or convert a string to upper- or lowercase letters, and more.

Special Functions

These miscellaneous functions offer information about cells, ranges, or the operating system. Two functions let you find out about the attributes of a given cell, such as its address or format. Others let you count the number or rows, columns, or worksheets in a specified range. The @INFO function supplies information about your current 1-2-3 session, such as how much memory is available, how many files are open, and which version of 1-2-3 you're using.

PART

9

Working with Macros

61 LESSON

Creating Macros

FEATURING

- Storing a Macro
- Documenting a Macro
- Running a Macro

ONCE YOU BEGIN WORKING WITH 1-2-3 ON A REGULAR basis, chances are good you'll find yourself carrying out similar or identical tasks over and over again. Maybe you format all your column labels in 14-point bold italic Arial type, with underlining. Perhaps you regularly print a particular range of cells on each of the 50 worksheets you use to track sales figures state by state. Or it could be you just type a label such as *ABC Inc.* many times every day. Wouldn't it be great if you could automate all the keystrokes, commands, and procedures these jobs require?

Macros give you the means to do just that. A macro records a series of instructions of your choice that together accomplish a specific task. Whenever you need to perform that task, you can "play back" the entire macro—no matter how many separate commands it contains—by tapping as few as two keys or by picking the macro by name from a list.

Macros can store and play back almost anything you can type from the keyboard. They can select any command from 1-2-3's menus, with a few exceptions. They can enter or change data, labels, or formulas in your worksheet cells.

But macros can do more than automate repetitive typing chores. For instance, a single macro can carry out the same operation on different parts of a worksheet or on different worksheets, deciding "for itself" where to do its work—and where not to. Or how about using a macro to display your own dialog box, from which you can select customized commands with the mouse? Macros are also great for creating automated "guided tours" of sample worksheets that show new users how to work with your own data in 1-2-3.

Guided-tour worksheets aside, there are two main reasons to create a macro:

- When you frequently execute the same series of two or more commands or repetitively type the same label, value, or formula, even if the entry is short

- When you use a long or complicated series of commands and keyboard entries, even if only occasionally

Once you decide to build a macro, here are the steps you'll follow:

① Plan the macro.

② Decide where to store the macro.

③ Type the macro into your worksheet.

④ Add an explanation of what the macro does.

⑤ Assign a name to the macro.

⑥ Test the macro and correct any errors.

When you've completed these six steps, you'll have a finished, working macro you can use as often as you need it. Let's see how the process works with a simple macro, one that changes the format of the current cell to currency and then displays the value in bold type.

LESSON 61

Planning Your Macro

Before you actually begin entering a new macro, it's always best to give some thought to how to accomplish the task at hand most efficiently. If the macro will simply type out *antidisestablishmentarianism* or some other long label for you, no real planning is necessary. With short, simple command macros it may be enough to simply think them through ahead of time.

For example, you can probably keep the command sequence needed for the sample macro in your head—it's Range/Format/Currency, followed by Style/Font/Bold. To plan this macro, you'd need to remember only a few keystrokes:

Alt R F C Enter

then

Alt S F Alt-B Enter

More complex macros require more careful planning. One good way to proceed is to manually step through the commands your macro will contain, writing them down as you go. Once you have a command sequence that actually does what you intend it to, you can type the equivalent macro into a cell. Another option is to use the Transcript window, which automatically stores all the keystrokes and commands you execute. Lesson 63 covers using the Transcript window to record macros.

Macros are limited to 512 typed characters, so you must be sure not to exceed that limit. If the operation you're planning requires more, you can break it into separate macros and have one macro trigger the next in sequence.

Storing Your Macro

Macros are always entered into worksheet cells. If a macro is too long for a single cell, you can break it up into consecutive cells in a column. You should choose a location that is out of the way of your worksheet data, so that the macro won't be altered if you insert or delete rows or columns or make other wholesale changes.

The safest parking place is in a separate worksheet that contains no data. But a convenient alternative for short, simple macros is in the top corners of any active worksheet. Either way, allow three columns for each macro: one for the macro itself, and one on either side for descriptive comments (see "Documenting the Macro" below).

You'll probably want to use some macros in many different worksheets. Instead of retyping the macro commands or copying them from one sheet to the next, you can store such macros in a *macro library,* a special worksheet containing only macros. You'll learn to use macro libraries in Lesson 64.

Entering the Macro

Enough theory for now—let's enter that sample macro.

① Create a new worksheet (E) with Worksheet/Insert/Sheet. In cell A1, enter **Macros Are Easy**.

② Move the cell pointer to cell B3.

③ The first keystroke you want to record is Alt, which activates 1-2-3's menu system. But since the Alt key doesn't have a corresponding one-character symbol, you must represent it in the macro by typing a special *macro key name.* Type

   {ALT}

All macro key names and special commands must be entered inside curly brackets in this way.

④ Type the keystrokes you would use to select Range/Format/Currency:

   RFC

⑤ To indicate the Enter key in a 1-2-3 macro, type ˜ (the tilde).

⑥ Press ↓ to move the cell pointer to cell B4.

⑦ Again, begin the entry with **{ALT}**.

LESSON 61

⑧ Type the keystrokes for Style/Font/Bold. Since you select the Bold option by typing Alt-B, you must again enter the {ALT} key name:

SF{ALT "B"}

⑨ Type ˜ (to indicate Enter) and then press Enter.

That completes the macro. Your work should look like Figure 61.1. (I've increased the point size for visibility in this and the following figures.)

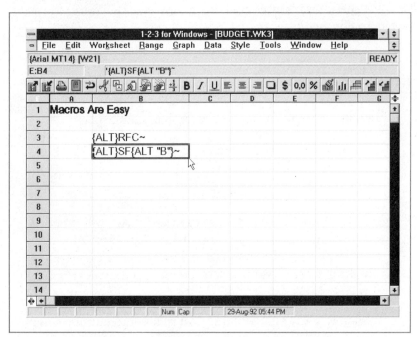

Figure 61.1: The sample macro

Notice in the edit line that 1-2-3 has recorded an apostrophe (') at the beginning of the macro. Since 1-2-3 treats macros as a special kind of label, each macro starts with a label prefix. Also, notice that the second Alt-key combination in the cell (Alt-B) must be written as *{ALT "B"}*. When you use the {ALT} key name to select a menu name, you place the underlined letter in the menu name after the second curly brace. When you use {ALT} to select a dialog box option, however, you place the letter of the option within quotation marks *within* the braces, leaving a space after ALT.

Documenting the Macro

Since the macro itself looks like gibberish, it's prudent to add an explanatory comment to remind you of its function and how to activate it. This is called documenting the macro. By convention, the description goes in the column to the right of the macro itself. To document the sample macro, move to cell C3 and type the following label:

Boldface currency format

It's wise to document the keystroke sequence or command with which you'll activate the macro. First, though, you have to decide on what that will be—and that's the subject of the next section.

Naming the Macro

In order to play back, or run, a macro you must first give it a name. This is easy—since macros occupy ranges of cells, they can be named with Range/Name/Create like any other range, as you learned to do in Lesson 25.

However, the name you choose is important, since it affects the way you run the macro. Each worksheet can create up to 26 macros that you run by pressing Ctrl and a letter key at the same time. For example, you might want execute the sample macro by pressing Ctrl-C (for *currency*).

To set up a macro of this type, you must give it a two-character name beginning with a backslash (\) and ending with the activation letter. To do this with the sample macro:

1. Move the cell pointer back to cell B3.

2. Choose Range/Name/Create.

3. When the dialog box appears, type in \C. (A backslash stands for the Ctrl key.) Since a macro continues executing

LESSON 61

down a column until it reaches a blank cell or the {QUIT} command, you need only name the first cell in the Range area. You don't need to explicitly enter the entire range of a multiple-cell macro.

④ Click on OK.

Now that the macro has a name, you can type the name into the worksheet for future reference. By convention, macro names go in the column immediately to the left of the macro. Move to cell A3 and type '\C (you must type the apostrophe to indicate that you're entering a label, not a value).

Running and Testing Your Macro

Before you try out any new macro, always save your worksheet. That way, if the macro doesn't work as you expected it to and changes something in the worksheet, you can return things to their original state with the File/Open command.

Now you're ready to test your new macro.

① Move to cell A6. Type in a numeric value, say **425**, and press Enter.

② Without moving the cell pointer, press Ctrl-C.

Because you named the macro \C, 1-2-3 executes the macro immediately. The cell contents should appear in boldface type as $425. If that doesn't happen, go back to cells B3 and B4 with the cursor keys. Check that you typed in the macro exactly as instructed, including the ~ characters at the end of each cell. Make any necessary corrections, then try again.

With more complex macros you can use 1-2-3's Tools/Macros/Debug command, covered in the *Lotus 1-2-3 for Windows User's Guide,* to help you discover and correct errors. Till then, remember this one simple trick for dealing with problem macros: You can stop any macro dead in its tracks by pressing Ctrl-Break.

LESSON | 62

Naming and Running Macros

FEATURING

- Naming Macros
- Creating Multiple Macros

ALTHOUGH MACROS WITH ONE-LETTER NAMES ARE easy to activate from the keyboard, you may well need more than 26 macros in a file. Besides, if you store a macro in a separate worksheet or a macro library, you may not remember what keystroke runs it, or what its cryptic name, \C, stands for.

Using Tools/Macro/Run

For the above reasons, 1-2-3 gives you an alternative method for naming and running macros. All you have to do is start the name with any character other than the backslash (\). Or, if you want to use the backslash as the first character, you must use more than one letter for the rest of the name. In this system, valid macro names might include BOLD/CURRENCY, PRINT_A_RANGE, or TODAY'S_DATE.

The Tools/Macro/Run command lets you activate any macro by its name. Let's build a few more sample macros to see how this works.

① Move the cell pointer to cell E3 of worksheet E.

② Type **ABC Inc.** and press Enter.

③ With the cell pointer still in E3, name this cell "ABC" with Range/Name/Create.

④ Run the new macro. Move to cell A7 and choose Tools/ Macro/Run. Select the name ABC in the list that appears, and 1-2-3 will type out the entire label in the edit line. You'll have to press Enter to enter it into the cell.

You can make a macro out of any label or value you've already entered. Move to the cell where you entered the title for this worksheet and use Range/Name/Create to name it "BIG MAC." Then move to an empty cell. When you execute the new macro with Tools/Macro/ Run and select BIG MAC from the list, 1-2-3 types *Macros Are Easy* into the current cell.

Tools/Macro/Run works just as well to execute macros with two- character names such as \C, the type you worked with in the previous lesson. And here's a tip about choosing macro names: All named ranges, including named ranges of data, appear in the list displayed when you press Tools/Macro/Run. If you have named more than two or three data ranges in your worksheet, it may be hard to tell them apart from the macro names. The best way to avoid confusion is to begin all macro names with a backslash (\)—that way they'll appear together in the list.

Creating and Naming Multiple Macros

If you are building several macros at the same time, you can save time and effort by naming them "automatically" with Range/Name/ Labels/Create. Give it a try:

① Enter the macros as shown in Figure 62.1. Starting in row 3, place the names in column H, the macros in column I, and their descriptions in column J. Skip a row between each macro. Remember to enter an apostrophe before the /N in cell H8, or 1-2-3 will think you're trying to enter a repeating character and fill the cell with *N's*.

② Select the range containing the names in column H (H3..H8).

③ Select Range/Name/Labels/Create. In the dialog box, choose Right. This indicates you want 1-2-3 to assign the labels in column H as range names for the cells to the right.

④ Click on OK. When you do, 1-2-3 matches up the names in column H—ignoring the blank cells—with the macros in column I. You can immediately use the new macros. To prove it, move to an empty cell and press Ctrl-N.

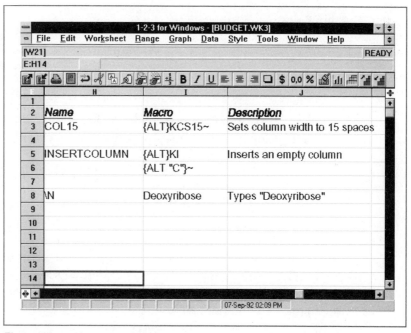

Figure 62.1: Naming multiple macros

63 LESSON

Using the
Transcript Window

FEATURING

- Creating Macros with the Transcript Window
- Editing the Transcript Window

AS YOU BECOME MORE SKILLED WITH 1-2-3, YOU'LL begin to attempt more complex procedures, and you'll want macros to match. But instead of typing a long macro yourself, you can simply execute the series of commands you want in your macro, then use the Transcript window to turn them into a macro for you.

The Transcript window keeps a record of the keystrokes you type and the commands you use, whether you activate them from the keyboard or by selecting them with the mouse. The Transcript window stores your keystrokes and commands in the same format used in 1-2-3 macros. It's a simple matter to copy the desired sequence from the Transcript window to a cell or columnar range. Then you just name the range, and you have an instant macro.

The Transcript window comes in very handy when you realize in the middle of a convoluted procedure that the command series you're executing would make a great macro. You haven't wasted any effort—just finish the procedure, open the Transcript window, and extract your new macro.

*C*reating a Macro with the *Transcript Window*

For practice, use the Transcript window to create a simple macro that inserts your name and department into the top left corner, cells A1 and A2, in the current worksheet. Later, you can apply the same technique to make much more sophisticated macros.

(1) Activate worksheet E in the Budget file, the one called "Macros Are Easy," if it isn't already visible. Move to any cell other than A1.

(2) Since you know ahead of time that you're going to be making a macro, clear the Transcript window before you start. Use Tools/Macro/Show Transcript to open the Transcript window, click once on the Transcript window to make it active, then choose Edit/Clear All to remove the current contents. If you don't clear the window now, you'll have to edit out unwanted commands and keystrokes later.

(3) Click once on the Budget worksheet to activate it, and adjust the Transcript and Budget windows so you can see them both, as shown in Figure 63.1.

(4) Tap Home to move the cell pointer to cell A1. If you can still see the Transcript window, notice that {*HOME*} appears in the window.

(5) Type your name, then press ↓. Your name appears in A1, replacing the words *Macros Are Easy*. The cell pointer moves to A2.

(6) Type your department name and press Enter.

(7) To turn your work into a macro, click on the Transcript window again. Notice that it displays all the keystrokes you've entered, as shown in Figure 63.1. Keys other than Enter that have no corresponding symbols are shown as key names between curly braces: {HOME} for the Home key and {D} for the down-arrow cursor key.

LESSON 63

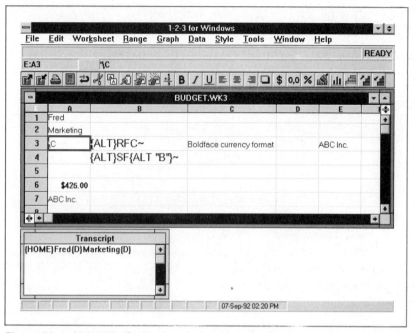

Figure 63.1: Using the Transcript window to create macros

⑧ Select all the text in the Transcript window, then choose Edit/Copy.

⑨ Return to the worksheet by clicking on its title bar. Move the cell pointer to cell I10, then choose Edit/Paste. The text from the Transcript window appears in the cell and the one immediately below it.

⑩ Use Range/Name/Create to name cell I10 "MY_NAME." That completes the macro itself. For good form, document the macro by entering its name in cell H10 and a brief description in cell J10.

⑪ Try out the macro. Switch to worksheet B and put the cell pointer in any cell besides A1. Use Tools/Macro/Run and choose MY_NAME from the list. You should see your name and department in the top left corner of the worksheet.

Remember, you can use the mouse or the keyboard in any combination to open menus and select commands and dialog box options. The Transcript window records all mouse actions as the equivalent keystrokes and key names. For instance, if you open the Windows menu with the mouse, then click on the Cascade option, the Transcript window records {ALT}WC.

Editing the Transcript Window

The material in the Transcript window is ordinary text and can be edited using 1-2-3's standard text editing techniques. You can remove keystrokes and commands you typed by mistake, or add new ones by typing them in, using key names in curly braces where necessary.

If you decide after the fact that some of the commands you recently used would make a good macro, you can edit the Transcript window to remove the unwanted text using Edit/Cut or Edit/Clear, then copy what's left to a worksheet with Edit/Copy. Alternatively, you can select and copy only that portion of the text you want to use as a macro. Of course, you can also make changes after you've copied the keystrokes and commands into the worksheet.

Playing Back Macros from the Transcript Window

You can play back any series of keystrokes and commands recorded in the Transcript window, just as if it were a macro. This gives you a handy way to test the waters when you're not sure whether a given set of instructions you've executed would make a good macro. It's also useful when you want to repeat a keystroke and command series just once or twice. The technique is simple.

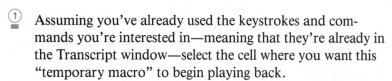

① Assuming you've already used the keystrokes and commands you're interested in—meaning that they're already in the Transcript window—select the cell where you want this "temporary macro" to begin playing back.

(2) Open the Transcript window with Tools/Macro/Show Transcript.

(3) Using the mouse or the keyboard technique, select whatever sequence you want to play back. Or, if you want to play back the entire contents of the window, leave all the text unselected.

(4) To play back the sequence, choose Tools/Macro/Run.

LESSON 64

Macro Libraries

FEATURING

- Using a Macro Library
- Loading Macros Automatically

WHILE IT'S EASIEST TO STORE A NEW MACRO IN THE current worksheet, it's often more efficient in the long run to keep your macros in a separate macro library file. That way, you can access them from any of your worksheets without having to retype or copy them into each file.

Creating a macro library is simple. Start a new worksheet file, then define your macros using the techniques you've learned in earlier lessons. You can also copy existing macros from other files to the new one as long as you remember to name the macro ranges in the library worksheet. Save the finished macro library as an ordinary file, but use a name such as MYMACROS.WK3 to remind you of its contents.

Using Macros from a Macro Library

To use a macro library, all you have to do is open the macro library file along with whatever worksheet files you're working with.

When you open it, 1-2-3 scans the library file for range names, including those of macros.

Once you've opened the file, all macros in the library are immediately available for use in any of your other open worksheets. You activate the macros using the ordinary methods—either by pressing Ctrl while you tap the macro's letter name or by selecting the macro name from the list displayed by Tools/Macro/Run.

You can actually have two or more macro libraries open at the same time. The Tools/Macro/Run list displays macro range names from one file at a time. At the bottom of the list, however, the names of any other open files are displayed in double angle brackets, like this:

<<**MACROS1.WK3**>>

<<**MACROS2.WK3**>>

<<**MACROS3.WK3**>>

The list displays the macros in only one library file at a time. To see macros from a different file, simply double-click on the file's name.

Organizing Your Macro Libraries

Some macros are specialized for tasks that you perform in particular types of worksheets. It makes sense to divide your macro collection into separate library files, each containing the macros you commonly use with a given set of worksheets. Name each library file according to its function, or give it a name similar to the associated worksheet file.

On the other hand, odds are good that you'll develop a core set of macros that you use with nearly every worksheet. You should store all these macros in one file that you load every time you work.

Loading Macro Libraries Automatically

The most efficient way to take advantage of 1-2-3's macro libraries is to load them automatically. It's easy to do, and I strongly recommend this technique.

To load your "universal" macro library automatically whenever you start 1-2-3, all you have to do is name the library file AUTO123.WK3 when you save it on disk, and place it in the default directory for your 1-2-3 files. When you first start the program, 1-2-3 always checks for the presence of this file name and loads the file if it's there. Your core macros will always be available to you, and they'll seem to become a part of 1-2-3.

The method for automatically loading a macro library when you open a particular worksheet is just a little trickier. In this case, you have to create a special macro within the worksheet file itself. Whenever you open a file, 1-2-3 checks for the presence of a macro named \0 (backslash-zero). If the program finds this autoexecute macro, it executes it immediately.

An automatic macro can do many things. For instance, you might create one that locates the next empty pair of cells in a given column and then places the current date and time there, providing a log of each time the worksheet was opened. But in this case, you simply want it to open a specific file, the matching macro library. Here's how to build the macro:

① Find a place in the worksheet for the macro. You need three empty adjacent columns.

② Type the macro's name, '**\0**, in the first column.

③ In the second column, same row, type {**ALT**}**FO**{**CE**}*filename.ext*, substituting the name of the macro library file, including the entire path, for *filename.ext*. (The macro command {CE} clears the entry in the text box.)

④ Name the macro "\0" using the Range/Name/Create command.

Once these steps are complete, your special-purpose macro library will load automatically the next time you open the associated worksheet file.

LESSON

Using Advanced Macro Features

FEATURING

- Controlling the Execution of a Macro

YOU'VE ALREADY LEARNED ENOUGH ABOUT MACROS to simplify and speed up many of your regular chores in 1-2-3. Even so, we've only scratched the surface of what you can do with macros. In this lesson, I'll introduce you to one of the more sophisticated operations that macros make possible. When you're ready for more detail, you'll find it in the *Lotus 1-2-3 for Windows User's Guide*.

Pausing for User Input

One of the most useful features of 1-2-3 macros is their ability to pause while they run to ask you to type something on the keyboard or make choices with the mouse. This lets you set up very flexible macros whose specific actions you can control as they run.

As a simple example, let's say you've built a macro that computes a monthly payment for a loan based on the prevailing interest rate. You could set up the macro to stop and ask you for the current rate so that it can complete its work. Or how about a macro that inserts a calculated value in a cell, displays the Style Font dialog box, and then pauses so that you can choose an appropriate font and style for the new value? After that, the macro could continue to perform other calculations.

To build these and similar macros, you'll need the services of one or more macro commands designed for this purpose. *Macro commands* are special 1-2-3 commands that work only within macros. They're used to access and manipulate data in worksheets, on the Clipboard, in other Windows programs, or in text files; alter the screen display during macro execution; communicate with the user; and to control the execution of the macro itself. The 1-2-3 Help system offers a Macro Command Index that describes the use of each macro command.

You can use any of five macro commands to pause a macro for user input: {?}, {GET}, {GETLABEL}, {GETNUMBER}, and {FORM} (you type in all macro commands within curly braces). Let's try a working macro that opens the Style Font dialog box, pauses for input using the {?} command, and then stops.

① Find an empty cell for the new macro.

② Type {**ALT**}**SF**{**?**}.

③ Press Enter to complete the macro.

④ Name the macro cell "\S" (for style).

⑤ Move to another empty cell and type in some text. Leave the cell selected.

⑥ Press Ctrl-S. The Font dialog box appears. From the keyboard, make any typeface or type style selections you like, then press Enter. The text you typed takes on the new style.

The {?} command accepts any keyboard input until you press Enter. For instance, you're free to select Cancel when the sample macro above displays the Font dialog box. You have to be careful not to perform any action that would interfere with the rest of the macro.

PART

10

What If?
Solving Business
Problems with 1-2-3

66 LESSON

Creating What-If Tables

FEATURING

- One-Way Tables

AS YOU'VE SEEN, 1-2-3 IS A GREAT TOOL FOR ORGANIZING and displaying numeric information. It makes a wonderful customized calculating and charting machine for determining totals and tracking trends. But for experienced users, 1-2-3 is perhaps even more valuable for its help in making business decisions.

Any successful enterprise must plan for the future based on a range of plausible scenarios. Putting it simply, you need to know the answer to the question "What if?" What if we sell 10,000 more units next quarter—what will our profits be? Equally important, what if we increase production that much—how much cash will we need? Or what will happen to housing starts in New England if interest rates rise above 10%?

Users of earlier 1-2-3 releases spent untold hours "what-iffing" manually. First, you would set up a worksheet "model" of the problem at hand—the obvious example is a worksheet that calculates bottom-line profit from total expenses and income. You'd then type in sets of alternative values to see how changing key values such as sales, labor costs, or energy prices affected the calculated results.

With 1-2-3 for Windows, all that work is unnecessary. Of course, you still have to define your problem by entering the formula that, say, calculates your bottom line. But after that, 1-2-3 can take over the what-if part of the process. On your command, it can plug a variety of values into one or more of the cells referred to in your formula, recalculating the formula for each different value. After completing these calculations, 1-2-3 gives you a full report on the results.

Three separate features of 1-2-3 for Windows solve problems of this sort: what-if data tables, the Solver, and the Backsolver.

Creating a What-If Table

What-if data tables are the basic what-if tool. You specify one or more formulas that calculate some result, like the bottom line profit for your business, the cost of goods for an item you're manufacturing, or your expected return on an investment. You then enter several different values for one or more variables in your formula. If you're calculating the expected return on an stock investment, for example, one variable is the stock's dividend, and you list a range of plausible dividend amounts. Once you've finished entering your data, 1-2-3 simply plugs these values into your formula one at a time, displaying all the calculated results when it finishes.

You can use three types of what-if data tables: one-way, two-way, and three-way tables. A one-way table analyzes how changes in one variable affect the results of one or more formulas; two- and three-way tables analyze the affect of two or three variables on a single formula.

Let's say you want to see how changes in the prime interest rate would affect your monthly mortgage payments and your income from two investments. Here's how to set up a sample one-way what-if data table to solve this problem efficiently:

① Make a new worksheet (F) with Worksheet/Insert/Sheet. Title it "What If?" in the first row. (Throughout this exercise, you can look ahead to Figure 66.1 to see where to place your data.)

② Move to cell B3 and enter **Input Cell** – – > as a label. What-if data tables require an input cell outside of the table

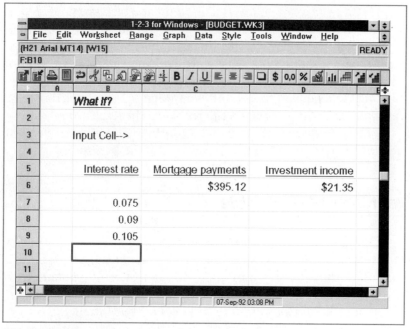

Figure 66.1: The sample what-if table before calculation

itself. This cell temporarily holds the current value of the variable—in this case the prime rate—as the computations proceed.

③ The actual input cell will be C3. Use Range/Name/Create to assign the name PRIME to C3.

④ Pick a range of cells for the what-if table itself. You need enough rows for all the test values, or input values, you want to try, plus one additional row. For this example, you'll need four rows so you can input three different interest rates. Set aside one more column than the number of formulas you want to calculate—in this case you'll need three columns for the two formulas, plus one more. Cell B6 will make a good first cell for this 4-by-3 range. You can use row 5 for column titles for the table.

⑤ Enter the formula for calculating your mortgage payment in cell C6. Assume the mortgage principal is $100,000 and the term is 30 years, or 360 months, and that the interest rate will be 2.5% higher than the prime rate. Remembering the method for computing payments you learned in Lesson 59, you would type in the following formula:

@PMT(100000,(PRIME + .025)/12,360)

Notice that the one variable value in the formula, PRIME, is a reference to cell C3—the input cell. Every formula you test in a what-if table must include the input cell.

⑥ In cell D6, enter the second formula, which calculates your monthly return on two variable-rate savings accounts. Say you have $10,000 in one account that earns 1% over the prime rate, plus $12,500 in a second account that earns 1.25% over prime. The formula to enter is

(10000*(PRIME + .01)/12) + (12500*(PRIME + .0125)/12)

⑦ Format the range C6..D9 as currency.

⑧ Starting in cell B7, enter the three interest rate input values in the first column of the table:

.075
.09
.105

for prime rates of 7.5%, 9% and 10.5%. Be sure to leave empty B6, the first cell in the table. Your table should now look like Figure 66.1.

⑨ Calculate the table. Begin by selecting the entire table range, cells B6 to D9. Remember, the table range includes only your test values formulas and input values—do not include the input cell, C3, or the column titles in the range. Then choose Data/What-if Table/1-Way.

⑩ In the dialog box that appears, the correct table range should already be entered in the Table range text box. If not, type in **B6..D9**.

⑪ Type in **PRIME** as the input cell in the Input cell text box.

⑫ Click on OK.

Now 1-2-3 will temporarily move the first input value to the input cell and then calculate each formula with that value. The result of each what-if calculation appears in the column for the corresponding formula, in the same row as the input value used. Then, 1-2-3 puts the second input value into the input cell and repeats the calculations, proceeding in this way until it has used all the input values. After the calculations are complete, the table should look like the one in Figure 66.2.

Two- and three-way tables are similar, but they give you results for two or three variables per calculation, and you can only calculate one formula at a time. For instance, you might use a two-way table to figure your monthly mortgage payments for different interest rates and different loan amounts.

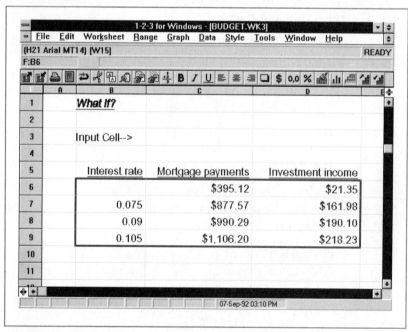

Figure 66.2: The sample what-if table after calculations

LESSON 67

Using the Solver

FEATURING

- Solving for the Maximum
- Solver Reports

WHAT-IF TABLES ARE FINE WHEN YOU'RE WORKING
with calculations having no more than three variables. For more complex what-if problems, however, you need the Solver, a completely separate feature in 1-2-3 for Windows.

The Solver lets you set up problems with as many formulas and variables as you like, within the limits of your computer's memory. To extend the example you worked with in the last lesson, a single Solver session can evaluate the impact of changes in interest rates, mortgage principal, loan term, loan fees and your own income on your monthly payments, the total cost of the loan, and your ability to afford the home.

Solver works with an entire worksheet at a time, recalculating all the formulas in the worksheet each time it tries a new set of values for the variables. That means that you don't have to set up your formulas in a special table—you can use an existing worksheet, with a few modifications. And you don't have to specify the particular values that 1-2-3 uses when calculating the formulas. Instead, 1-2-3 thinks up the test values itself, within limits or constraints that you set. For example, if you think interest rates are unlikely to fall below 9%

or rise above 11%, you can tell Solver to choose values between these two figures for the interest rate variable.

The Solver can do better than just tell you what will happen to your worksheet results as the values change. If you ask it to, Solver will give you direct advice like "here's how to maximize your profit" (in numbers, not in words). It does this by determining which values give the maximum or minimum possible result for a given formula. If you were planning on advertising budget, for instance, you'd probably like to know what mix of radio, television, and newspaper ads will bring you the most sales. The Solver could give you the answer.

Using the Solver to Maximize Income

Let's use this advertising budget problem as our sample to learn how the Solver works. Set up the problem as follows:

① Start a new worksheet (G) with Worksheet/Insert/Sheet.

② Enter the data shown in Figure 67.1 into your worksheet.

③ Now enter the following formulas into the worksheet.

In cell B5:	+ B4 + C4 + D4 = 80000
In cell B6:	+ B4 > = 10000
In cell B7:	+ C4 > = 12500
In cell B8:	+ D4 > = 25000
In cell B9:	(B4/B3*B2) + (C4/C3*C2) + (D4/D3*D2)

Let's say that you know from past research that the values in row 3, the gross dollar sales per ad, are accurate, at least for the current ad campaign. The cost per ad is also fixed. On the other hand, you can decide how much to spend on radio, how much on TV, and how much on newspaper. Therefore, cells B4, C4, and D4 are variables, or in the Solver's terminology, *adjustable cells.*

You have a maximum total budget of $80,000 for all three types of ads. What's more, because your company wants to maintain a

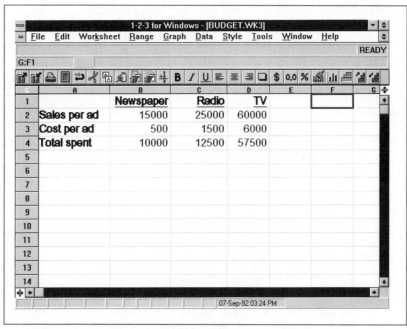

Figure 67.1:The Advertising Budget worksheet

noticeable presence in each medium, you must spend a certain minimum amount on each type. You work these minimum values into the worksheet as *constraints*. With the Solver, a constraint is a logical formula—one that evaluates to either true or false— that refers to one or more of the cells in the worksheet. The symbol > = means greater than or equal to.

④ Choose Tools/Solver.

⑤ The first text box in the Solver dialog box is for the adjustable cells. Enter the range **B4..D4**, which holds the values for amounts you will spend on each medium.

⑥ In the Constraint cells text box, enter the range **B5..B8** for all four constraints.

If you choose Solve now, the Solver performs a classic what-if series of calculations, trying several values for each of the adjustable cells. It selects "representative" values of its own choosing, though the values may not meet the criteria set by the constraints.

However, you probably want to know how to apportion your advertising budget to generate the greatest possible sales. This is a problem you could never hope to solve what-iffing by trial and error. Instead, you have the Solver solve for the optimal mix of the three variables.

⑦ Enter **B9** in the Optimal cell text box, and then choose Max (for maximum). The Solver will find the values for the adjustable cells that produce the maximum in cell B9. In other words, you'll know how much to spend on each type of advertising to generate the most possible sales.

⑧ Click on the Solve button. There'll be a rather lengthy pause as the Solver analyzes the problem and performs its calculations. When these are complete it reports an "answer" for each set of variables. The answer is a complete copy of the worksheet, showing the values of the variables used, and, in cell B9, the total sales generated by advertising calculated from those values. The Solver Answer dialog box appears.

⑨ The Solver usually comes up with more than one answer. The Solver Answer dialog box tells you how many answers were found and which answer you're currently viewing. Move the dialog box so you can see cells B4, C4, D4, and B9. To see the next answer (actually, the next copy of the worksheet), choose Next in the Solver Answer dialog box.

⑩ Once you've browsed through the answers, you can save any answer you're interested in as a worksheet file. Activate the worksheet and save it with File/Save As. Give it a new name so you don't erase the original.

Alternatively, you can prepare a complete summary of all of the Solver's work. Choose Report in the Solver Answer dialog box. When the Solver Report dialog box appears, choose Answer Table for Type and Table for Format. When you click on OK, 1-2-3 prepares a new worksheet summarizing all of the answers. For each answer, this report worksheet lists the highest and lowest values used in the adjustable cells and calculated for the optimal cell and for other cells containing formulas. It then lists the actual values for each of the cells for every answer. You can modify or save this report worksheet just like any other 1-2-3 worksheet.

The Solver may be a very powerful tool, but it does have some important limitations. It takes much longer than a what-if table to do its work, even on comparable calculations. Worse yet, the Solver takes over your computer while it's solving, so you can't do anything else in 1-2-3 or Windows. In addition, you can't use formulas in the adjustable cells.

LESSON

Using Backsolver

FEATURING

- Solving for a Specific Value

THOUGH SIMILAR TO THE WHAT-IF TOOLS IN MANY ways, the 1-2-3 Backsolver answers different questions, such as "What do I need?" or "How much can I afford?" It's simpler than either what-if tables or the Solver. All you do is specify what the result of a formula should be, and Backsolver figures out the value of one variable that would be needed to produce that result.

Say your company makes computers, and you've built a worksheet that tells you how many computers you can build based on the number of memory chips in stock. It might look like Figure 68.1.

The value in cells B3 and B5 were calculated from formulas. The formula for cell B3 is

+B1 – (B1*B2)

and the formula for cell B5 is

+B3/B4

Your firm now gets a rush order for 500 computers. You call up the worksheet, which tells you that you don't have enough memory chips to build that many. The Backsolver can tell you how many chips to order.

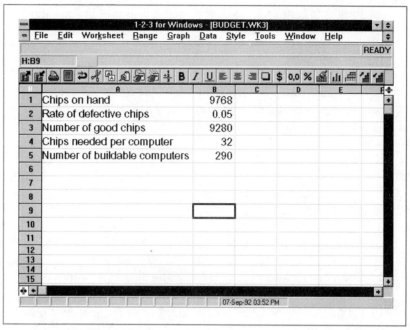

Figure 68.1: The Inventory worksheet

① To try this out, start a new worksheet (H) and enter the labels and values shown in Figure 68.1. In cells B3 and B5, enter the formulas listed above.

② Save the current worksheet, assuming you want to keep a copy with the current values. Backsolver replaces the previous contents of one of the cells with the value it calculates. Other cells that refer to that cell will be changed as well.

③ Choose Tools/Backsolver. You'll be presented with the Backsolver dialog box. This dialog has text boxes for the Make cell, Equal to, and the By changing cell. These peculiar names make more sense if you read them together, with the contents of the text boxes, like this: "Make cell B5 equal to 500 by changing cell B1."

④ The Make cell is the cell that contains the formula you're calculating. Enter the address of this cell, **B5**, in the first text box.

⑤ Enter the result you want the formula to give in the Equal to value text box. You want enough chips to build 210 additional computers, so enter **210** here.

⑥ The last text box is for the By changing box. Enter the address of the cell containing the value to be calculated in this box. You're asking the question "How many chips should I order?" so enter **B1**.

Notice that the formula in the Make cell, B5, doesn't directly refer to the By changing cell, B1. But it does refer to B3, which in turn contains a formula based on B1. The Backsolver can handle any formula that refers directly or indirectly to the By changing cell.

⑦ Select Solve. Move the dialog box down a bit so you can see cells B1, B3, B5. In a moment, you'll have your answer—the Backsolver replaces the current value in cell B1 with 7073.8, the number of chips required for the formula in B5 to give you 210 more computers. You need to order at least 7074 more chips.

To keep a copy of the new values, use File/Save As to save the worksheet with a different name. You can then use File/Open to bring back the original worksheet containing the number of chips you actually have on hand.

If you thought this process through, you've probably noticed that you could solve the same problem without the Backsolver by setting up a different worksheet. In general, you should use the Backsolver for situations like this, in which you've already built a formula containing the variable you want to solve for.

APPENDIX

Installation

APPENDIX

Installation

BEFORE YOU CAN USE 1-2-3 FOR WINDOWS, YOU MUST install it. If you or someone else has done so already, then you can skip this appendix and move to Lesson 1 to begin learning how to use the program. If you are in doubt about whether the program is installed, bring up the Windows Program Manager window, and look for a program group icon called Lotus Applications. Open the window and there should be a triangular 1-2-3 icon in there. Or, open the Program Manager's Window menu and see if Lotus Applications is one of the choices. If you don't have the group or the program icon in your Program Manager, then 1-2-3 hasn't been installed.

System Requirements

To run 1-2-3 for Windows, you must have the following:

- An 80286, 80386, or 80486 (or higher) system running Windows version 3.0 or higher, running with DOS 3.1 or higher
- A minimum of 2 megabytes of RAM
- A Windows-compatible monitor
- At least 5 megabytes of free disk space for installing 1-2-3

It's recommended you have a mouse. This book assumes you have a mouse, though some of the shortcut keys that allow you to control 1-2-3 from the keyboard are discussed.

Installing

An automated install program takes care of most of the installation process. All you have to do is tell it where you want 1-2-3 stored. You can optionally elect to alter certain convenience settings during the installation. For the purposes of this book, you should confirm that certain of these settings are set properly.

The installation described here is for single-user computers. If you are installing 1-2-3 on a network server or node, follow the instructions for network installation supplied with 1-2-3.

Before following these instructions, you may want to look at the end of the Introduction to this book, which explains the typographic conventions used to describe procedures. It's pretty self-explanatory here, but if you get stuck, you might want to refer to that.

① Boot up your computer, and run Windows.

② Find the Install disk (disk 1) in the set of disks that came with the 1-2-3 package. Insert it into drive A, or if the size of the disk is wrong for drive A, then in drive B, assuming the size is correct.

③ Open the Program Manager window if it isn't already open.

④ Open the File menu and choose Run.

⑤ In the dialog box that appears, type

   A:INSTALL.EXE

   and click on OK, or press Enter. (If your Install disk is in drive B, use a *B:* instead of the *A*.) The install program now runs.

⑥ First you will see a little window telling you that files are being copied to your hard disk. Just watch and wait.

⑦ Then you will see a copyright screen window with information to read. Click on OK after you have finished reading, or on Exit Install if you want to stop the installation process.

⑧ Next you will be asked to type in your name and your company name. This information will be recorded on your Install master disk so that any copies of it made later will come up on the screen with your name and company name displayed. Type in the appropriate names and press Enter. This request only occurs during the initial installation of 1-2-3.

⑨ You're now asked to confirm that the names are correct. Click on Yes, if they are. If they are not, click on No; you can go back and alter them. Use the Backspace key to fix any typos, then click on OK again, then on Yes.

⑩ Now you see an installation screen asking if you want to install 1-2-3, read product updates, or change international options. Click on Install 1-2-3. If you want more information, you can click on Help.

   Note: You can later rerun the install program to read the updates if you like. The international options probably don't need changing unless you exchange worksheets with people who use other forms of currency or numeric and date conventions other than those used in the country where you bought the software.

⑪ The install program now gives you two icons (small pictures) to choose from: Install with Defaults or Install with Options. To choose one of these, you click on it. Click on Install with Options, since we'll want to set a couple of options for use with this book.

⑫ The install program now examines your hard disk(s), looking for space to install 1-2-3. If there isn't enough space, you'll have to make some more, then run Install again.

⑬ Assuming there is enough room, a screen looking like Figure A.1 will appear. This screen will report what it has

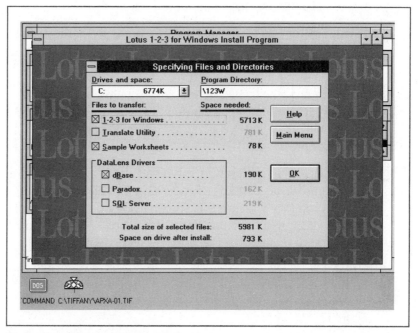

Figure A.1: *Specifying files and directories*

found, suggest a directory in which to install 1-2-3, and indicate which extra programs and files it will copy to your hard
disk. I suggest you leave the drive and directory settings as
they are. If you want to change the directory, click in the
Program Directory text area, and type in the new directory.
If you want to change the drive, click on the little down
arrow under Drives and Space to open the drives list and
choose one from the list by clicking on it.

⑭ By default, the sample worksheets supplied with 1-2-3 are
copied to your hard disk. For the purpose of this book, omit
these. Click on the little square box to the left of Sample
Worksheets. The X should disappear. You can install them
later if you want by running the install program again.

⑮ If you don't plan to use 1-2-3 with databases that are in
dBASE, Paradox, or on an SQL Server, remove any X's in
the boxes to the left of those words in the DataLens Drivers
section by clicking on them.

⑯ Finally, click on OK to continue.

⑰ If the directory you indicated didn't already exist, the install program asks if you want to create it. Press **Y**, press Enter, or click on Yes.

⑱ Now you are asked which group and icons you want to add to the Program Manager's windows. The boxes next to 1-2-3 and Install are already set on. Leave them that way, and click on OK or press Enter.

⑲ Next, the default preferences will be displayed. Here is where you want to make a change. Notice that Enable Edit Undo is not checked (no X). Turn this on by clicking on its box or typing Alt-E. An X should appear in the box. This will later allow you to undo accidental erasures and commands that you would otherwise not be able to reverse.

⑳ At the bottom of the box you'll see the directory in which 1-2-3 will store new spreadsheets you create. This should read

C:\123W\WORK

If it doesn't, edit it so that it does by clicking on the end of the name and using the Backspace key and the arrow keys (← and →) to delete the incorrect directory name. Type in the correct name.

㉑ Click on OK.

㉒ If the directory specified in step 20 doesn't already exist, you're asked if you want the install program to create it for you. Click on Yes.

㉓ A window now appears that reports the progress of the installation process. This part takes a while. You'll be prompted to insert disks from time to time as the installation progresses. Just follow the instructions on the screen, and click on OK (or press Enter after switching each disk).

㉔ When the installation is complete, a little box tells you so. Move ahead by clicking on OK.

㉕ Now you'll be advised to install the Adobe Type Manager, which is supplied with 1-2-3. ATM is a program that makes text look better both on your screen and when you print it. You should install it, as the dialog box suggests. You'll be prompted to insert the ATM Program Disk. Do so, and click on OK.

㉖ The ATM Install program now runs. A dialog box comes up, telling you what directories it's going to install fonts in. They are probably

C:\PSFONTS
C:\PSFONTS\PFM

though the disk drive letter may be different for you (other than C:). Just accept them as they are, and click on Install (or press Enter).

㉗ When the installation is complete, you'll be told about it and be advised to start Windows again. Click on OK. You're returned to the 1-2-3 Install Main menu.

㉘ Click on Exit Install.

㉙ You're returned to the Windows Program Manager.

㉚ Exit Windows by opening the Program Manager's File menu and choosing Exit Windows. Click on OK when the Exit dialog box appears.

You're done installing! (Whew.) Now turn to the Introduction (or to Lesson 1) to learn how to run 1-2-3.

INDEX

Selections from
The SYBEX Library

SPREADSHEETS AND INTEGRATED SOFTWARE

1-2-3 for Scientists and Engineers
William J. Orvis
371pp. Ref. 733-9
This up-to-date edition offers fast, elegant solutions to common problems in science and engineering. Complete, carefully explained techniques for plotting, curve fitting, statistics, derivatives, integrals and differentials, solving systems of equations, and more; plus useful Lotus add-ins.

The ABC's of 1-2-3 (Second Edition)
Chris Gilbert
Laurie Williams
245pp. Ref. 355-4
Online Today recommends it as "an easy and comfortable way to get started with the program." An essential tutorial for novices, it will remain on your desk as a valuable source of ongoing reference and support. For Release 2.

The ABC's of 1-2-3 Release 2.2
Chris Gilbert
Laurie Williams
340pp. Ref. 623-5
New Lotus 1-2-3 users delight in this book's step-by-step approach to building trouble-free spreadsheets, displaying graphs, and efficiently building databases. The authors cover the ins and outs of the latest version including easier calculations, file linking, and better graphic presentation.

The ABC's of 1-2-3 Release 2.3
Chris Gilbert
Laurie Williams
350pp. Ref. 837-8
Computer Currents called it "one of the best tutorials available." This new edition provides easy-to-follow, hands-on lessons tailored specifically for computer and spreadsheet newcomers—or for anyone seeking a quick and easy guide to the basics. Covers everything from switching on the computer to charts, functions, macros, and important new features.

The ABC's of 1-2-3 Release 3
Judd Robbins
290pp. Ref. 519-0
The ideal book for beginners who are new to Lotus or new to Release 3. This step-by-step approach to the 1-2-3 spreadsheet software gets the reader up and running with spreadsheet, database, graphics, and macro functions.

The ABC's of Excel on the IBM PC
Douglas Hergert
326pp. Ref. 567-0
This book is a brisk and friendly introduction to the most important features of Microsoft Excel for PC's. This beginner's book discusses worksheets, charts, database operations, and macros, all with hands-on examples. Written for all versions through Version 2.

The ABC's of Quattro Pro 3
Alan Simpson
Douglas Wolf
338pp. Ref. 836-6
This popular beginner's tutorial on Quattro Pro 2 shows first-time computer and

spreadsheet users the essentials of electronic number-crunching. Topics range from business spreadsheet design to error-free formulas, presentation slide shows, the database, macros, more.

The Complete Lotus 1-2-3 Release 2.2 Handbook
Greg Harvey
750pp. Ref. 625-1

This comprehensive handbook discusses every 1-2-3 operation with clear instructions and practical tips. This volume especially emphasizes the new improved graphics, high-speed recalculation techniques, and spreadsheet linking available with Release 2.2.

The Complete Lotus 1-2-3 Release 3 Handbook
Greg Harvey
700pp. Ref. 600-6

Everything you ever wanted to know about 1-2-3 is in this definitive handbook. As a Release 3 guide, it features the design and use of 3D worksheets, and improved graphics, along with using Lotus under DOS or OS/2. Problems, exercises, and helpful insights are included.

Lotus 1-2-3 2.2 On-Line Advisor Version 1.1
SYBAR, Software Division of SYBEX, Inc.
Ref. 935-8

Need Help fast? With a touch of a key, the Advisor pops up right on top of your Lotus 1-2-3 program to answer your spreadsheet questions. With over 4000 index citations and 1600 pre-linked cross-references, help has never been so easy to find. Just start typing your topic and the Lotus 1-2-3 Advisor does all the look-up for you. Covers versions 2.01 and 2.2. Software package comes with 3½" and 5¼" disks. **System Requirements:** IBM compatible with DOS 2.0 or higher, runs with Windows 3.0, uses 90K of RAM.

Lotus 1-2-3 Desktop Companion SYBEX Ready Reference Series
Greg Harvey
976pp. Ref. 501-8

A full-time consultant, right on your desk. Hundreds of self-contained entries cover every 1-2-3 feature, organized by topic, indexed and cross-referenced, and supplemented by tips, macros and working examples. For Release 2.

Lotus 1-2-3 Instant Reference Release 2.2 SYBEX Prompter Series
Greg Harvey
Kay Yarborough Nelson
254pp. Ref. 635-9

The reader gets quick and easy access to any operation in 1-2-3 Version 2.2 in this handy pocket-sized encyclopedia. Organized by menu function, each command and function has a summary description, the exact key sequence, and a discussion of the options.

Lotus 1-2-3 Tips and Tricks (2nd edition)
Gene Weisskopf
425pp. Ref. 668-5

This outstanding collection of tips, shortcuts and cautions for longtime Lotus users is in an expanded new edition covering Release 2.2. Topics include macros, range names, spreadsheet design, hardware and operating system tips, data analysis, printing, data interchange, applications development, and more.

Mastering 1-2-3 (Second Edition)
Carolyn Jorgensen
702pp. Ref. 528-X

Get the most from 1-2-3 Release 2.01 with this step-by-step guide emphasizing advanced features and practical uses. Topics include data sharing, macros, spreadsheet security, expanded memory, and graphics enhancements.

Mastering 1-2-3 Release 3
Carolyn Jorgensen
682pp. Ref. 517-4

For new Release 3 and experienced Release 2 users, "Mastering" starts with a basic spreadsheet, then introduces spreadsheet and database commands, functions, and macros, and then tells how to analyze 3D spreadsheets and make high-impact reports and graphs. Lotus add-ons are discussed and Fast Tracks are included.

Mastering Enable/OA
Christopher Van Buren
Robert Bixby
540pp. Ref 637-5

This is a structured, hands-on guide to integrated business computing, for users who want to achieve productivity in the shortest possible time. Separate in-depth sections cover word processing, spreadsheets, databases, telecommunications, task integration and macros.

Mastering Excel on the IBM PC
Carl Townsend
628pp. Ref. 403-8

A complete Excel handbook with step-by-step tutorials, sample applications and an extensive reference section. Topics include worksheet fundamentals, formulas and windows, graphics, database techniques, special features, macros and more.

Mastering Excel 3 for Windows
Carl Townsend
625pp. Ref. 643-X

A new edition of SYBEX's highly praised guide to the Excel super spreadsheet, under Windows 3.0. Includes full coverage of new features; dozens of tips and examples; in-depth treatment of specialized topics, including presentation graphics and macros; and sample applications for inventory control, financial management, trend analysis, and more.

Mastering Framework III
Douglas Hergert
Jonathan Kamin
613pp. Ref. 513-1

Thorough, hands-on treatment of the latest Framework release. An outstanding introduction to integrated software applications, with examples for outlining, spreadsheets, word processing, databases, and more; plus an introduction to FRED programming.

Mastering Freelance Plus
Donald Richard Read
411pp. Ref. 701-0

A detailed guide to high-powered graphing and charting with Freelance Plus. Part I is a practical overview of the software. Part II offers concise tutorials on creating specific chart types. Part III covers drawing functions in depth. Part IV shows how to organize and generate output, including printing and on-screen shows.

Mastering Quattro Pro 2
Gene Weisskopf
575pp. Ref. 792-4

This hands-on guide and reference takes readers from basic spreadsheets to creating three-dimensional graphs, spreadsheet databases, macros and advanced data analysis. Also covers Paradox Access and translating Lotus 1-2-3 2.2 work sheets. A great tutorial for beginning and intermediate users, this book also serves as a reference for users at all levels.

Mastering Quattro Pro 3
Gene Weisskopf
618pp. Ref. 841-6

A complete hands-on guide and on-the-job reference, offering practical tutorials on the basics; up-to-date treatment of advanced capabilities; highlighted coverage of new software features, and expert advice from author Gene Weisskopf, a seasoned spreadsheet specialist.

Mastering Smartware II
Jonathan Paul Bacon
634pp. Ref. 651-0

An easy-to-read, self-paced introduction to a powerful program. This book offers separate treatment of word processing, data file management, spreadsheets, and communications, with special sections on data integration between modules. Concrete examples from business are used throughout.

Mastering SuperCalc5
Greg Harvey
Mary Beth Andrasak
500pp. Ref. 624-3

This book offers a complete and unintimidating guided tour through each feature. With step-by-step lessons, readers learn about the full capabilities of spreadsheet, graphics, and data management functions. Multiple spreadsheets, linked spreadsheets, 3D graphics, and macros are also discussed.

Mastering Symphony
(Fourth Edition)
Douglas Cobb
857pp. Ref. 494-1

Thoroughly revised to cover all aspects of the major upgrade of Symphony Version 2, this Fourth Edition of Doug Cobb's classic is still "the Symphony bible" to this complex but even more powerful package. All the new features are discussed and placed in context with prior versions so that both new and previous users will benefit from Cobb's insights.

Teach Yourself Lotus 1-2-3
Release 2.2
Jeff Woodward
250pp. Ref. 641-3

Readers match what they see on the screen with the book's screen-by-screen action sequences. For new Lotus users, topics include computer fundamentals, opening and editing a worksheet, using graphs, macros, and printing typeset-quality reports. For Release 2.2.

Understanding 1-2-3 Release 2.3
Rebecca Bridge Altman
700pp. Ref. 856-4

This comprehensive guide to 1-2-3 spreadsheet power covers everything from basic concepts to sophisticated business applications. New users will build a solid foundation; intermediate and experienced users will learn how to refine their spreadsheets, manage large projects,

create effective graphics, analyze databases, master graphics, more.

Understanding PFS:
First Choice
Gerry Litton
489pp. Ref. 568-9

From basic commands to complex features, this complete guide to the popular integrated package is loaded with step-by-step instructions. Lessons cover creating attractive documents, setting up easy-to-use databases, working with spreadsheets and graphics, and smoothly integrating tasks from different First Choice modules. For Version 3.0.

Up & Running with Lotus 1-2-3
Release 2.2
Rainer Bartel
139pp. Ref 748-7

Start using 1-2-3 in the shortest time possible with this concise 20-step guide to the major features of the software. Each "step" is a self-contained, time-coded lesson (taking 15, 30, 45 or 60 minutes to complete) focused on a single aspect of 1-2-3 operations.

Up & Running with 1-2-3
Release 2.3
Robert M. Thomas
140pp. Ref. 872-6

Get a fast start with this 20-step guide to 1-2-3 release 2.3. Each step takes just 15 minutes to an hour, and is preceded by a clock icon, so you know how much time to budget for each lesson. This book is great for people who want to start using the program right away, as well as for potential 1-2-3 users who want to evaluate the program before purchase.

Up & Running with Lotus 1-2-3
Release 3.1
Kris Jamsa
141pp. Ref. 813-0

A 20-step overview of the new 3.1 version of 1-2-3. The first twelve steps take you through the fundamentals of creating, using and graphing worksheets. Steps 13 through 15 explain the database, and the balance of the book is dedicated to 3.1's powerful WYSIWYG capabilities.

Up & Running with Quattro Pro 3
Peter Aitken
140pp. Ref.857-2
Get a fast start with this 20-step guide to Quattro Pro 3. Each step takes just 15 minutes to an hour, and is preceded by a clock icon, so you know how much time to budget for each lesson. This book is great for people who want to start using the program right away, as well as for potential Quattro Pro 3 users who want to evaluate the program before purchase.

HOME MONEY MANAGEMENT

Mastering Quicken 3
Steve Cummings
350pp. Ref. 662-6
With tips on personal financial planning by Pauline Tai of *Money Magazine*, this hands-on guide to both Quicken and Stock! portfolio manager centers on a variety of valuable examples. Covers simple check writing, budgeting, tax accounting, cash flow management, even payroll.

Understanding Managing Your Money
Gerry Litton
372pp. Ref. 751-7
A complete guide to the principal features of this practical software package. Replete with valuable examples and useful illustrations. Learn how various screens should be handled, and how to avoid trouble spots. Topics include: using the word processor and the calculator; managing a budget; maintaining a checkbook; estimating tax liabilities; calculating net worth; and more.

Will Builder™
The Complete Will-Writing Program
SYBAR, Software Division of SYBEX, Inc.
3½″ and 5¼″ disks Ref. 906-4
Designed by two experienced lawyers, Will Builder software provides you with all the information you need to create a solid, legally-binding will. Save on legal fees, write your will on your own computer in the privacy of your own home. On-Line Expertise leads you through the process step-by-step. PLUS, you can create a Living Will and a Medical Power of Attorney to express your wishes in advance in case you ever need to be placed on a life-support system. You can also create a Financial Power of Attorney and Letter to Executor. Software program uses state-specific forms for powers of attorney and living wills. **System requirements:** IBM compatible with hard disk, minimum 512K RAM, DOS 2.0 or higher.

ACCOUNTING

Mastering DacEasy Accounting (Second Edition)
Darleen Hartley Yourzek
463pp. Ref. 679-0
This new edition focuses on version 4.0 (with notes on using 3.0), and includes an introduction to DacEasy Payroll. Packed with real-world accounting examples, it covers everything from installing DacEasy to converting data, setting up applications, processing work and printing custom reports.

Mastering Peachtree Complete III
Darleen Hartley Yourzek
601pp. Ref. 723-1
Presented from the business user's perspective, this practical, task-oriented guide can be used as a step-by-step tutorial or an easy reference guide. Detailed

topics include: preparing your records for computer conversion; setting up and maintaining files; managing accounts payable and receivable; tracking inventory, and more. With a glossary of accounting and computer terms.

Up & Running with Quicken 4
Darleen Hartley Yourzek
139pp. Ref. 783-5

Enjoy a fast-paced introduction to this popular financial management program. In just 20 steps—each taking only 15 minutes to an hour—you can begin computerized management of all your financial transactions. Includes a special chapter for small business.

Understanding Quicken 4
Steve Cummings
506pp. Ref. 787-8

A practical guide to managing personal and business finances. Readers build a solid financial recordkeeping system, as they learn the ins and outs of using Quicken 4 to print checks; manage monthly bills; keep tax records; track credit cards, investments, and loans; produce financial statements, and much more.

OPERATING SYSTEMS

The ABC's of DOS 4
Alan R. Miller
275pp. Ref. 583-2

This step-by-step introduction to using DOS 4 is written especially for beginners. Filled with simple examples, *The ABC's of DOS 4* covers the basics of hardware, software, disks, the system editor EDLIN, DOS commands, and more.

The ABC's of DOS 5
Alan Miller
267pp. Ref. 770-3

This straightforward guide will haven even first-time computer users working comfortably with DOS 5 in no time. Step-by-step lessons lead users from switching on the PC, through exploring the DOS Shell, working with directories and files, using

essential commands, customizing the system, and trouble shooting. Includes a tear-out quick reference card and function key template.

ABC's of MS-DOS (Second Edition)
Alan R. Miller
233pp. Ref. 493-3

This handy guide to MS-DOS is all many PC users need to manage their computer files, organize floppy and hard disks, use EDLIN, and keep their computers organized. Additional information is given about utilities like Sidekick, and there is a DOS command and program summary. The second edition is fully updated for Version 3.3.

The ABC's of SCO UNIX
Tom Cuthbertson
263pp. Re. 715-0

A guide especially for beginners who want to get to work fast. Includes hands-on tutorials on logging in and out; creating and editing files; using electronic mail; organizing files into directories; printing; text formatting; and more.

The ABC's of Windows 3.0
Kris Jamsa
327pp. Ref. 760-6

A user-friendly introduction to the essentials of Windows 3.0. Presented in 64 short lessons. Beginners start with lesson one, while more advanced readers can skip ahead. Learn to use File Manager, the accessory programs, customization features, Program Manager, and more.

DESQview Instant Reference
Paul J. Perry
175pp. Ref. 809-2

This complete quick-reference command guide covers version 2.3 and DESQview 386, as well as QEMM (for managing expanded memory) and Manifest Memory Analyzer. Concise, alphabetized entries provide exact syntax, options, usage, and brief examples for every command. A handy source for on-the-job reminders and tips.

DOS 3.3 On-Line Advisor Version 1.1
SYBAR, Software Division of SYBEX, Inc.
Ref. 933-1

The answer to all your DOS problems. The DOS On-Line Advisor is an on-screen reference that explains over 200 DOS error messages. 2300 other citations cover all you ever needed to know about DOS. The DOS On-Line Advisor pops up on top of your working program to give you quick, easy help when you need it, and disappears when you don't. Covers thru version 3.3. Software package comes with 3½" and 5¼" disks. **System Requirements:** IBM compatible with DOS 2.0 or higher, runs with Windows 3.0, uses 90K of RAM.

DOS Instant Reference
SYBEX Prompter Series
Greg Harvey
Kay Yarborough Nelson
220pp. Ref. 477-1

A complete fingertip reference for fast, easy on-line help:command summaries, syntax, usage and error messages. Organized by function—system commands, file commands, disk management, directories, batch files, I/O, networking, programming, and more. Through Version 3.3.

DOS 5 Instant Reference
Robert M. Thomas
200pp. Ref. 804-1

The comprehensive quick guide to DOS—all its features, commands, options, and versions—now including DOS 5, with the new graphical interface. Concise, alphabetized command entries provide exact syntax, options, usage, brief examples, and applicable version numbers. Fully cross-referenced; ideal for quick review or on-the-job reference.

The DOS 5 User's Handbook
Gary Masters
Richard Allen King
400pp. Ref. 777-0

This is the DOS 5 book for users who are already familiar with an earlier version of DOS. Part I is a quick, friendly guide to DOS. Part I is a quick, friendly guide to new features; topics include the graphical interface, new and enhanced commands, and much more. Part II is a complete DOS 5 quick reference, with command summaries, in-depth explanations, and examples.

Encyclopedia DOS
Judd Robbins
1030pp. Ref. 699-5

A comprehensive reference and user's guide to all versions of DOS through 4.0. Offers complete information on every DOS command, with all possible switches and parameters—plus examples of effective usage. An invaluable tool.

Essential OS/2
(Second Edition)
Judd Robbins
445pp. Ref. 609-X

Written by an OS/2 expert, this is the guide to the powerful new resources of the OS/2 operating system standard edition 1.1 with presentation manager. Robbins introduces the standard edition, and details multitasking under OS/2, and the range of commands for installing, starting up, configuring, and running applications. For Version 1.1 Standard Edition.

Essential PC-DOS
(Second Edition)
Myril Clement Shaw
Susan Soltis Shaw
332pp. Ref. 413-5

An authoritative guide to PC-DOS, including version 3.2. Designed to make experts out of beginners, it explores everything from disk management to batch file programming. Includes an 85-page command summary. Through Version 3.2.

Graphics Programming
Under Windows
Brian Myers
Chris Doner
646pp. Ref. 448-8

Straightforward discussion, abundant examples, and a concise reference guide to graphics commands make this book a must for Windows programmers. Topics range from how Windows works to programming for business, animation, CAD, and desktop publishing. For Version 2.

Hard Disk Instant Reference
SYBEX Prompter Series
Judd Robbins

256pp. Ref. 587-5

Compact yet comprehensive, this pocket-sized reference presents the essential information on DOS commands used in managing directories and files, and in optimizing disk configuration. Includes a survey of third-party utility capabilities. Through DOS 4.0.

Inside DOS: A Programmer's Guide
Michael J. Young

490pp. Ref. 710-X

A collection of practical techniques (with source code listings) designed to help you take advantage of the rich resources intrinsic to MS-DOS machines. Designed for the experienced programmer with a basic understanding of C and 8086 assembly language, and DOS fundamentals.

Mastering DOS (Second Edition)
Judd Robbins

722pp. Ref. 555-7

"The most useful DOS book." This seven-part, in-depth tutorial addresses the needs of users at all levels. Topics range from running applications, to managing files and directories, configuring the system, batch file programming, and techniques for system developers. Through Version 4.

Mastering DOS 5
Judd Robbins

800pp. Ref.767-3

"The DOS reference to keep next to your computer," according to PC Week, this highly acclaimed text is now revised and expanded for DOS 5. Comprehensive tutorials cover everything from first steps for beginners, to advanced tools for systems developers—with emphasis on the new graphics interface. Includes tips, tricks, and a tear-out quick reference card and function key template.

Mastering SunOS
Brent D. Heslop
David Angell

588pp. Ref. 683-9

Learn to configure and manage your system; use essential commands; manage files; perform editing, formatting, and printing tasks; master E-mail and external communication; and use the SunView and new Open Window graphic interfaces.

Mastering Windows 3.0
Robert Cowart

592pp. Ref.458-5

Every Windows user will find valuable how-to and reference information here. With full details on the desktop utilities; manipulating files; running applications (including non-Windows programs); sharing data between DOS, OS/2, and Windows; hardware and software efficiency tips; and more.

Understanding DOS 3.3
Judd Robbins

678pp. Ref. 648-0

This best selling, in-depth tutorial addresses the needs of users at all levels with many examples and hands-on exercises. Robbins discusses the fundamentals of DOS, then covers manipulating files and directories, using the DOS editor, printing, communicating, and finishes with a full section on batch files.

Understanding Hard Disk Management on the PC
Jonathan Kamin

500pp. Ref. 561-1

This title is a key productivity tool for all hard disk users who want efficient, error-free file management and organization. Includes details on the best ways to conserve hard disk space when using several memory-guzzling programs. Through DOS 4.

SYBEX ®

FREE BROCHURE!

Complete this form today, and we'll send you a full-color brochure of Sybex bestsellers.

Please supply the name of the Sybex book purchased.

_____

How would you rate it?

_____ Excellent _____ Very Good _____ Average _____ Poor

Why did you select this particular book?

_____ Recommended to me by a friend

_____ Recommended to me by store personnel

_____ Saw an advertisement in _____

_____ Author's reputation

_____ Saw in Sybex catalog

_____ Required textbook

_____ Sybex reputation

_____ Read book review in _____

_____ In-store display

_____ Other _____

Where did you buy it?

_____ Bookstore

_____ Computer Store or Software Store

_____ Catalog (name: _____)

_____ Direct from Sybex

_____ Other: _____

Did you buy this book with your personal funds?

_____ Yes _____ No

About how many computer books do you buy each year?

_____ 1-3 _____ 3-5 _____ 5-7 _____ 7-9 _____ 10+

About how many Sybex books do you own?

_____ 1-3 _____ 3-5 _____ 5-7 _____ 7-9 _____ 10+

Please indicate your level of experience with the software covered in this book:

_____ Beginner _____ Intermediate _____ Advanced

Which types of software packages do you use regularly?

_____ Accounting	_____ Databases	_____ Networks
_____ Amiga	_____ Desktop Publishing	_____ Operating Systems
_____ Apple/Mac	_____ File Utilities	_____ Spreadsheets
_____ CAD	_____ Money Management	_____ Word Processing
_____ Communications	_____ Languages	_____ Other _____

(please specify)

Which of the following best describes your job title?

_____ Administrative/Secretarial   _____ President/CEO

_____ Director   _____ Manager/Supervisor

_____ Engineer/Technician   _____ Other _____
                                                   (please specify)

Comments on the weaknesses/strengths of this book: _____

_____

_____

_____

_____

Name _____

Street _____

City/State/Zip _____

Phone _____

PLEASE FOLD, SEAL, AND MAIL TO SYBEX

SYBEX, INC.
Department M
2021 CHALLENGER DR.
ALAMEDA, CALIFORNIA USA
94501

SYBEX ®

SEAL

FUNCTION KEYS

F1 (HELP)	Displays Help information about the command or dialog box you are using.
F2 (EDIT)	Switches between EDIT and READY, POINT, VALUE, or LABEL mode. When in EDIT mode, you can edit the data in the current cell.
F3 (NAME)	Lists names of files, graphs, ranges, @functions, macro key names, and macro commands.
F4	In READY mode, F4 anchors the cell pointer so you can select a range using the arrow keys. In EDIT, POINT or VALUE mode, F4 changes the cell references in formulas from absolute to mixed to relative.
F5 (GOTO)	Moves the cell pointer to a cell, named range, worksheet, or active file. Pressing F5 (GOTO) is equivalent to choosing Range/Go To.
F6 (PANE)	Moves between panes and between worksheets you display in perspective view.
F7 (QUERY)	Repeats the most recent Data Query command.
F8 (TABLE)	Repeats the most recent Data What-if Table command.
F9 (CALC)	In READY mode, recalculates formulas. In EDIT or VALUE mode, converts a cell's formula to its current value.
F10 (MENU)	Activates the menu bar. F10 (MENU) is equivalent to Alt.
Alt + F1 (COMPOSE)	Enters characters into cells that you can't enter directly from your keyboard.
Alt + F2 (STEP)	Turns macro STEP mode on or off.
Alt + F3 (RUN)	Displays a list of the macros in the active files. Alt + F3 (RUN) is equivalent to choosing Tools/Macro/Run.
Alt + F6 (ZOOM)	Enlarges the current horizontal, vertical, or perspective pane to the full size of the window or shrinks it to its original size.
Alt + F7 (add-in 1), **Alt + F8 (add-in 2),** **Alt + F9 (add-in 3)**	Starts the 1-2-3 add-in assigned to the key F7, F8, or F9.